Wolfgang Obenaus/Josef Weidacher

This is the Manager Speaking

Erfolgreich kommunizieren im Alltags- und Geschäftsleben

unter Mitarbeit von
Rowena Catherine Prewett

Ueberreuter

Die Deutsche Bibliothek – CIP-Einheitsaufnahme

Obenaus, Wolfgang:
This is the manager speaking : erfolgreich kommunizieren im Alltags- und Geschäftsleben / Wolfgang Obenaus ; Josef Weidacher. – Wien : Ueberreuter, 1992
ISBN 3-8000-3458-1
NE: Weidacher, Josef:

S 10/1

Umschlag von Beate Dorfinger
unter Verwendung eines Fotos von Buenos Dias Bildagentur

Druck und Bindung: Ueberreuter Buchproduktion, Korneuburg
Printed in Austria

VORWORT

Das vorliegende Buch, das sich hauptsächlich an den internationalen Manager und alle, die es noch werden wollen, wendet, ist das dritte Werk im Rahmen unserer Publikationsreihe „Wirtschaftsenglisch“. Während sich die beiden ersten mit den grammatikalischen Aspekten von Wirtschaftstexten bzw. mit der Wirtschaftsterminologie und -phraseologie befassen, ist **This is the Manager Speaking** der mündlichen Kommunikation in Alltags- und Wirtschaftssituationen gewidmet. Es erübrigt sich wohl, lange zu erklären, warum mündliche Kommunikation im Zeitalter der zunehmenden Verflechtung der Nationalwirtschaften und der zunehmenden Dominanz des Englischen als Lingua franca des internationalen Geschäftslebens für den Manager von zentraler Bedeutung ist. Auf eine Kurzformel gebracht: „Ohne Englisch – und besonders ohne mündliches Englisch – geht im Management nichts mehr.“

Auch der Aufbau des Buches erfordert keine langatmigen Erklärungen. Die wesentlichen kommunikativen Situationen werden in Form von Einzelsätzen und Kurzdialogen abgedeckt. Zu jedem der Sätze bzw. Dialoge werden ausreichend Übersetzungshilfen geboten, so daß das Buch auch für den Interessenten mit relativ bescheidenen Englischkenntnissen nutzbar sein sollte. Dabei ist zu beachten, daß die deutschen Entsprechungen nur für den jeweiligen sprachlichen oder situativen Zusammenhang gelten und nicht notwendigerweise auf andere Kontexte übertragbar sind. Um die Benutzerfreundlichkeit des Buches zu erhöhen, wurde die Anzahl der Abkürzungen auf ein Minimum beschränkt. Eine Liste findet sich im Anschluß an dieses Vorwort.

Zur intensiven und effizienten Nutzung des Buches sollten auch die begleitenden Tonbandkassetten beitragen, die voraussichtlich ab Herbst 1992 angeboten werden.

Abschließend möchten wir uns herzlich bei allen bedanken, die direkt oder indirekt mitgeholfen haben, dieses Buch zu ermöglichen. Dazu gehören Mag. Elisabeth Eder, Mag. Martin Herles, Sandra Lang B.A., Keith Oliff B.A. Honours und Susan Tapply. Unser besonderer Dank gilt Rowena Catherine Prewett B.A., die bei der Ausarbeitung und Überprüfung des Textes einen wertvollen Beitrag geleistet hat und deren freundliches Wesen und kooperative Einstellung uns die Arbeit sehr erleichtert hat.

Wien, im März 1992

Wolfgang Obenaus
Sepp Weidacher

ABKÜRZUNGEN

brit. – britisch
sbdy. – somebody
sthg. – something
U.S. – United States / amerikanisch

jmdm. – jemandem
jmdn. – jemanden

INHALTSVERZEICHNIS

Meeting People (Vorstellung) 17
Introducing Yourself (Sich selbst vorstellen) 17
Introducing Other People (Jemand anderen vorstellen) 19

Greeting People (Begrüßung) 22

Saying Goodbye (Verabschiedung) 26

Requests and Replies (Bitten/Aufforderungen und wie man darauf reagiert) 30

How to Say "bitte" and "danke" in English 34

Apologies and Reactions (Entschuldigungen und wie man darauf reagiert) 41

Congratulations and Good Wishes (Gratulationen, Genesungs- und sonstige Wünsche) 44

Season's Greetings (Weihnachts- und Neujahrswünsche) 48

Sympathy, Regrets and Consolation, Condolences (Mitgefühl, Bedauern und Beileid) 49

Exclamations (Ausrufe) 53

Language Problems (Sprachliche Probleme) 55

Jokes (Witze) 62

My Family (Meine Familie) 63

Weather (Wetter) 66

Politics (Politik) 74
Political System (Politisches System) 74
Present Political Situation and Attitudes (Gegenwärtige politische Lage und persönliche Einstellung) 76
Political Parties (Politische Parteien) 78
Elections (Wahlen) 79
Political Past (Politische Vergangenheit) 80
International Aspects (Internationale Aspekte) 81

Health (Befinden und Gesundheit) 83
General; Minor Illnesses (Allgemeines Befinden; kleinere Wehwehchen) 83
At the Chemist's (In der Apotheke) 86
At the Doctor's (Beim Arzt) 87
At the Dentist's (Beim Zahnarzt) 88

Emergencies (Notfälle) 90
Lost Property (Verlust von Sachen) 90
In Hospital (Im Krankenhaus) 91
Accidents (Unfälle) 92
Car Accidents (Autounfälle) 92

Time (Zeit und Zeitangaben) 94
Appointments (Terminvereinbarungen und Verabredungen) 94
Deadlines (Termine und Fristen) 99
Pressed for Time (Unter Zeitdruck) 100
Time of Day (Tageszeitangaben) 102
Other Expressions Indicating Time (Sonstige Zeitangaben) 103
Age (Altersangaben) 107
Miscellaneous (Sonstiges) 108

Asking the Way and Public Transport (Erkundigung nach dem Weg und öffentliche Transportmittel) 110
Asking the Way – General (Erkundigung nach dem Weg – allgemein) 110
Underground (U-Bahn) 113
Bus/Coach (Bus/Überlandbus) 115
Tram (Straßenbahn) 118

Air Travel (Mit dem Flugzeug) 119
Booking and Other Arrangements (Buchungen und alles, was dazugehört) 119
Check-in (Einchecken) 123
Between Check-in and Departure (Zwischen Einchecken und Abflug) 125
On Board the Aircraft (Im Flugzeug) 126
Post Flight (Nach dem Flug) 128

Rail Travel (Mit der Eisenbahn) 130
Inquiries and Tickets (Auskünfte und Fahrkarten) 130
At the Station (Auf dem Bahnhof) 133
In the Train (Im Zug) 134
General (Allgemeines) 136

Motoring (Mit dem Auto unterwegs) 137
Car Rental (Autovermietung) 137

Asking the Way (Erkundigung nach dem Weg) 140
At the Petrol Station (An der Tankstelle) 141
Breakdowns and Minor Repairs (Pannen und kleinere Reparaturen) 143
Parking (Parken) 145
Car Ferry (Autofähre) 147
Miscellaneous (Sonstiges) 148
Taxi (Taxi) 149

Hotel (Hotel) 151
Inquiries, Reservations, etc. (Anfragen, Zimmerreservierungen usw.) 151
At the Reception (Am Empfang) 155
Hotel Services 158
Breakfast (Frühstück) 160
Complaints (Beschwerden) 161
Checking out (Abreise) 162
Business Facilities (Leistungsangebot für Geschäftsleute) 164

Visits and Parties (Besuche und Parties) 166
Invitations (Einladungen) 166
Arrival (Eintreffen) 168
Drinks (Getränke) 169
Tea/Coffee 170
At the Table (Bei Tisch) 171
After the Meal (Nach dem Essen) 173
At a Party 174
Leaving and Thanking for Hospitality (Verabschiedung und Dank für die Gastfreundschaft) 175

Restaurants, Bars, etc. (Restaurants, Bars usw.) 177
Invitations (Einladungen) 177
Pubs/Pub Lunch 179
Booking a Table (Tischreservierung) 181
At the Reception 182
At the Bar 183
Ordering (Bestellung) 183
During the Meal (Während des Essens) 187
Smoking 189
Complaints (Beschwerden) 190
The Bill (Die Rechnung) 190
After the Meal (Nach dem Essen) 192
Out on the Town (Nachtleben) 193

Formal Occasions (Offizielle Anlässe) 195
Toasts – General (Allgemeine Toasts) 195

Toasts – Thanking Somebody (Toasts in Verbindung mit einem Dank) 195
Toasts – Best Wishes for the Future (Toasts in Verbindung mit besten Wünschen für die Zukunft) 196
Toasts – Congratulating People (Toasts in Verbindung mit Gratulationen) 197
Announcements (Ankündigungen und Verlautbarungen) 197
Celebrations (Feiern) 198
Welcoming People (Jemanden begrüßen) 199
Thanking for Invitation (Dank für Einladung) 199
Thanking People (Wie man sich bedankt) 200

TV, Radio, Video, etc. (Fernsehen, Radio, Video usw.) 202

Cinema, Theatre, Opera, Concerts and Museums (Kino, Theater, Oper, Konzerte und Museen) 207
Cinema 207
Theatre 211
Opera 215
Concerts 216
Museums 218

Sports and Other Leisure Time Activities (Sport und andere Freizeitbeschäftigungen) 219

Shopping (Einkaufen) 224

At the Post Office (Auf der Post) 231

Telephoning (Telefonieren) 235
Answering the Switchboard (Telefonzentrale meldet sich) 235
Requesting Identity (Bitte um Namensnennung) 235
Person/Company Called Requests Identity (Angerufene Person oder Firma bittet um Namensnennung)
Person Calling Requests Identity (Anrufer/in bittet um Namensnennung)
Caller Identifies himself/herself in Reply to a Request for Identity (Anrufer/in nennt auf Ersuchen hin seinen/ihren Namen) 236
Person Called Answers the Phone (Angerufene/r meldet sich) 236
Caller Requests a Particular Person or Service (Anrufer/in verlangt eine bestimmte Person oder Abteilung) 237
Reaction to Caller's Request for a Particular Person (Reaktion auf den Wunsch eines Anrufers/einer Anruferin, jemanden bestimmten zu sprechen) 238
Caller States his/her Business (Anrufer/in gibt den Grund für seinen/ihren Anruf an) 239

The Person Wanted is not Available (Die gewünschte Person ist nicht erreichbar) 240
Reacting to Unavailability of Party Called (Reaktion auf Nichterreichbarkeit des/der Angerufenen) 241
Difficulties in Understanding the Other Party (Schwierigkeiten, den Gesprächspartner zu verstehen) 242
Spelling Words, Numbers and Other Details (Buchstabieren von Wörtern, Zahlen und anderen Details) 243
Ringing off (Beendigung des Telefongesprächs) 244
Talking about the Telephone (Gespräche rund um das Telefon) 245

Personal Banking (Persönliche Bankgeschäfte) 247
Opening Hours (Öffnungszeiten) 247
Travellers' Cheques (Reiseschecks) 247
Eurocheques (Euroschecks) 249
Ordinary Cheques 249
Changing Money (Geld wechseln) 250
Opening and Closing an Account (Eröffnung und Schließung eines Kontos) 252
Deposits (Einzahlungen) 253
Withdrawals (Abhebungen) 254
Transfers (Überweisungen) 255
Overdrafts (Kontoüberziehungen) 257
Statements and Balance of Account (Kontoauszüge und Kontostand) 257
Credit Cards (Kreditkarten) 258

My Job (Mein Job) 259
What do you Do for a Living? (Wie verdienen Sie sich Ihren Lebensunterhalt?) 259
Joining the Company (Eintritt in die Firma) 259
Working Hours and Working Conditions (Arbeitszeit und Arbeitsbedingungen) 260
Superiors, Subordinates and Colleagues (Vorgesetzte, Untergebene und Kollegen) 261
Job Description and Duties (Beschreibung des Arbeitsplatzes und Aufgaben) 262
Job Satisfaction (Arbeitszufriedenheit) 264
Leaving the Company and Looking for a New Job (Ausscheiden aus der Firma und Suche nach einem neuen Arbeitsplatz) 265
Compensation (Entlohnung) 266
Promotion (Beförderung) 268
Your Business here in Britain (Zweck Ihres Aufenthaltes in Großbritannien) 269

Educational Background (Bildungsweg) 271
Secondary Education (Höhere Schulen, „Mittelschulen") 271
Access to Universities (Zulassung zum Universitätsstudium) 272
Degrees (Akademische Grade) 273
Studies and Examinations (Studium und Prüfungen) 274
Finance (Finanzierung des Studiums) 276
Conditions at University (Studienbedingungen) 278
Study Record (Studienergebnisse) 278
Studying Abroad (Studium im Ausland) 279
Extracurricular Activities (Außeruniversitäre Aktivitäten) 280
Post University (Nach dem Studienabschluß) 280

My Company (Meine Firma) 282
Type, Size, Location, Ownership, History, etc. (Art, Größe, Standort, Eigentumsverhältnisse, Geschichte usw.) 282
Products and Activities (Produkte und Tätigkeitsbereiche) 285
Organisational Structure and Management (Organisationsstruktur und Management) 286
Current Conditions (Gegenwärtige Lage) 288
Orders and Capacity Utilisation (Aufträge und Kapazitätsauslastung)
Competition (Konkurrenz)
Sales (Umsatz/Absatz)
Profits and Losses (Gewinn und Verlust)
Costs (Kosten)
Financing (Finanzierung)
Human Resources/Employees (Personalressourcen/Mitarbeiter) 296
Premises (Räumlichkeiten, Betriebsstätten) 298

Computers (Computer) 300

Negotiating Contracts (Vertragsverhandlungen) 303
Chat Phase (Vorgeplänkel) 303
Opening the Discussion (Eröffnung der Diskussion) 304
Delivery, Delivery Dates and Transport (Lieferung, Liefertermine und Transport) 305
Quantities (Mengen) 308
Products, Quality and Modifications (Produkte, Qualität und Modifikationen) 309
Terms of Payment (Zahlungsbedingungen) 310
Prices and Commissions (Preise und Provisionen) 313
Discounts (Preisnachlässe) 317
Term and Termination (Vertragslaufzeit und Beendigung des Vertragsverhältnisses) 319
Draft Contracts, Legal and Technical Points (Vertragsentwürfe, juristische und technische Details) 320

Breaks, Next Meeting, Finishing (Pausen, die nächste Sitzung, Abschluß der Verhandlungen) 322

Meetings (Sitzungen) 324
Starting the Meeting (Sitzungseröffnung) 324
Setting the Agenda (Festlegung der Tagesordnung) 325
Inviting Contributions and Asking for Opinions (Bitte um Diskussionsbeiträge und Meinungsäußerungen) 326
Agreeing and Disagreeing (Zustimmung und Ablehnung) 327
Persuading and Convincing (Überreden und überzeugen) 329
Suggestions and Reactions (Vorschläge und Reaktionen darauf) 330
Conceding Points (Zugeständnisse machen) 332
Clarifying (Klarstellungen) 332
Interruptions and Dealing with Interruptions (Unterbrechungen und wie man damit umgeht) 333
Moving the Discussion Forward (Überleitung zum nächsten Tagesordnungspunkt) 335
Keeping the Discussion on Track (Wie man Abweichungen vom Thema verhindert) 336
Handling Awkward Questions and Being Evasive (Wie man mit unangenehmen Fragen umgeht und Ausflüchte macht) 336
Summarising (Zusammenfassungen) 337
Formal Motions and Voting (Formelle Anträge und Abstimmungen) 338
Minutes (Das Protokoll) 340
Closing the Meeting (Wie man eine Sitzung schließt) 341
Post Meeting (Nach der Sitzung) 341

Conferences (Konferenzen) 343
Registration and General Information (Anmeldung und allgemeine Informationen) 343
Opening Conferences and Introducing Speakers (Eröffnung von Konferenzen und Vorstellung von Vortragenden) 345
Speaker Thanks Chairman (Vortragende/r dankt Vorsitzendem) 346
Speaker Introduces Subject (Vortragende/r stellt ihr/sein Thema vor) 346
Speaker Introduces First Point (Vortragende/r präsentiert ersten Punkt) 347
Speaker Moves on to Next Point/s (Vortragende/r leitet zum nächsten Punkt/zu den nächsten Punkten über) 347
Concluding Remarks (Schlußbemerkungen) 348
Thanking Speaker, Initiating Discussion, Closing Conference or Session (Dank an die/den Vortragende/n, Eröffnung der Diskussion, Abschluß der Konferenz oder Sitzung) 349

General Presentations [Including Quantitative Statements and Diagrams] (Allgemeine Präsentationen [unter besonderer Berücksichtigung von quantitativen Aussagen und Diagrammen]) 350
Introductions (Einleitende Worte) 350
Technical Aspects (Technische Aspekte) 352
Quantitative Statements and Diagrams (Quantitative Aussagen und Diagramme) 353
Introducing Diagrams (Einführung von Diagrammen)
Breakdowns and Percentage Shares (Aufgliederungen und Prozentanteile)
Variable Changes or Remains Constant (Änderung oder Gleichbleiben einer Variablen)
Rankings (Rangordnungen)
Miscellaneous (Sonstiges)
Moving the Presentation Forward (Überleitung zum nächsten Punkt der Präsentation) 360
Closing the Presentation (Abschluß der Präsentation) 360

Product Presentations (Produktpräsentationen) 362
Introduction (Einleitung) 362
Materials and Composition (Materialien und Zusammensetzung) 363
Properties and Quality (Eigenschaften und Qualität) 364
Handy Size and Flexibility (Praktische Größe und Flexibilität) 365
Beneficial Environmental Consequences (Positive ökologische Auswirkungen) 366
Customer Acceptance (Kundenakzeptanz) 367
Price and Performance (Preis und Leistung) 368
Packing (Verpackung) 368
Measurements and Weights (Abmessungen und Gewichte) 369
Improvements (Verbesserungen) 369
Variety (Vielfalt des Angebots) 370
Suitability and Modifications (Eignung und Modifikationen) 371
Comparison with Competing Products (Vergleich mit Konkurrenzprodukten) 371
Demonstrations and Illustrations (Vorführungen und Illustrationen) 372

Trade Fairs (Messen) 374
About Fairs and Fair Preparations (Gespräche über Messen und Vorbereitungsarbeiten) 374
On the Stand (Am Messestand) 376
Conversations with Other Staff Members (Gespräche mit anderen Mitarbeitern)
Conversations with Visitors (Gespräche mit Besuchern)

Conversations with Fair Contractors and Workers (Gespräche mit Messebaufirmen und -arbeitern)
Post Mortem (Nach der Messe - Analyse und Bewertung) ____ 379

Contacts with Advertising Agencies (Kontakte mit Werbeagenturen) ____ 381
Reactions to Suggestions and Concepts (Reaktionen auf Vorschläge und Konzepte) ____ 381
Discussing Advertising Policies - Media Selection (Diskussion werbepolitischer Konzepte - Medienauswahl) ____ 382
Technical Details, Schedules and Deadlines (Technische Details, Zeitpläne und Termine) ____ 384
Terminating Agreement with Agency (Beendigung des Vertragsverhältnisses mit der Agentur) ____ 385

Complaints (Reklamationen) ____ 386
Buyer Makes a Complaint (Käufer beschwert sich/reklamiert) ____ 386
General/Unspecific Complaints (Allgemeine/Unbestimmte Reklamationen)
Faulty or Damaged Goods (Mangelhafte oder beschädigte Ware)
Wrong Goods (Falsche Ware)
Wrong Quantity (Falsche Menge)
Delays in Delivery (Lieferverzug)
Packing (Verpackung)
Buyer Suggests Plan of Action (Käufer schlägt Regelung vor) ____ 391
Buyer Makes Threats (Käufer droht) ____ 392
Seller's Reaction to Complaint, Investigation and Inspection (Reaktion des Verkäufers auf Reklamation, Untersuchung und Inspektion) ____ 393
Seller's Admission of Fault and Apologies (Verkäufer nimmt Schuld auf sich und entschuldigt sich) ____ 394
Seller Suggests or Announces Settlement (Verkäufer schlägt Regelung vor oder kündigt eine an) ____ 395
Buyer Reacts to Seller's Suggestions (Käufer reagiert auf Vorschläge des Verkäufers) ____ 396
Seller does not Accept Complaint (Verkäufer weist Reklamation zurück) ____ 397
Seller's or Buyer's Suggestions if there is no Agreement (Vorschläge seitens des Verkäufers oder Käufers im Falle der Nichteinigung) ____ 398
Buyer Accepts Responsibility (Käufer übernimmt Verantwortung) ____ 399

The Austrian Economy (Die österreichische Wirtschaft) ____ 401
Economic Situation (Konjunkturlage) ____ 401

Economic System and Industrial Structure (Wirtschaftssystem und Wirtschaftsstruktur) 402
Private Sector and Nationalised Industries (Privatwirtschaft und verstaatlichte Industrie) 404
Various Industries (Verschiedene Wirtschaftszweige) 406
International Economic Relations (Internationale Wirtschaftsbeziehungen) 407
Joining the EC (Beitritt zur EG) 410
Financial Markets (Finanzmärkte) 411
Economic and Social Policies (Wirtschafts- und Sozialpolitik) 412
Taxes (Steuern) 414

Environmental Matters (Umweltaspekte) 416
Environmental Regulations (Umweltvorschriften) 416
Waste (Abfall) 418
Promotional Aspects (Kommunikationspolitische Aspekte) 420
Products (Produkte) 421
Transport (Transport) 422

MEETING PEOPLE

Vorstellung

INTRODUCING YOURSELF

Sich selbst vorstellen

* A: **May I introduce myself: My name is Fred Artner and I'm Head of Marketing here.**
(introduce – vorstellen / Head of Marketing – Leiter der Marketingabteilung; Marketingleiter)
B: **How do you do. My name is Mary Bell.**
(Im britischen Englisch wird mit 'How do you do' nicht nach dem Befinden der angesprochenen Person gefragt. Es ist eine mehr oder minder inhaltslose Grußformel, die im Deutschen je nach Kontext etwa mit „Sehr erfreut" oder „Guten Tag" wiedergegeben werden kann.)

* **Hello, let me introduce myself. I'm Norbert Teufelberger from Casinos Austria. I'm in charge of Controlling.**
(be in charge of – Leiter sein von)

* **Good morning. Allow me to introduce myself. Hannes Dopsch from Vienna. Here's my business card.**
(business card – Visitenkarte)

* **I'd like to introduce myself: Hans-Jörg Ertl, Raiffeisen-Zentralbank, Vienna.**

* **A: How do you do. I'm Thomas Auer.**
B: How do you do. My name is Brown, Neil Brown.

* **A: How do you do. My name is Philipp Aigner, Advertising Manager for General Motors Austria.**
(advertising – Werbung)
B: Pleased to meet you, Mr. Aigner. I'm Gary Baker, Assistant Marketing Manager of Electrovans PLC, London.
(Freut mich, Sie kennenzulernen, ... / Assistant Marketing Manager – stellvertretender Marketingleiter)

* **A: I'm sorry. I didn't catch your name.**
(catch – verstehen)
B: Baker, Gary Baker.

* **A: Excuse me. I don't think we've met before. My name is Tom Abbey. I work with Mr. Smith.**
(meet – sich begegnen; sich kennenlernen)
B: How do you do, Mr. Abbey. I'm Karl Bender from Austrian Industries.
A: How do you do, Mr. Bender. How long are you going to be here?

* **A: Good morning. My name's Adams.**
B: Good morning, Mr. Adams, I'm Fritz Baumann. May I introduce our Sales Manager for Eastern Europe, Mr. Wagner?
(Sales Manager – Verkaufsleiter)

* **A: Hello, my name's Adrian.**
B: Mine's Barbara. Nice to meet you.
A: You're Austrian, aren't you?
(aren't you? – nicht wahr?)
B: Yes, that's right. I come from Vienna.

* **Hi! I'm Paul. I'm a friend of John's.**

* **A: Excuse me. Are you Mr. Brown, by any chance?**
(by any chance – zufällig)
B: Yes, that's me.
A: It's nice to meet you. Anger's my name.
B: Nice to meet you too.

* **You're not Miss Kelly by any chance, are you?**
(are you? – oder?)

* **A: Mr. Brand, isn't it?**
(isn't it – nicht wahr?)
B: Yes, that's right. Walter Brand.
A: How do you do. I'm Tony Adams.
B: How do you do, Mr. Adams. I hope I'm not putting you to any trouble.
(.... Ich hoffe, daß ich Ihnen keine Umstände mache.)
A: Not at all.
(Nein, überhaupt nicht.)

* **A: Miss Brannigan?**
B: Yes, that's right, I'm Donna Brannigan.
A: Hello, I'm Robert Achatz. Welcome to Voest Alpine AG. It's great to have you with us.
B: Pleased to meet you Mr. Achatz.
A: How long are you planning to stay?
(stay – bleiben)

* **A: Hello! You must be Charles Bolder.**
B: Yes, that's right.
A: I'm Werner Aumann. Pleased to meet you.
B: Pleased to meet you too.

* **A: Hello. You're the new export clerk, aren't you? My name is Sarah Adlington. I do most of the secretarial work in the office.**
(export clerk – Exportsachbearbeiter / aren't you? – nicht wahr? / office – Büro)
B: It's very nice to meet you, Miss Adlington. I'm Peter Baumer.
A: Please call me Sarah.
(Dies entspricht etwa dem Anbieten des Du-Wortes. Beachten Sie, daß in England diese Art des Du-Wortes oft schon bei der ersten Begegnung angeboten wird.)
B: And I'm Peter.

INTRODUCING OTHER PEOPLE

Jemand anderen vorstellen

* **A: Let me introduce you to my wife. Brigitte, this is Chris Carter.**
(introduce – vorstellen)
B: Hello, Chris. Nice to meet you.
C: How do you do, Mrs. Auer.
B: Oh, do call me Brigitte.
C: Oh, right.

* **A: I'd like to introduce you to Mrs. Chlepac. She's from Austria.**
B: Nice to meet you, Mrs. Chlepac. My name's Boyd, James Boyd.
C: Very nice to meet you too.

* A: **Dr. Beer, may I introduce you to Dr. Crimson? Dr. Crimson, Dr. Beer.**
B: **How do you do.**
C: **How do you do.**
B: **I'm pleased to meet you at long last. I've heard so much about you from Dr. Aliber.**
(at long last – endlich)

* A: **Mr. Bond, allow me to introduce one of our consultants, Jane Colby from New York.**
(consultant – Konsulent)
B: **Pleased to meet you, Miss Colby.**
C: **The pleasure's all mine. And please call me Jane.**
(Ganz meinerseits. … .)

* A: **Mr. Bacher, I'd like you to meet Linda Clemence. She's our new Advertising Manager.**
(… , ich möchte Sie gerne mit … bekannt machen. … .)
B: **How do you do.**
C: **How do you do. I'm very pleased to meet you, Mr. Bacher.**

* A: **Barbara, I want you to meet a business colleague of mine, Carol Simpson. Carol, this is Barbara Baxter. I don't think you've met.**
(business colleague – Kollegin aus der Firma)
B: **Hello, Carol.**
C: **Hello.**

* A: **Bruno, I'd like you to meet Miss Taylor. She has just arrived from London and is going to work as a management trainee.**
(just – gerade / arrive – ankommen / trainee – Praktikantin, Trainee)
B: **How do you do. I'm delighted to meet you, Miss Taylor. I hope you had a good flight.**
(be delighted – sich sehr freuen)

* A: **Bob, have you met Peter Cromwell, my new assistant, yet?**
(yet – schon)
B: **No, I don't think I have. How do you do, Mr. Cromwell.**
C: **How do you do.**

* A: **I don't think you've met Dr. Randolph yet, have you?**
(have you? – oder?)

B: No, I haven't yet had the pleasure.
(Nein, ich hatte noch nicht das Vergnügen.)

* **A: Have you two already met?**
B: Yes, I think we have, haven't we?
(haven't we? – oder?)

* **A: By the way, do you know Mr. Redford?**
(Übrigens, ... ?)
B: No, I don't think so. Pleased to meet you.

* **No, I don't actually. But I've heard a lot about you. How do you do, Mr. Redford. I'm delighted to meet you.**
(a lot – viel)

* **A: I don't think you know Mr. Crane, our Production Manager, do you?**
(do you? – oder?)
B: No, we haven't met. How do you do, Mr. Crane.
C: How do you do. I'm very pleased to meet you, Mr. Benson.

* **A: Do you two know each other?**
B: I don't believe we do. Nice to meet you.
(believe – glauben)

* **A: Mrs. Böhm, this is Brian Clough. He's visiting us from England.**
B: How do you do, Mr. Clough.
C: How do you do.
B: Which part of England are you from?

* **A: Brian, this is Wolfgang Cech from Austria. He's over here on business. Wolfgang, Brian Baxter, our Export Manager.**
(on business – geschäftlich)
B: Nice to have you with us.
C: How do you do, Mr. Baxter.
B: Have you been to London before, Mr. Cech?
C: No, this is my first time. I went to Brighton a year ago, but I didn't come here.

* **George, this is Mary. Mary, this is George. He's a friend of mine.**

GREETING PEOPLE

Begrüßung

* **A: Good morning, Mr. Brown!**
  B: Morning, Ann.

* **A: Hi, Betty.**
  B: Hello, Adrian.

* **Hello you two.**

* **Hi there, Trevor!**

* **A: Morning, Barbara. How did you enjoy your holiday?**
  (.... Wie war's im Urlaub?)
  B: Oh, hello, Andy. It was wonderful. Just what I needed.
  (just – genau)

* **A: Hi, Bill.**
  B: Hello, Alex. You're back?
  A: Yes, I got back this afternoon.
  B: Did you have a good crossing?
  (crossing – Überfahrt)
  A: The sea was a bit choppy, but otherwise it was fine.
  (sea – Meer / choppy – unruhig / otherwise – sonst)

* **Hello, Tony. How was your trip to Brazil?**

* **Hello, Jane. I'm afraid I'm rather late. Have you been waiting long?**
  (.... Tut mir leid, ich bin ziemlich spät dran. Wartest du schon lange?)

* **A: Morning, Bill. Nice to see you!**
  B: Hello Ann. You're looking very well.

* **A: Hello, Brian. How nice to see you again!**
  B: Hello Arnold. Haven't seen you for ages. Where've you been?
  (for ages – ewig; seit einer Ewigkeit)
  A: I've been back in Austria as a matter of fact.

* **A: Good evening, Mrs. Bracknell.**
  B: Good evening. It's good to see you again.
  A: It's good to see you too.

* **A: Hello, Bill.**
  B: Hello. This is a pleasant surprise.
  (pleasant surprise – freudige Überraschung)
  A: It's very nice to see you again, Bill. It's been a long time.
  (.... Es ist lange her, seit wir uns das letzte Mal gesehen haben.)

* **A: Good morning, Mr. Beeston. Come along in. Do sit down.**
  B: Thank you.
  A: Well, now. I'm pleased to see you again. You don't smoke, do you?
  (do you? – oder?)
  B: No, I don't.

* **A: Hello, Mr. Bauer, I don't know if you remember me. David Allen, we met at ...**
  (remember sbdy. – sich an jemanden erinnern)
  B: Of course! It's nice to meet you again, Mr. Allen.

* **I'm very pleased to meet you again, Mr. Allen.**

* **A: Hello, Miss Brenner. I'm delighted to meet you again. Did you have a good journey?**
  (be delighted – sich sehr freuen / journey – Reise)
  B: Yes, it was fine, thanks.
  A: So, what are you doing in London?
  B: Well, I'm here on business for a few days. I've got quite a few meetings here.
  (on business – geschäftlich / quite a few – ziemlich viele / meeting – Sitzung)
  A: And when are you going back to Vienna?
  B: Well, I'm staying till the end of the week. My flight's on Friday morning.

——— ❖ ———

* **A: Good evening, Mr. Bloch. How are you?**
  (.... Wie geht es Ihnen?)
  B: Very well, thank you. And how are you?
  A: I'm very well, too, thank you.

* **A: Nice to see you again, Mrs. Bear. How are you?**
B: Very well, thank you, Mr. Auer. I hope you are well too.

* **A: Hello, Mr. Berger. How are you?**
B: I'm fine, thank you. And you?
(I'm fine – mir geht es gut)
A: All right, thank you.

* **A: Good afternoon, Miss Brophy.**
B: Good afternoon. How are you today, Mr. Alber?
A: Not too well, I'm afraid. Must've caught a bit of a cold I think.
(Leider nicht allzu gut. Ich muß wohl eine leichte Verkühlung erwischt haben.)
B: Oh, I'm sorry to hear that.

* **A: Bill! Good to see you again! How are you?**
B: I'm fine, thanks. How are you?
A: I'm okay, thanks. Nice of you to come.

* **A: Hi, Ben, how are things?**
(. . . , wie läuft's denn so?)
B: Great, thanks. I've got a really interesting new job. What about you?
(great – super)
A: I'm all right, thanks.

* **A: Hello, Betty! How are you doing?**
B: Fine, thanks. And you?
A: Oh, not so bad.

* **A: Good morning, Berta. How're you getting on?**
(. . . . Wie geht's dir denn so?)
B: Fine, thanks.
A: And how's the family?
B: Oh, the usual problems. But they're all well, thanks.
(well – gesund)

* **A: Morning. How are things with you, Brigitte?**
B: Oh, not too bad, thanks.
A: How are you enjoying your stay in London?
(Wie gefällt es dir in London?)
B: Very much. I love it here.

* **A: Barbara! It's great to see you again. So – how's life?**
(great – schön / how's life – wie geht's denn so)
B: Oh, pretty good, thanks.
(pretty – ganz)

* **A: Hi, Brian! How's it going?**
(.... Wie läuft's denn so?)
B: Oh, mustn't grumble.
(Kann mich nicht beklagen.)

* **A: How's life treating you?**
(Wie geht's dir denn so?)
B: Can't complain, thanks.
(Kann mich nicht beklagen, ...)

* **A: Hello, Bettina, I haven't seen you for a while. How's everything going?**
(.... Wie läuft's denn so bei dir?)
B: Quite well, thanks. And yourself? I heard you got a new job. How are you enjoying it?
(quite – ganz)
A: Okay, so far. Everything's going very smoothly and I'm enjoying the challenge.
(go very smoothly – wie geschmiert laufen / challenge – Herausforderung)

SAYING GOODBYE

Verabschiedung

* **A: Goodbye, Dr. Benson.**
(Auf Wiedersehen, … !)
B: Goodbye.

* **A: I'll see you then, Bill. Bye!**
(Bis dann, Bill. Grüß dich!)
B: See you, Ann.
(Servus, Ann!)

* **A: See you on Friday!**
(Bis Freitag!)
B: OK. Bye for now!
(… . Bis dann also. Servus!)

* **A: See you later, bye!**
(Bis später. | Bis nachher. … !)
B: Take care. Bye now!
(take care – mach's gut)

* **A: I'll be seeing you!**
(Bis dann!)
B: Look after yourself. Bye-bye!
(Paß gut auf dich auf! … !)

* **A: Goodbye. It's been nice meeting you.**
(… . Es war nett, Sie kennenzulernen.)
B: Goodbye, and thank you very much for coming!

* **Goodbye. I have enjoyed talking to you.**
(… . War nett, mit Ihnen zu plaudern.)

* **A: Bye, Berta, and thanks for the lift.**
(… , und danke fürs Mitnehmen.)
B: Goodbye, Mr. Abraham. Best of luck!
(… . Viel Glück!)

* **A: Goodbye, Barbara. Have a good holiday and I'll see you when you get back.**
B: Yes, bye, and I hope your meeting goes well this afternoon.
(meeting – Sitzung)

* **A: Cheerio, Bob. Have a good trip!**
(Servus, Bob! Gute Reise!)
B: Thanks, and you!
(Danke, dir auch!)

* **A: Goodbye, Dr. Brown, I trust you have a pleasant journey.**
(trust – hoffen / pleasant journey – angenehme Reise)
B: Thank you, and have a good weekend!

* **A: Goodbye and all the best. It's been a pleasure meeting you.**
(.... Es war mir ein Vergnügen, Ihre Bekanntschaft zu machen.)
B: Yes, I've thoroughly enjoyed my stay. I hope to see you again soon. Goodbye.
(Ganz meinerseits, mir hat es hier wirklich sehr gut gefallen. ...)

* **A: Good night, Elisabeth. Have a good evening. I'll see you tomorrow, before you go back to England, won't I?**
(won't I – ohnehin noch)
B: Yes, indeed. See you tomorrow!
(indeed – sicher)
A: Good night.

—— ❖ ——

* **A: I'll see you again tonight, Brian.**
(tonight – heute abend)
B: Yes, I'm looking forward to the party. Bye.
(look forward to – sich freuen auf)
A: Bye!

* **A: Well, thanks very much, Bill. Very pleased to have met you.**
(be pleased – sich freuen)
B: It's been most enjoyable. I'll look forward to seeing you next week. Goodbye for now.
(War wirklich sehr nett. ... .)
A: Bye, Bill.

* A: **You're going back to Austria tomorrow, aren't you?**
(aren't you? – nicht wahr?)
B: **That's right. We won't be seeing each other for a while.**
(won't – will not)
A: **Well, take care of yourself and do keep in touch.**
(Paß gut auf dich auf und bleibe auf alle Fälle in Kontakt!)
B: **Right, bye.**

* A: **I've come to say goodbye.**
B: **When are you off?**
(be off – abreisen)
A: **Tomorrow morning, first thing.**
(Gleich morgen in der Früh.)
B: **Goodbye then, and all the very best.**

* A: **I'd like to say goodbye to you all.**
B: **Oh, are you off now? Have a good journey!**
A: **Thanks. Goodbye and remember to look me up if ever you're in Vienna.**
(remember – nicht vergessen / look sbdy. up – jemanden aufsuchen; bei jemandem vorbeischauen)

* A: **I think, that's everything, Mr. Bene. We've covered all the points we need to discuss for the moment.**
(cover – sich befassen mit / need – müssen)
B: **Fine, I'll say goodbye for now then, and thank you. It's been a useful meeting.**

* A: **Well, I must go. Goodbye then, Betty.**
B: **Bye then. Come again soon!**

* **I think, I'd better be going or I'll be late. Goodbye.**
(Ich glaube, ich sollte lieber gehen, sonst komme ich zu spät. ... .)

* **Must dash – I'm meeting Paul at eight thirty.**
(dash – rennen, sausen / meet – treffen)

* **Sorry, I must be off now.**
(Tut mir leid, ich muß nun weg.)

* **I think I really ought to be going.**
(Ich glaube, ich sollte jetzt wirklich gehen.)

* **I really should be getting back to my hotel. It's getting very late and I've got an early morning flight.**

* **A: I hope you don't mind but I really have to go now.**
  (Ich hoffe, daß es Ihnen nichts ausmacht, aber … .)
  B: That's OK, see you again soon.

* **It's been very nice talking to you, but I'm afraid I can't stay any longer.**
  (I'm afraid – leider)

—— ❖ ——

* **A: Goodbye then, and remember me to your parents.**
  (… , und schöne Grüße an Ihre Eltern!)
  B: Thank you, I certainly will. Goodbye. See you next year!
  (certainly – sicher)

* **A: Give my best wishes to John Carter.**
  (wishes – Grüße)
  B: Thank you, I will.

* **Please give my kind regards to your wife.**
  (kind regards – schöne Grüße)

* **Give my love to Doris. Hope to see her here next year.**
  (Grüß Doris von mir! … .)

* **Say hello to Simon for me.**

REQUESTS AND REPLIES

Bitten/Aufforderungen und wie man darauf reagiert

* **A: Could you send a price-list, please?**
B: I'll send one straight away.
(straight away – gleich)

* **A: Could you possibly lend me your dictating machine for a couple of hours? I've got a report to dictate.**
(possibly – vielleicht / lend – leihen, borgen / dictating machine – Diktiergerät / a couple of – ein paar / report – Bericht)
B: I'm sorry but I'll be needing it myself this afternoon. You can have it as soon as I've finished, though.
(I'm sorry – tut mir leid / need – brauchen / have finished – fertig sein / though – aber)

* **A: Do you think you could come back later, Mr. Bretschneider?**
(come back – nochmals kommen)
B: OK, no problem.

* **A: I wonder if you could have a look at this letter and check it for grammatical errors and spelling mistakes, please.**
(Könnten Sie bitte … / check for – überprüfen auf … hin / error – Fehler / spelling mistake – Rechtschreibfehler)
B: With pleasure.
(Aber gern.)

* **A: You couldn't just help me for a minute, could you?**
(could you? – oder?)
B: All right.

* **A: I'd be very grateful if you could get me a spare key.**
(grateful – dankbar / get – besorgen / spare key – Ersatzschlüssel)
B: Of course, no problem.

* **A: Could you do me a favour and post this letter, please?**
(do favour – Gefallen tun / post letter – Brief aufgeben)
B: Yes, OK. I don't mind.
(… . Mach' ich schon.)

* **A: I wonder if I could possibly ask you to let us use your meeting room to discuss the details of our negotiations in confidence.**
(meeting room – Sitzungszimmer / negotiation – Verhandlung / in confidence – vertraulich)
B: I'm terribly sorry, Mr. Andrews, but it's not convenient at the moment.
(terrible – schrecklich, fürchterlich / …, aber es geht im Moment nicht gut.)

* **A: Excuse me, do you think I could have a look at your newspaper?**
B: Yes, here you are.
(Ja gern, hier bitte!)

* **Could I borrow your lighter a minute, please?**
(borrow – ausborgen / lighter – Feuerzeug)

* **Could I have a light, please?**
(light – Feuer)

* **Do you have a light, by any chance?**
(Haben Sie zufällig Feuer?)

* **You haven't got a cigarette by any chance, have you?**
(have you? – oder?)

* **A: Excuse me, can you give me a hand, please?**
(give sbdy. a hand – jemandem helfen)
B: Yes, of course.

* **A: Would you put me through to Daphne, please?**
(put through – verbinden)
B: I'm sorry that's not possible, she's on holiday today.

* **A: Mr. Brennan, would you kindly move your car? Our delivery van can't get past.**
(… , würden Sie bitte mit Ihrem Auto wegfahren? Unser Lieferwagen kommt nicht vorbei.)
B: I'll do it right away.
(right away – sofort)

* A: **Would you mind lending me your calculator for a minute?**
(Würde es Ihnen etwas ausmachen, mir kurz Ihren Rechner zu borgen?)
B: **Not at all, here you are.**
(Aber nein, hier bitte!)

* A: **Would you mind showing a group of representatives from Midwest Ltd. around tomorrow afternoon?**
(show around – herumführen / representatives – Firmenangehörige / Ltd. – private limited company | [brit.] etwa: Gesellschaft mit beschränkter Haftung)
B: **No, not at all. I'd be delighted to.**
(.... Sehr gerne.)

* A: **Mind if I join you?**
(Etwas dagegen, wenn ich mitkomme?)
B: **No, of course not.**

* A: **Would you be so kind as to send a telex to confirm that?**
(kind – freundlich / confirm – bestätigen)
B: **No problem at all.**
(Überhaupt kein Problem.)

* A: **I hope you don't mind me asking, but I wonder if it might be possible for you to get me a car for the weekend?**
(... , aber wäre es Ihnen vielleicht möglich, mir für das Wochenende ein Auto zu besorgen?)
B: **I'll see what I can do.**

* A: **Sorry, but would it be possible for you to shut the window? I'm in a draught here.**
(shut – schließen / draught – Luftzug)
B: **I'm afraid I can't. It's stuck.**
(Tut mir leid, es geht nicht. Es klemmt.)

* A: **I'd like you to inspect the machinery you delivered last Tuesday.**
(inspect sthg. – sich etwas anschauen / deliver – liefern)
B: **I'll send someone round at once.**
(at once – sofort)

* **A: Any chance of borrowing your car tonight, Ben? Mine's being serviced.**
(borrow – ausborgen / tonight – heute abend / .... Meines ist beim Service.)
B: I'm afraid not. Cath needs it tonight.
(Geht leider nicht. ....)

HOW TO SAY "BITTE" AND "DANKE" IN ENGLISH

* **Please sit down.**

* **I'd like a double room for two nights, please.**
(double room – Doppelzimmer)

* **A: What would you like?**
B: A gin and tonic, please.

* **Sign here, please.**
(sign – unterschreiben)

* **A: Would you like tea or coffee, Barbara?**
B: Oh, I'll have tea, please.

* **A: Could I speak to Mr. Wright, please?**
B: Just a moment, please.

* **Could you please send me a quotation?**
(quotation – Angebot)

* **Could you show me how to work the photocopier, please?**
(work – bedienen)

* **Would you please come this way?**
(Würden Sie mir bitte hier folgen?)

* **Can you help me, please?**

* **May I leave at 4 o'clock, please, Mr. Telford? I've got to be at the dentist's at a quarter past.**
(leave – weggehen)

———— ❖ ————

* **Thank you for your attention.**
(attention – Aufmerksamkeit)

* **A: Is your office all right?**
  B: Yes, it's fine, thanks.

* **A: Have you had any lunch, Ben?**
  B: Yes, thanks.

* **A: Have a good weekend!**
  B: Thanks a lot. You too!

* **A: Merry Christmas!**
  B: Thanks very much. Same to you!

—— ❖ ——

* **A: Thank you for all your help.**
  B: That's quite all right.
  (Bitte sehr! I Nichts zu danken! I Gern geschehen!)

* **A: Thank you very much for standing by me in this difficult situation.**
  (stand by – beistehen)
  B: Don't mention it.
  (Das war doch selbstverständlich!)

* **A: Thanks very much for letting me use your office.**
  B: That's okay.
  (Gern geschehen!)

* **A: Thanks a lot for the information.**
  B: You're welcome.
  (Bitte!)

* **A: It was a good party, thanks for inviting me.**
  (invite – einladen)
  B: My pleasure.
  (Es war mir ein Vergnügen!)

* **A: Thanks for everything.**
  B: That's all right.

* **A: Thank you very much for showing me around.**
  (show sbdy. around – jemanden herumführen)
  B: It was a pleasure. Hope to see you again next year.

* **A: Thank you very much for finding out about the theatre.**
B: That's okay. It was no trouble.
(trouble – Problem)

* **A: I really can't thank you enough for all you've done.**
B: Not at all, it was a pleasure.
(not at all – nichts zu danken)

* **A: Well, many thanks for lunch, Bill. It really was very good.**
B: Good, glad you enjoyed it.
(Freut mich, daß es dir geschmeckt hat.)

* **A: Thank you very much for the lift.**
(Vielen Dank fürs Mitnehmen.)
B: Delighted I was able to help.
(be delighted – erfreut sein; sehr froh sein)

* **A: Thank you very much indeed for the delicious meal.**
(delicious meal – ausgezeichnetes Essen)
B: Thank <u>you</u> for coming.

* **A: Could I have a light, please?**
(light – Feuer)
B: Yes, here you are.
(Hier, bitte!)
A: Thanks.
B: That's all right.

* **A: Where is the information desk, please?**
(information desk – Informationsschalter)
B: It's just round that corner over there.
(Er ist gleich um die Ecke dort drüben.)
A: Thank you very much.
B: It's a pleasure.

* **A: The cab will be here in about ten minutes.**
(cab – Taxi)
B: Oh, thank you so much, Ann.
A: Not at all.

* **A: There is a telegram for you, Mr. Baxter. Here you are.**
(.... Hier, bitte! | Da haben Sie es! | Hier ist es!)
B: Thank you very much indeed.

A: That's quite all right.

* **A: Here's my car. Let me give you a lift.**
B: Thank you. That's very kind of you.
(kind – freundlich)
A: Not at all.

* **A: Here's a copy of "Time". I thought you might like to have a look at it on the plane.**
(copy – Ausgabe, Nummer / plane – Flugzeug)
B: Thanks very much. That's very kind of you.
A: You're welcome.

* **A: Oh, I'll take your suitcase.**
(suitcase – Koffer)
B: Many thanks. That is really nice of you.
(nice – nett, freundlich)
A: Not at all.

——— ❖ ———

* **A: The success of my trip was in large part due to your efforts, and I am most grateful to you.**
(Der Erfolg meiner Reise war großteils auf Ihre Bemühungen zurückzuführen, und ich bin Ihnen sehr dankbar dafür.)
B: It was a pleasure to help you.

* **Oh, that's excellent. I'm really very grateful.**

* **Tony, I'm extremely grateful to you for all your help.**
(extremely grateful – wirklich dankbar)

——— ❖ ———

* **A: May I help you?**
B: Yes, please.

* **A: Would you like a cup of tea?**
B: Yes, please. I'd love one.
(Ja bitte, gerne!)

* **A: Would you like us to deliver the flowers to your home?**
  (Wollen Sie, daß wir die Blumen zu Ihnen nach Hause schicken?)
  B: Oh yes, please. That would be lovely.
  (lovely – nett; sehr freundlich)

* **A: Do you want me to photocopy this for you?**
  B: Yes, that's very kind of you.

* **A: Could you come to a party at my place next Wednesday?**
  (at my place – bei mir zu Hause)
  B: Yes, with pleasure.

* **A: Could I tempt you with another piece of cake?**
  (tempt – verführen / piece – Stück)
  B: Thank you, yes. I'd very much like to have another one. The cake's delicious.
  (delicious – köstlich, ausgezeichnet)

* **A: Would you like to come and watch a game of cricket with me?**
  (watch – anschauen)
  B: Thank you, I'd like to very much.
  (Danke, sehr gerne!)

* **A: Would you like to come to a concert with me tonight?**
  B: I'd love to. Thanks very much.
  (Sehr gerne, danke!)

* **A: Cigarette?**
  B: No, thank you. I've given up, you know.
  (give up – aufgeben, aufhören)

* **A: Brian, can I get you another coffee?**
  (get – holen, bringen)
  B: No, thank you very much. Not at the moment.

* **A: Would you like anything else?**
  B: No, thanks. That'll be all.

* **A: Would you like some more soup?**
  B: Thank you, no. I'd rather not.
  (I'd rather not – eher nicht)

* **A: Would you like to sit down?**
B: No, I'm all right, thanks.
(Nein danke, es geht schon!)

* **A: Are you sure you won't have a scotch?**
(won't – will not)
B: Thanks very much, but I'm driving.
(drive – mit dem Auto fahren)

* **A: Will you have a cigar?**
(Möchten Sie eine Zigarre haben?)
B: That's very kind, but I won't, thank you.

* **A: Would you like to leave a message, or can I ask him to call you back?**
(leave message – Nachricht hinterlassen / call back – zurückrufen)
B: No, it's all right, I'll call back.
(Nein danke, ich werde nochmals anrufen.)

❖

* **A: These fast trains are very noi ....**
B: Pardon?
(Wie bitte?)

* **A: The paper says the price of petrol is going up.**
(paper – Zeitung / petrol – Benzin)
B: I beg your pardon?
(Wie bitte?)

❖

* **A: Oh, I'm so sorry Mr. Brewer.**
(Es tut mir wirklich leid, ...)
B: That's quite all right.
(Aber bitte, macht doch nichts!)

* **A: I'm terribly sorry.**
(Es tut mir schrecklich leid!)
B: It's all right.
(Aber bitte, schon gut!)

* **A: Sorry to trouble you.**
(trouble – belästigen, stören)
B: That's all right.

* **A: Oh! I'm sorry to disturb you.**
(disturb – stören)
B: That's okay, Ann.

APOLOGIES AND REACTIONS

Entschuldigungen und wie man darauf reagiert

* **A: Sorry!**
  (Verzeihung! | Entschuldigung! | Tut mir leid!)
  B: That's all right.
  (Schon gut! | Nichts passiert!)

* **A: I'm awfully sorry for being late.**
  (Es tut mir schrecklich leid, daß ich zu spät komme.)
  B: That doesn't matter.
  (Das macht doch nichts!)

* **A: Sorry if I'm disturbing you.**
  (Tut mir leid, wenn ich Sie störe.)
  B: Not at all. I'm not doing anything that can't wait until later.
  (Sie stören überhaupt nicht. ... .)

* **A: Sorry to bother you.**
  (bother – belästigen, stören)
  B: It's all right, it's no trouble at all.
  (Aber bitte, überhaupt kein Problem!)

* **A: I really am very sorry to have kept you waiting. I got stuck in the traffic on the way down here.**
  (keep sbdy. waiting – jemanden warten lassen / get stuck – steckenbleiben / traffic – Verkehr)
  B: Oh, that's quite all right.
  (Aber bitte, macht doch nichts!)

* **I'm sorry but I didn't quite catch what you were saying.**
  (Es tut mir leid, aber ich habe Sie nicht recht verstanden.)

* **A: I can't tell you how sorry I am for not preparing the report in time.**
  (prepare report – Bericht erstellen / in time – rechtzeitig)
  B: Well, that kind of thing really shouldn't happen, you know. But let's forget it this once.
  (that kind of thing – so etwas / happen – passieren / this once – dieses eine Mal)

* **A: I didn't mean to do it. Sorry.**
(Ich habe das nicht absichtlich gemacht. Tut mir leid.)
B: It's not your fault. I'm entirely to blame.
(.... Es ist einzig und allein meine Schuld.)

* **Joanna has asked me to say she's sorry she can't be with us but she's tied up elsewhere all day.**
(be tied up elsewhere – unabkömmlich sein / all day – den ganzen Tag)

* **A: I'm so sorry about this afternoon. I'm afraid it was my fault.**
(Es tut mir wirklich leid .... / Tut mir leid, es war meine Schuld.)
B: Never mind.
(Ist schon in Ordnung!)

* **A: I'm afraid I'm rather late.**
(Tut mir leid, daß ich so spät komme.)
B: Don't worry, we haven't started yet anyway.
(Kein Grund zur Aufregung, wir haben ohnehin noch nicht begonnen.)

* **A: I'm afraid I can't make it on Sunday.**
(Ich kann leider am Sonntag nicht.)
B: Oh dear, that's a pity!
(Das ist aber schade!)

* **I'm afraid I've forgotten your name, sorry.**
(Ich habe leider Ihren Namen vergessen.)

* **A: Could you give me a hand with a few things tomorrow afternoon, please?**
(give sbdy. a hand – jemandem helfen)
B: I'm afraid not. I'm away on business for the rest of this week.
(Geht leider nicht. / on business – geschäftlich)

* **A: I'd like to apologise for being late.**
(apologise – sich entschuldigen)
B: That's O.K.

* **A: I really must apologise to you for what happened.**
B: There's no need to apologise, it's just one of those things.
(Sie brauchen sich nicht zu entschuldigen, so etwas kann schon einmal passieren.)

* **A: Please accept my apologies.**
(apology – Entschuldigung)
B: I quite understand. Please don't worry.
(So etwas kann schon einmal passieren. Bitte machen Sie sich keine Sorgen.)

* **A: I've got an apology to make. I seem to have lost that umbrella you lent me.**
(... . Ich dürfte den Schirm, den Sie mir geborgt haben, verloren haben.)
B: Not to worry. It was only an old one anyway.
(not to worry – macht nichts; lassen Sie sich darüber keine grauen Haare wachsen / anyway – ohnehin)

* **Excuse me, but I must go and find Bill.**
(Entschuldigen Sie mich, ...)

* **Excuse me for interrupting, but this is very urgent.**
(Verzeihen Sie mir, daß ich Sie unterbreche, aber es ist sehr dringend.)

* **A: I hope you will excuse me for not calling in earlier.**
(call in – vorbeikommen)
B: It really doesn't matter at all.
(Das macht überhaupt nichts.)

* **A: Please forgive me for having caused you any inconvenience.**
(Ich möchte mich für die Unannehmlichkeiten, die ich Ihnen bereitet habe, entschuldigen.)
B: Don't give it another thought.
(Verschwenden Sie keinen weiteren Gedanken mehr daran.)

* **Forgive me for asking again, but where did you say you came from?**

* **I do beg your pardon. I've found out that what you said was in fact absolutely correct.**
(Ich muß mich wirklich entschuldigen. ... .)

* **A: Oh dear, my mistake!**
(mistake – Fehler)
B: Well, these things happen.
(So etwas kann schon einmal passieren.)

CONGRATULATIONS AND GOOD WISHES

Gratulationen, Genesungs- und sonstige Wünsche

* **A: I'd like to congratulate you on your promotion. And the best of luck in your new position.**
(congratulate on – gratulieren zu / promotion – Beförderung / best of luck – alles Gute / position – Position, Stellung)
B: Thank you. That's very kind of you.
(kind – freundlich)

* **A: May I congratulate you on being nominated salesman of the year.**
(salesman – Verkäufer)
B: Thanks.

* **A: I didn't get a chance to congratulate you on being appointed Marketing Manager. Your board made a very wise decision I must say.**
(appoint – ernennen, bestellen / board – Verwaltungsrat; Führungsgremium einer britischen/amerikanischen Kapitalgesellschaft)
B: Thank you. That's very kind of you to say so.

* **By the way, I must congratulate you on your new job.**
(by the way – übrigens)

* **Congratulations on winning the IBM contract.**
(win contract – Auftrag erhalten)

* **A: That was a super performance. Congratulations!**
(performance – Leistung)
B: Thank you.

* **A: I passed my driving test.**
(Ich habe meine Fahrprüfung bestanden.)
B: That's great. Congratulations!
(great – super, toll)
A: Thank you.

* **That's really good news. Well done!**
  (Das ist wirklich eine gute Nachricht. Gratuliere! | Gut gemacht! | Bravo! | Sehr gut! | Super!)

* **A: Well done, Betty!**
  B: Thanks.

* **A: I haven't had time to congratulate you yet. Well done!**
  B: Thanks. Although I was quite lucky.
  A: Well, fortune favours the brave.
  (Glück hat nur der Tüchtige.)

——— ❖ ———

* **A: Happy birthday!**
  (Alles Gute zum Geburtstag.)
  B: Thanks.

* **A: Many happy returns of the day!**
  (Alles Gute zum Geburtstag.)
  B: Thank you.

* **A: I'd like to wish you many happy returns of the day, Barbara.**
  B: Oh, thank you very much.

* **A: I'd like to wish you a happy birthday.**
  B: Thank you. That's very kind of you.

* **A: Hello Bill. Many happy returns!**
  B: Oh, thank you. How did you know?
  A: Ah, a little bird told me.
  (Jemand hat es mir geflüstert.)

——— ❖ ———

* **I hope you get better soon.**
  (Ich hoffe, daß es Ihnen bald besser geht. | Ich wünsche Ihnen baldige Besserung.)

* **I do hope you get well soon.**
  (Ich hoffe sehr, daß Sie bald gesund werden. | Ich wünsche Ihnen baldige Genesung.)

* **Have fun!**
  (Viel Vergnügen!)

* **A: Enjoy yourself!**
(Viel Spaß!)
B: Thanks. I'm sure I will.

* **A: Have a good time!**
(Viel Vergnügen!)
B: Thanks, Andrew. You too!

* **A: Have a good weekend!**
(Schönes Wochenende!)
B: Thank you. The same to you!

* **A: Have a nice day!**
B: Thanks. You too!

* **Have a good trip, Peter! I hope everything goes well.**
(Gute Reise, Peter! … .)

* **I hope you have a nice holiday.**

* **A: Well, I do hope you have a nice journey.**
B: Thank you very much.

* **I wish you a pleasant journey.**
(Ich wünsche Ihnen eine angenehme Reise.)

* **A: All the best, Mr. Bail!**
B: Thank you. I'll see you next year sometime.
(sometime – irgendwann einmal)

* **A: All the very best!**
B: Thank you.

* **All the best, Keith! And give my best wishes to your mother.**

* **I wish you all the best for the future.**
(future – Zukunft)

* **A: Good luck!**
(Viel Glück!)
B: Thanks.

* **A: Best of luck with the IBM deal!**
(deal – Geschäft)
B: Thank you very much.

* **A: I'd like to wish you every success in your new company.**
(success – Erfolg / company – Firma)
B: Thank you very much. It'll be a challenge, anyway.
(challenge – Herausforderung / anyway – ohnehin)

SEASON'S GREETINGS

Weihnachts- und Neujahrswünsche

* A: Merry Christmas!
  B: Merry Christmas!

* A: A merry Christmas to you, Mr. Brown!
  B: A merry Christmas to you too!

* A: Merry Christmas to you, Miss Bell!
  B: And to you too!

* A: Have a good Christmas!
  B: Thank you. Same to you!

* A: Happy Christmas!
  B: Thanks, the same to you!

* A: A merry Christmas and a happy New Year!
  B: Thank you. And the same to you!

* A: A happy New Year to you!
  B: Thank you. And a happy New Year to you too!

* A: Happy New Year!
  B: Thank you very much. You too!

* A: A very happy New Year!
  B: Thanks. And you, too!

SYMPATHY, REGRETS AND CONSOLATION, CONDOLENCES

Mitgefühl, Bedauern und Beileid

* **A: What's wrong?**
(Ist etwas nicht in Ordnung? | Fehlt Ihnen etwas?)
B: Oh, it's nothing really.

* **A: What's the matter?**
(Was ist los mit dir?)
B: I'm just not feeling too well.
(Nichts Besonderes, ich fühl' mich nur nicht ganz gut.)

* **You don't look too well. What's the matter?**
(look well – gesund aussehen)

* **A: I can't stay long I'm afraid.**
(Ich kann leider nicht lange bleiben.)
B: Oh, what a pity!
(Das ist aber schade!)

* **A: I have to leave tomorrow.**
(leave – wegfahren)
B: Oh, what a shame!
(Das ist aber wirklich schade!)

* **A: My wife and I would like to invite you for a meal on Saturday. Can you come?**
(invite sbdy. for a meal – jemanden zum Essen einladen)
B: What a pity! I don't think I can. We've got some friends staying all weekend.
(all weekend – das ganze Wochenende)

* **A: I'm going back to Canada on Sunday.**
B: Sunday? Oh, that's a shame.
(that's a shame – das ist schade)

* **It really is a shame that you didn't get the job.**

* **It's a great pity that you can only stay two days.**
  (Es ist sehr schade, daß … .)

* **A: I missed the bus, so I was late for the interview.**
  (miss – versäumen)
  B: How annoying! That was too bad, wasn't it?
  (how annoying – wie ärgerlich)

* **A: John's mother died in that air crash last week.**
  (air crash – Flugzeugabsturz)
  B: How terrible!
  (Furchtbar!)

* **Craig, I was so sorry to hear about your wife. How is she?**
  (how is she – wie geht es ihr)

* **A: I'm afraid she's broken both her legs.**
  (I'm afraid – leider)
  B: Oh no, how awful! I am sorry. Is there anything you'd like me to do?
  (awful – furchtbar, schrecklich)

* **A: I've lost my wallet somewhere. It's got over £300 in it.**
  (wallet – Brieftasche / somewhere – irgendwo)
  B: Oh, I'm very sorry to hear that. Do you remember when you had it last?
  (last – zuletzt; das letzte Mal)

* **A: The bad news is I lost my job.**
  B: Oh dear, I'm sorry to hear that. What a terrible situation for you.

* **I feel sorry for you, Paul. That's a terrible blow.**
  (blow – Schlag)

* **That's really a shame. They shouldn't have done that to you.**
  (shame – Schande)

* **No, this can't be true! They can't have fired you after 20 years.**
  (fire – feuern, hinauswerfen, entlassen)

* **I'm awfully sorry to hear that your wife is in hospital. Is there anything I can do?**

* **A: We've broken off our engagement.**
(break off engagement – Verlobung lösen)
B: Oh dear, I am sorry. That's too bad.

* **I really sympathise with you.**
(Ich kann mir gut vorstellen, wie Sie sich fühlen.)

——— ❖ ———

* **A: I need the draft contract, but I can't find it.**
(draft contract – Vertragsentwurf)
B: Don't worry. I'll find it for you.
(don't worry – reg dich nicht auf)

* **A: I'm sure I'm going to fail my exam.**
(Ich bin sicher, daß ich bei der Prüfung durchfallen werde.)
B: There's nothing to worry about. Your German seems very good to me.
(Du brauchst dich doch nicht zu ängstigen. .... /seem – scheinen)

* **Don't worry, there's plenty of time.**
(Keine Angst, es ist noch genug Zeit.)

* **A: I'm afraid I've made a mess of your desk.**
(Tut mir leid, ich habe Ihren Schreibtisch in Unordnung gebracht.)
B: Oh, that doesn't matter.
(Das macht doch nichts!)

* **A: Oh dear, I've forgotten my umbrella.**
(umbrella – Regenschirm)
B: Well, never mind. I don't suppose it will rain.
(never mind – das macht nichts / suppose – annehmen)

* **A: I didn't manage to get a ticket.**
(manage – es schaffen)
B: Oh, bad luck!
(So ein Pech! / Pech gehabt!)

* A: **There was so much traffic that we didn't get back till after midnight.**
(Der Verkehr war so stark, daß wir erst nach Mitternacht heimgekommen sind.)
B: **Well, it could have been worse. At least you got home safely.**
(Nun, es hätte schlimmer sein können. Wenigstens sind Sie sicher nach Hause gekommen.)

* **Hard luck, Tom!**
(So ein Pech, Tom!)

* **How silly of me to leave my brief-case on the bus!**
(leave – liegenlassen / brief-case – Aktenkoffer)

——— ❖ ———

* **Sorry to hear that your father has died, Mr. Redford. I'd like to express my heartfelt sympathy.**
(.... Ich möchte Ihnen mein aufrichtiges Beileid ausdrücken.)

* **My heartfelt sympathy, Mr. Ryan.**

* **I really don't know what to say, but I know how you must feel.**

EXCLAMATIONS

Ausrufe

* **What a nuisance! I've lost a button off my coat.**
(Wie ärgerlich! Ich habe einen Knopf von meinem Mantel verloren.)

* **A: What's the name of that pub where we're supposed to be meeting Joseph?**
(... , wo wir Joseph treffen sollen?)
B: For heaven's sake, I've told you three times already. It's the Red Lion.
(for heaven's sake – du meine Güte; das darf doch nicht wahr sein)

* **Oh my god, you don't mean to say they're not going to be able to pay, do you?**
(... , du willst doch damit nicht sagen, daß sie nicht zahlen können, oder?)

* **Oh my goodness, it's two o'clock already! It'll be a tough job meeting the deadline.**
(oh my goodness – du meine Güte / Es wird sehr schwer werden, den Termin einzuhalten.)

* **For Christ's sake, Tom, can't you just stop talking for one minute? I can't hear a word Nigel's saying.**
(for Christ's sake – verdammt noch mal)

* **ATG is up for sale again. Just imagine! They were taken over by STF just two months ago.**
(ATG wird schon wieder zum Verkauf angeboten. Stellen Sie sich das nur vor! Die Gesellschaft wurde erst vor zwei Monaten von STF übernommen.)

* **Goodness me, what's happening out there? There's a hell of a noise!**
(Du meine Güte, was ist da draußen los? Das ist aber ein fürchterlicher Lärm.)

* A: **Steven's been promoted to department head.**
(Steven ist zum Abteilungsleiter befördert worden.)
B: **Well I never! I thought that position was reserved for Rachel.**
(Nein, so was! … .)

* **Fancy meeting you here of all people. I thought you'd gone to live in Sweden.**
(Na so was, daß ich gerade dich hier treffe! … .)

* **Fancy meeting you here of all places. I didn't know you liked jazz.**
(Na so was, daß ich dich gerade hier treffe! … .)

* A: **Ronnie said AFK were going to place another order with us.**
(place another order with sbdy. – jemandem einen weiteren Auftrag erteilen)
B: **My foot! They went bust last week!**
(Quatsch! … ./go bust – pleite gehen)

* **Good heavens! Have you seen the latest news? Interest rates are going up by another 1/2%.**
(Du lieber Himmel! Hast du die letzten Nachrichten gesehen?/ interest rate – Zinssatz)

* **Damn! I can't find that customer file anywhere!**
(Verflixt! Ich kann diesen Kundenordner nirgends finden.)

* **What the hell did he think he was doing? He's ruined everything now.**
(Was zum Teufel hat er sich denn dabei gedacht? … .)

* A: **We lost another order to Finland last week.**
B: **Oh dear! That's the second in three weeks, isn't it?**
(Du meine Güte!/isn't it? – nicht?)

* A: **Did you know Jack Trilby's having a retirement party next Thursday?**
(retirement – Pensionierung)
B: **Good gracious! Is he 65 already?**
(Na so was! … ?)

LANGUAGE PROBLEMS

Sprachliche Probleme

* **Excuse me, how do you pronounce this word?**
(pronounce – aussprechen)

* **[...] – is that the right pronunciation?**
(pronunciation – Aussprache)

* **That's very difficult to pronounce.**

* **That's a real tongue-twister.**
(tongue-twister – Zungenbrecher)

* **Will you correct me if I pronounce something wrongly, please?**
(Würden Sie mich bitte korrigieren, wenn ... .)

——— ❖ ———

* **How do you spell 'accommodation'?**
(spell – buchstabieren, schreiben / accommodation – Unterkunft, Unterbringung)

* **How do you spell it, please?**

* **Could you spell that word, please?**

* **I'm not sure if I've spelt this name correctly. Can you check it for me, please?**
(check – überprüfen)

* **Do you spell 'transferred' with one or two r's?**
(transfer – übertragen, überweisen)

* **Do the Americans spell this word in the same way as the British?**

* **Is this the right spelling of 'separate'?**
(spelling – Schreibweise, Rechtschreibung / separate – separat, getrennt)

——— ❖ ———

* **Can I use 'Hello' when I meet someone for the first time?**
  (meet – treffen, begegnen)

* **What should I say if I want to attract someone's attention?**
  (attract attention – Aufmerksamkeit erregen)

* **In German, when friends drink together, we say 'Prost!'. How would you say that in English?**

* **What would you say for this in English?**

* **What is that in English?**

* **What do you call that in English?**
  (Wie heißt das auf englisch?)

——— ❖ ———

* **Is it correct to say, 'I have been waiting for one hour'?**
  (… , ‚Ich warte schon seit einer Stunde'?)

* **Is this sentence correct?**

* **Is that the right word?**

* **I'm trying to find the right word, perhaps you can help me?**

* **What is the plural of 'crisis'?**
  (plural – Mehrzahl)

* **What is the singular of 'media'?**
  (singular – Einzahl / media – Medien)

* **Which is correct: 'at a low price' or 'on a low price'?**

* **Can I say, 'The current account is in the red'?**
  (current account – Leistungsbilanz / in the red – in den roten Zahlen; in der Verlustzone; passiv)

* **Will you tell me if I make a mistake, please?**
  (Würden Sie mir bitte sagen, wenn … .)

* **When do you use 'economical'? Can you give me an example?**
  (economical – wirtschaftlich, sparsam / example – Beispiel)

❖

* **Could you speak a bit more slowly?**
(a bit – ein bißchen; ein wenig)

* **Could you possibly speak a little more slowly?**
(a little – ein bißchen; ein wenig)

* **Could you speak a little louder, please?**

* **I wonder if you could speak up a little?**
(Könnten Sie etwas lauter sprechen?)

* **Please don't speak so fast, I can't follow you.**
(fast – schnell / follow – folgen)

❖

* **If we don't meet these deadlines, our customers will lose faith in us. Do you see what I mean?**
(meet deadline – Termin einhalten / customer – Kunde / faith – Vertrauen / see – verstehen)

* **Do you know what I mean?**

* **If there's anything you haven't understood, please say so.**

❖

* **I'm not sure I understand. Does that mean you've lost your job?**
(mean – heißen, bedeuten)

* **Does that mean 'no'?**

* **Do you mean you can't come tomorrow evening?**

* **If I understand you correctly, you think we need to do a market survey first.**
(market survey – Marktstudie, Markterhebung, Marktuntersuchung)

❖

* **Sorry, but I didn't catch the last word.**
(catch – verstehen)

* **I'm sorry, I didn't hear what you said.**

* **I'm sorry, I'm not with you.**
  (… , ich kann Ihnen nicht folgen.)

* **A: I'm sorry, what did you say?**
  B: I said, could - you - turn - the - music - down.
  (turn down - leiser stellen)

* **What was his name again please?**
  (Wie war noch eben sein Name, bitte?)

* **What was that again? I didn't quite catch what you said.**
  (Was war das eben? Ich habe nicht ganz verstanden, was Sie gesagt haben.)

* **Could you repeat what you just said, please?**
  (repeat - wiederholen / just - gerade)

* **Would you please repeat that last remark?**
  (remark - Bemerkung)

* **Sorry, can you say that again, please?**

* **Would you mind repeating your last point, please?**
  (Würden Sie bitte so freundlich sein und den letzten Punkt wiederholen.)

* **A: Strictly speaking, you can't say that.**
  (Strenggenommen … .)
  B: Pardon?
  (Wie bitte?)

——— ❖ ———

* **Could you explain it in simple terms?**
  (explain - erklären / in simple terms - mit einfachen Worten)

* **Excuse me, could you explain that in more detail?**
  (in more detail - detaillierter)

* **Would you please elaborate on that?**
  (Würden Sie das bitte näher ausführen?)

——— ❖ ———

* **A: What exactly do you mean by 'turnover' in this context?**
  (mean by – meinen mit / turnover – Fluktuation / context – Zusammenhang)
  B: Well, it refers to the employees of our firm. It's a ratio which shows the percentage of people leaving the firm.
  (refer to – sich beziehen auf / employee – Arbeitnehmer, Mitarbeiter / ratio – Verhältniszahl, Kennzahl / percentage – Prozentsatz / leave – ausscheiden aus)

* **I'm sorry ... I don't quite understand what you mean by irresponsible.**
  (irresponsible – unverantwortlich, verantwortungslos)

* **What does 'factoring' mean?**
  (mean – bedeuten)

* **A: What is the exact meaning of this word?**
  (exact meaning – genaue Bedeutung)
  B: Sorry, I don't know that word.

* **What's the meaning of 'clean floating'?**
  (clean floating – sauberes Floaten der Wechselkurse)

* **I don't understand this expression. Can you help me?**
  (expression – Ausdruck)

* **What is the opposite of 'polite'?**
  (opposite – Gegenteil / polite – höflich)

* **What is another word for 'exposure'?**
  (exposure – Risikoposition)

* **What other words are there for 'depreciation-prone'?**
  (depreciation-prone – abwertungsanfällig, abwertungsverdächtig, abwertungsbedroht)

* **What is another way of saying 'prices sky-rocket'?**
  (way – Möglichkeit, Art, Weise / sky-rocket – stark in die Höhe schnellen)

* **Do 'drop' and 'decline' mean the same thing?**
  (drop – fallen, zurückgehen / decline – fallen, zurückgehen)

* **What's the difference between 'franchising' and 'licensing'?**
  (difference – Unterschied / licensing – Lizenzvergabe)

* **Is there a difference in meaning between 'force majeure' and 'act of god'?**
  (force majeure – höhere Gewalt / act of god – Naturereignis)

* **A: What is the word for people who always think that they are ill?**
  B: Oh, it's on the tip of my tongue – hypochondriacs, that's it.
  (it's on the tip of my tongue – es liegt mir auf der Zunge / hypochondriac – Hypochonder)

* **Is there an English word to describe the fact that unit costs come down the more you produce?**
  (describe – bezeichnen / unit costs – Stückkosten / come down – zurückgehen, abnehmen)

* **What do you call someone who makes out a bill of exchange?**
  (Wie bezeichnet man jemanden, der einen Wechsel ausstellt?)

* **A: What do you call a cheque which cannot be cashed over the bank counter, but must be paid into an account?**
  (cash cheque – Scheck einlösen / bank counter – Bankschalter / account – Konto)
  B: Um, let me think – it's called a crossed cheque.
  (crossed cheque – gekreuzter Scheck; Verrechnungsscheck)

* **When would you use the word 'underwriting'?**
  (underwriting – Emissionsgarantie)

* **When would you use the expression 'once bitten, twice shy'?**
  (once bitten, twice shy – ein gebranntes Kind scheut das Feuer)

* **Does 'turnover' have more than one meaning?**
  (turnover – Umschlagshäufigkeit, Umsatz, Fluktuation)

* **A: I'm sorry, but I don't quite see what you mean.**
  (see – verstehen)
  B: What I mean is, we can't offer you more than our normal 10% discount on the list price.
  (offer – anbieten / discount – Rabatt / list price – Listenpreis)

* **What does this abbreviation stand for?**
(abbreviation - Abkürzung)

* **Could you translate that word into German?**
(translate - übersetzen)

—— ❖ ——

* **Could you put it in a different way?**
(Könnten Sie es anders ausdrücken?)

* **Would you mind putting that in different words?**
(Würde es Ihnen etwas ausmachen, das mit anderen Worten auszudrücken?)

* **To put it another way: it's too expensive.**
(expensive - teuer)

—— ❖ ——

* **Your German is very good. Where did you learn it?**

* **That goes without saying.**
(Das versteht sich von selbst. | Das ist doch selbstverständlich.)

* **I can't make head or tail of it.**
(Ich werde daraus überhaupt nicht klug.)

* **You're telling me.**
(Wem sagen Sie das.)

* **You must be joking!**
(Das können Sie doch wohl nicht ernst meinen.)

JOKES

Witze

* **Have you heard any good jokes recently?**
  (joke – Witz / recently – in der letzten Zeit)

* **Do you know any good jokes?**

* **A: Have you heard the one about ... ?**
  B: No, go on.
  (Nein, erzähl weiter! I erzähl schon!)

* **While we're on the subject of animals, do you know the one about the little monkey?**
  (Da wir gerade über Tiere sprechen, kennen Sie den über den kleinen Affen schon?)

* **Let me tell you a good joke I heard the other day.**
  (the other day – neulich)

* **In Austria we make fun of the people from Burgenland in the east of Austria – a bit like you with the Irish!**
  (make fun of sbdy. – sich über jemanden lustig machen)

* **I know a good one. There was this man ... .**

* **I like that one.**

* **I know a similar joke, but it's actually a dirty one.**
  (dirty – unanständig)

* **I can never remember the best jokes.**

* **I'm sorry, I didn't catch the punch line.**
  (... , ich habe die Pointe nicht verstanden.)

MY FAMILY

Meine Familie

* **A: Do you have a family?**
B: Yes, I'm married and have two boys and one girl.

* **Have you got a family?**

* **A: Do you come from a big family?**
B: Yes, as a matter of fact, I've got two elder brothers and two younger sisters.

* **A: Have you any brothers and sisters?**
B: No, I'm an only child.
(only child – Einzelkind)

* **A: Are your parents still alive?**
(Leben Ihre Eltern noch?)
B: My mother is, but unfortunately my father died three years ago.
(unfortunately – leider)

* **A: Both my parents have been dead for a long time.**
(Meine Eltern sind beide schon seit langem tot.)
B: Oh, I'm sorry to hear that.

* **A: So I see you're married.**
B: Yes, I've been married for ten years now.
(Ja, ich bin nun schon seit zehn Jahren verheiratet.)

* **A: Are you married?**
B: No, but I'll be getting married next year – I'm engaged.
(get married – heiraten / engaged – verlobt)

* **I'm still single.**
(Ich bin noch immer ledig.)

* **I used to be married, but now I'm divorced.**
(Ich war früher einmal verheiratet, aber nun bin ich geschieden.)

* **I got married two years ago.**

* **A: What does your wife do, Brian?**
  (do – [beruflich] machen)
  B: She's a journalist.

* **She's a teacher.**

* **She's a full-time mother.**

* **A: What does your husband do, Betty?**
  B: He works for IBM.

* **A: Do you have any children?**
  B: No, but we would like to have some.

* **A: How old are your children?**
  B: My eldest is 21 and my youngest is 12.

* **A: Do your children still live at home?**
  B: Oh yes, they are still at school.

* **My daughter has just started university.**

* **A: Are your children still living at home?**
  B: No, not any more – my son is doing his military service and my daughters are married and have their own families.
  (do military service – Militärdienst ableisten)

* **Did you bring any of your family over with you?**
  (Haben Sie wen von Ihrer Familie mitgebracht?)

* **A: Have you got any pets, Bill?**
  (pet – Haustier)
  B: Yes, I've got a dog.

* **We used to have a dog, but it was too much of a bind when we wanted to go away.**
  (it was too much of a bind – wir waren zu sehr gebunden)

* **We've got a couple of cats.**
  (Wir haben ein paar Katzen.)

* **My sons have got a hamster, a guinea-pig and a rabbit.**
  (guinea-pig – Meerschweinchen)

* **My daughter has a pony.**
* **I keep tropical fish actually.**
* **Is it right that most people have a dog over here?**

WEATHER

Wetter

* **A: What's the weather like today?**
  (Wie ist das Wetter heute?)
  B: The sun is shining.

* **It's raining.**

* **It looks like rain.**
  (Es schaut nach Regen aus.)

* **It's cold, wet and very stormy.**
  (wet – naß / stormy – stürmisch)

* **It's drizzling.**
  (drizzle – nieseln)

* **It's coming down in buckets.**
  (Es gießt in Strömen.)

* **It's pouring.**
  (Es gießt in Strömen.)

* **It's snowing heavily.**
  (Es schneit stark.)

* **It's freezing.**
  (freeze – eiskalt sein)

* **The sky is overcast, and it is very sultry.**
  (overcast – bedeckt / sultry – schwül)

* **It's very close. I think there's going to be a thunderstorm this afternoon.**
  (close – schwül / there's going to be – es wird geben / thunderstorm – Gewitter)

* **The sky is clear, not a cloud in sight.**
  (cloud – Wolke / in sight – in Sicht; zu sehen)

* **It is snowing, but I'm sure it'll stop soon.**

* **It seems to be clearing up.**
(seem – scheinen / clear up – aufhellen, aufklaren)

* **It's a miserable day today.**

* **The sun is scorching. It's too hot to walk.**
(scorch – herunterbrennen)

* **It's bitterly cold.**

* **It's not as cold as I imagined it'd be.**
(imagine – sich etwas vorstellen)

* **Do you think the weather will stay like this?**
(stay like this – so bleiben)

* **A: What is the temperature today?**
B: It is 20 degrees centigrade.
(20 degrees centigrade – 20° Celsius)

* **It is minus twenty.**
(Wir haben 20° unter Null.)

* **A: What's the weather going to be like today?**
(Wie wird das Wetter heute?)
B: I think it's going to be fine.
(Ich glaube, es wird schön.)

* **What's the weather forecast for today?**
(weather forecast – Wetterprognose, Wettervorhersage)

* **It's going to stay fine.**
(Es bleibt schön.)

* **It's going to get colder.**
(Es wird kälter.)

* **I think we're going to have a fine day.**

* **It's going to be mainly cloudy with rainy spells.**
  (mainly cloudy with rainy spells – vorwiegend bewölkt mit vereinzelten Regenschauern)

* **There will be heavy showers in the afternoon.**
  (heavy showers – starke Schauer)

* **D'you think it'll rain?**

* **Is the fog going to lift?**
  (Wird sich der Nebel lichten?)

* **I don't think the weather is going to be very good.**

* **A: What is the weather forecast for tomorrow?**
  B: Very hazy and humid with scattered showers.
  (hazy – dunstig, diesig / humid – feucht / scattered showers – vereinzelte Regenschauer)

* **Mainly cloudy with sunny spells in the afternoon.**
  (sunny spells – einige sonnige Aufhellungen)

* **Light rain showers during the night, mostly cloudy sky in the early morning hours but sunny in the afternoon.**

* **The weathermen think that it is going to be bright and sunny tomorrow.**
  (weatherman – Wetterprophet, Meteorologe / bright – heiter)

* **Have you heard the weather forecast yet?**
  (yet – schon)

* **According to the weather forecast, it's going to get even hotter.**
  (according to – laut / get even hotter – noch heißer werden)

* **A: What does the weather report say?**
  (weather report – Wetterbericht)
  B: It doesn't look very promising.
  (promising – vielversprechend)

* **There is going to be a change in the weather.**
  (change in the weather – Wetterveränderung, Wetterumschwung)

* **We are in for changeable weather.**
  (Es ist unbeständiges Wetter zu erwarten.)

* **We are in for a spell of fine weather.**
  (spell of fine weather – Schönwetterperiode)

* **There'll be a heatwave.**
  (heatwave – Hitzewelle)

* **Drive slowly; the weather forecast says there will be patches of fog on the M4.**
  (drive – fahren / patches of fog – Nebelschwaden / M4 – Autobahnbezeichnung)

* **A: Do you think the weather will remain stable?**
  (remain – bleiben / stable – beständig)
  B: No, it looks very unsettled.
  (unsettled – unbeständig)

* **A: Looks a bit like rain, don't you think?**
  B: I think it may hold off.
  (hold off – aushalten)

* **What are the road conditions like?**
  (Wie ist der Straßenzustand?)

* **The roads are icy.**
  (icy – vereist)

* **A: What was the weather like when you were on holiday?**
  (holiday – Urlaub)
  B: We had a week of brilliant sunshine and yet not too hot.
  (brilliant sunshine – strahlender Sonnenschein / yet – trotzdem)

* **We had terrible weather every day.**
  (terrible – schrecklich, furchtbar, fürchterlich)

* **It rained all the time we were in Paris.**

* **The weather in California was splendid, just fantastic.**
  (splendid – prachtvoll, prächtig, herrlich)

* **A: How was the weather in Spain?**
  B: Well, not too good actually, we had quite a lot of rain.
  (quite a lot of – ziemlich viel)

* **It's raining all the time. I'll have to buy an umbrella or a raincoat.**
  (umbrella – Schirm / raincoat – Regenmantel)

* **It's not unusual for the temperature to remain below zero for weeks on end.**
  (unusual – ungewöhnlich / on end – ohne Unterbrechung)

* **I think the rain's over.**
  (over – vorbei, vorüber)

* **The wind has changed.**
  (Der Wind hat gedreht.)

* **The wind has dropped.**
  (Der Wind hat sich gelegt.)

* **The barometer's rising.**

* **I wish the weather was better.**

* **The weather can only get better.**

* **The weather is bound to get better soon.**
  (Das Wetter muß einfach bald besser werden.)

* **It's too wet to go on foot.**

* **We can't go out in this weather.**
  (Wir können bei diesem Wetter nicht hinausgehen.)

* **We'll go out in all weathers.**
  (in all weathers – bei jeder Witterung)

* **It's too chilly to sit outside.**
  (chilly – kühl, frostig)

* **I hope the weather will stay fine over the weekend. I want to go for a hike on the moors.**
(.... Ich will eine Wanderung auf dem Hochmoor machen.)

* **The weather looks pretty awful, John. Bet we have some rain before long.**
(pretty awful – ziemlich schlecht / bet – wetten / before long – bald)

* **Just look at that rain! The weather's terrible. I wish I was in Greece now.**
(Greece – Griechenland)

* **A: When does the tide come in?**
(Wann kommt die Flut? | Wann ist Flut?)
B: It is in at ten in the morning and at eight in the evening.

* **A: Does it rain a lot here at this time of year?**
B: No, not really. But we have had an exceptionally wet summer so far.
(exceptional – ungewöhnlich, außergewöhnlich / so far – bisher)

* **A: Is it always this windy here?**
B: Yes, there is usually a wind from the west.

* **There is always a breeze here. So it never gets really hot and sweltering.**
(breeze – Brise / sweltering – schwül)

* **A: Do you get any snow here in winter?**
B: Not down here in the valley. But there is snow up in the mountains. Not enough for skiing though.
(valley – Tal / though – aber)

* **You should go to Austria. We usually have plenty of snow there.**
(plenty of snow – sehr viel Schnee)

* **A: What kind of climate does your country have?**
B: Fairly mild, on the whole.
(fairly – ziemlich / on the whole – im großen und ganzen)

* **In Austria we have got what I suppose is called 'continental climate'. Fairly hot summers and quite cold winters with lots of snow.**
(suppose – vermuten / climate – Klima / quite – ziemlich)

* **It's pretty cold in your country in the winter, I suppose.**

* **We haven't had much luck with the weather so far.**

* **That hailstorm is said to have destroyed most of the crops.**
(Dieses Hagelgewitter soll angeblich den Großteil der Ernte zerstört haben.)

* **I wouldn't shelter under the tree. You might get struck by lightning.**
(shelter – sich unterstellen; Schutz suchen / get struck by lightning – von einem Blitz getroffen werden)

* **The snow seems to be turning into sleet.**
(Der Schnee scheint in Eisregen überzugehen.)

* **Don't drive so fast, the road looks pretty slippery.**
(slippery – rutschig)

* **The weather's driving me up the wall.**
(Das Wetter macht mich ganz verrückt.)

* **What awful weather!**
(awful – scheußlich)

* **What a lovely breeze!**
(lovely – angenehm, herrlich)

* **Nice and bright this morning, isn't it?**
(isn't it? – nicht wahr?)

* **It's a real scorcher today, isn't it?**
(scorcher – sehr heißer Tag)

* **It was pretty cold this morning, wasn't it?**
(wasn't it? – nicht wahr?)

* **What a dreadful day, isn't it?**
(Schrecklicher Tag heute, nicht wahr?)

* **It's getting cold, isn't it?**

* **A: Isn't it a lovely day?**
B: Yes, we're having beautiful weather.

* **A: Fairly mild for the time of year, isn't it?**
B: Yes. Quite different from the forecast.

* **A: Looks as if it's going to rain, doesn't it?**
(Es schaut so aus, als ob es regnen wird, nicht wahr?)
B: Yes, I'm afraid so.
(Ja, ich fürchte schon.)

* **A: What d'you think of this weather?**
B: It's very nice, isn't it?

POLITICS

Politik

(see also "The Austrian Economy")

POLITICAL SYSTEM

Politisches System

* A: **Austria is certainly less centralised than Great Britain. We have a number of federal states, called "Bundesländer".**
(certainly – sicher / number – Anzahl / federal state – Bundesland)
B: **That's similar to the German system, isn't it?**
(similar – ähnlich / isn't it? – nicht wahr?)
A: **Yes, only that in Germany the "Länder" are even more independent.**
(even – noch / independent – unabhängig, selbständig)

* **We also have a president, who is elected by popular vote.**
(. . . , der direkt vom Volk gewählt wird.)

* **No, he is not elected for life. His term of office is six years.**
(term of office – Amtszeit)

* **In theory, the president's powers are quite far-reaching. In practice, he is a mere figure-head, in fact not unlike your Queen.**
(power – Befugnis / quite – ziemlich / mere – bloß / be a figure-head – repräsentative Rolle spielen / unlike – unähnlich)

* **No, no, our president is much less powerful than, let's say, his American counterpart.**
(be powerful – Macht haben / counterpart – Pendent, Gegenstück)

* **You may not know that our election system is based on proportional representation. One constituency returns more than one member of parliament.**
(be based on – basieren auf / proportional representation – Verhältniswahlrecht / constituency – Wahlkreis / return – in das Parlament entsenden / member of parliament – Abgeordneter, Volksvertreter)

* **You seem to have a completely different system here in Britain. It's based on some kind of all-or-nothing principle, isn't it?**
(seem – scheinen / different – anders, verschieden / isn't it? – nicht wahr?)

* **In our system absolute majorities are much more difficult to achieve than here in Great Britain. That's probably why coalitions between parties are much more common in Austria.**
(majority – Mehrheit / achieve – erreichen / probably – wahrscheinlich / common – üblich)

* **Yes, we do have a second chamber, called the "Federal Council". It represents the federal element in our constitution, not unlike the US Senate. It's less powerful though, and the members are not elected by popular vote.**
(Doch, wir haben eine zweite Kammer, die sich Bundesrat nennt. Sie repräsentiert das föderative Element in unserer Verfassung, nicht ganz unähnlich dem US-Senat, obwohl sie weniger Macht hat und die Mitglieder nicht direkt vom Volk gewählt werden.)

* **No, there isn't much grass-roots democracy in Austria.**
(grass-roots – Basis...)

* A: **Apart from government and parliament, the so-called "social partners" have to be reckoned with.**
(apart from – abgesehen von / reckon – rechnen)
B: **I've heard of this system. Sounds interesting. But how does it work?**
(sound – klingen / work – funktionieren)
A: **Well, it's rather complicated. Basically it means that a lot of the political decisions are not taken by the government but by bodies composed of representatives of employers, employees, and farmers.**
(rather – ziemlich / basically – im wesentlichen / a lot of – eine Menge / decision – Entscheidung / body – Gremium / be composed – zusammengesetzt sein / employer – Arbeitgeber / employee – Arbeitnehmer)

* **I think you could safely say that our political system includes a fairly strong corporatist element.**
(safely – ohne Gefahr der Übertreibung / fairly – ziemlich / corporatist – ständestaatlich)

* **Is it true that you have no written constitution?**

* **Don't you think that the Crown is a bit of an anachronism?**
(Crown – Krone, Monarchie)

—— ❖ ——

* **Unlike you, we don't have a professional army. What we have is a kind of militia system based on general conscription.**
(unlike – im Gegensatz zu / militia – Miliz / general conscription – allgemeine Wehrpflicht)

* **Yes, basically all young men have to do a stint in the army. I think it's eight months at the moment. I was lucky, I didn't have to do military service.**
(basically – im Prinzip / do stint – Zeit abdienen / be lucky – Glück haben)

* **There is an alternative for conscientious objectors though. They may do community service in hospitals and so on instead.**
(conscientious objector – Wehrdienstverweigerer aus Gewissensgründen / though – jedoch / community service – Zivildienst / hospital – Krankenhaus / instead – statt dessen)

PRESENT POLITICAL SITUATION AND ATTITUDES

Gegenwärtige politische Lage und persönliche Einstellung

* **The head of our government is called the "Federal Chancellor". At present the man in charge is Dr. Vranitzky, a Socialist and a former banker.**
(head – Chef / government – Regierung / at present – zur Zeit / man in charge – Mann an der Spitze / former – ehemalig)

* **No, in Austria and in Germany the Chancellor is not the Minister of Finance but the Prime Minister. The terminology is a bit confusing.**
(confusing – verwirrend)

* **The country has been governed by a "Grand Coalition" between the Social Democrats and the Conservatives since 1986.**
(govern – regieren / grand – groß)

* **What's life in post-Thatcher Britain like? Does it make any difference now that she's gone?**
(difference – Unterschied)

* **How did the British people react to your Prime Minister's visit to China?**
(react to – reagieren auf)

* **There always seems to be some scandal or other brewing: it's either somebody bribing government officials or diverting public funds to numbered accounts in Switzerland, or turning a blind eye to smuggling weapons, or just plainly lying to the public.**
(brew – am Kochen sein / either – entweder / bribe – bestechen / official – Beamter / divert – verschieben / public funds – öffentliche Mittel / account – Konto / turn a blind eye to – wegschauen bei / weapon – Waffe / plain – einfach / lie – lügen)

* **Not surprisingly, a lot of people are becoming disaffected with politics.**
(Es kann wohl nicht überraschen, daß sich eine Menge Leute von der Politik abwenden.)

* **I'm not interested in politics. Wouldn't dream of joining a party, for instance.**
(dream – träumen / join – beitreten / for instance – zum Beispiel)

* **I think the present government have done quite a good job, considering the difficult circumstances. So I'm going to vote for them again.**
(do a good job – es gut machen / considering – wenn man bedenkt / difficult circumstances – schwierige Umstände / vote – wählen)

* **Personally I think it's time for a change. The present lot have been in office for too long. I'm all for giving the opposition a chance.**
(change – Wechsel, Änderung / present – jetzig / lot – Gruppe, Crew / office – Amt / all – sehr)

POLITICAL PARTIES
Politische Parteien

* **Our political culture is perhaps less adversarial than yours. Most people seem to prefer some form of co-operation between the two main parties. Although we had government by one party between 1966 and 1983.**
(adversarial – konfliktträchtig / seem – scheinen / prefer – vorziehen / main – wichtigst / although – obwohl)

* **We have four main parties: the Socialists, or rather Social Democrats as they are now called, the Conservatives, the so-called “People’s Party”, the Liberals, and the Greens.**
(rather – genauer)

* **A: The Liberal Party is headed by a popular young politician with nationalist leanings, the well-known Dr. Haider.**
(head – anführen / leaning – Tendenz)
B: Is he the one that attracted international attention by characterising Hitler’s employment policy as “sound”?
(attract attention – Aufmerksamkeit erregen / employment policy – Beschäftigungspolitik / sound – ordentlich)

* **The Greens have a lot of basically sound ideas, but you can’t always take them seriously. They always seem to be quarrelling among themselves.**
(sound – vernünftig / serious – ernst / quarrel – streiten / among – unter)

* **The main reason seems to be the rift between pragmatists and fundamentalists inside the Green party. It’s probably difficult to work with somebody who is radically anti-business and wants to change the present political system.**
(reason – Grund / rift – Riß / anti-business – wirtschaftsfeindlich)

* **Membership of parties is probably more important in Austria than in Great Britain, although its importance has declined a bit recently.**
(probably – wahrscheinlich / important – wichtig / although – obwohl / decline – fallen, zurückgehen / recently – in der letzten Zeit)

* **Yes, the Communists are still around, but they haven't won a seat for I don't know how long and so they aren't represented in parliament.**
(be around – existieren / still – noch / represent – vertreten)

* **I think the number of floating voters will go up.**
(floating voter – Wechselwähler)

* **Who do you normally vote for?**
(vote – wählen)

ELECTIONS
Wahlen

* **A: When are your next elections?**
(elections – Wahlen)
B: I really don't know. The Prime Minister can call an election at any time before next spring, when the five-year term of the present Parliament runs out.
(call an election – wählen lassen / spring – Frühling / term – Legislaturperiode / run out – auslaufen)

* **A: What are the odds of Labour winning the next election?**
(odds – Chancen)
B: If you can believe the polls, Labour's lead has fallen to three per cent. That's not much, considering that there's always a margin of error.
(believe – glauben / poll – Meinungsumfrage / lead – Vorsprung / considering – wenn man bedenkt / margin of error – Fehlerquote)

* **The latest poll gives the Social Democrats an eight per cent lead.**

* **A: Who do you think will be the next Prime Minister? Kinnock?**
B: No, not Kinnock. He hasn't got a chance.
A: Do you really think so?

* **No, there's no chance that Dr. Waldheim will be elected again and create a lot of difficulties for Austria. He's already gone on record that he won't be standing again.**
(go on record – offiziell erklären / won't – will not / stand – sich bewerben)

* **This time round the two main parties may agree on a joint candidate.**
(this time round – dieses Mal / agree – sich einigen / joint – gemeinsam)

* **In the last elections the party took only 35 per cent of the vote and lost three seats. It's expected to perform even worse this year.**
(vote – abgegebene Stimmen / seat – Sitz [z. B. im Parlament] / expect – erwarten / perform even worse – noch schlechter abschneiden)

* **On the whole we have a higher turnout at elections than most other European countries. But the percentage of people willing to go to the polls has been declining steadily.**
(on the whole – insgesamt gesehen / turnout at elections – Wahlbeteiligung / go to the polls – wählen gehen / decline – fallen)

POLITICAL PAST

Politische Vergangenheit

* **I'm not sure whether we have really come to terms with our recent political past.**
(whether – ob / come to terms with – zu Rande kommen mit; bewältigen / recent – jüngst / past – Vergangenheit)

* **Of course we have some skeletons in our cupboard. The way, for instance, we treated Jewish people in the 1930s and during World War II is nothing to write home about.**
(skeleton in cupboard – unbewältigtes Vergangenheitsproblem; Leiche im Keller / way – Art und Weise / treat – behandeln / Jewish - jüdisch / nothing to write home about – kein Ruhmesblatt)

* **It's true, quite a few Austrians welcomed Hitler when he occupied our country in 1938.**
(quite a few – ziemlich viele / occupy – besetzen)

* **The post-war period was very tough. I still remember when we had food-rationing and not enough to eat.**
(post-war period – Nachkriegszeit / tough – hart / remember – sich erinnern / food – Lebensmittel)

* **Yes, you're right. Austria was divided into four "Zones". The British Zone, for instance, covered Carinthia and parts of Styria in the south of Austria.**
(divide – teilen / for instance – zum Beispiel / cover – umfassen)

* **A: Do you remember the signing of the State Treaty?**
B: Not really. I was too young then.
(sign – unterzeichnen / treaty – völkerrechtlicher Vertrag)

INTERNATIONAL ASPECTS

Internationale Aspekte

* **The recent resurgence of nationalism is a bit frightening, isn't it?**
(recent – jüngst / resurgence – Neuaufflammen / frightening – beängstigend / isn't it? – nicht wahr?)

* **One unpleasant side-effect of the refugee problem is that it's working into the hands of right-wing groupings.**
(unpleasant – unangenehm / side-effect – Nebenwirkung / refugee – Flüchtling / right-wing – dem rechten Flügel zuzurechnen)

* **The fighting started without either country declaring war on the other.**
(either country – eines der beiden Länder / declare war – Krieg erklären)

* **I think the two countries are still at war.**
(be at war – im Kriegszustand sein)

* **Terrible what's happening in Yugoslavia, isn't it?**

* **Neither the EC nor the CSCE seems to be able to do much to stop the fighting there.**
(neither ... nor – weder ... noch / EC – European Community | Europäische Gemeinschaft / CSCE – Conference on Security and Cooperation in Europe | KSZE)

* **It is a pity that all attempts at mediation seem to have failed.**
  (it is a pity – es ist schade / attempt – Versuch / mediation – Vermittlung / fail – fehlschlagen)

* **Incredible, but this is the third cease-fire in four weeks.**
  (incredible – unglaublich / cease-fire – Waffenstillstand)

* **How do you see the Irish problem? Seems to be pretty intractable, doesn't it?**
  (pretty – ziemlich / intractable – verfahren / doesn't it? – nicht wahr?)

* **The pace of political change in the former East-bloc countries is breath-taking, isn't it?**
  (pace – Tempo / former – ehemalig / breath-taking – atemberaubend)

* **If you had predicted a couple of years ago that anything like this would happen, nobody would have believed you.**
  (predict – vorhersagen / couple of – paar / believe – glauben)

* **I can't imagine that our neutrality will be an obstacle to entry into the EC. After all Ireland – I mean Eire – is neutral as well, isn't it?**
  (imagine sthg. – sich etwas vorstellen / obstacle – Hindernis / entry – Eintritt / EC – European Community | Europäische Gemeinschaft / after all – schließlich / as well – auch, ebenso / isn't it? – nicht wahr?)

* **Are you in Britain afraid of a larger and more powerful Germany?**
  (be afraid of – sich fürchten vor / powerful – mächtig)

* **Yes, you're right, I think both Britain and Austria have an interest in slowing down the process of political union in the EC.**
  (both ... and – sowohl ... als auch / slow down – verlangsamen / union – Vereinigung)

* **Many Brits don't seem to relish the loss of sovereignty that a closer political union would imply.**
  (Brit – Brite / relish – Geschmack finden an / close – eng / imply – implizieren; mit sich bringen)

HEALTH

Befinden und Gesundheit

GENERAL; MINOR ILLNESSES

Allgemeines Befinden; kleinere Wehwehchen

* **A: How are you?**
(Wie geht es Ihnen?)
B: I'm fine, thanks.
(Mir geht es gut, danke.)

* **Very well, thanks.**
(Sehr gut, danke.)

* **I'm on top of the world.**
(Mir geht es ausgezeichnet. Ich könnte Bäume ausreißen.)

* **A: Hi, how are you feeling today?**
B: I feel a bit under the weather.
(Ich fühl' mich nicht ganz auf der Höhe.)

* **A: You don't look yourself, is anything the matter?**
(Du schaust heute aber gar nicht gut aus, ... ?)
B: As a matter of fact, I've got a splitting headache.
(splitting headache – rasende|stechende Kopfschmerzen)

* **A: How are things?**
(Wie geht's?)
B: I'm feeling completely run down.
(Ich fühl' mich völlig ausgebrannt.)

* **I'm under so much stress at work, I feel pretty lousy.**
(pretty lousy – ziemlich elend)

* **A: What's the matter, Barbara?**
(Was ist los mit dir, ... ?)
B: I'm not feeling very well to be honest.
(Ich fühl' mich nicht sehr wohl, um ehrlich zu sein.)

* **I'm feeling stressed.**

* **A: I'm not feeling myself at all. Do you mind if I call it a day?**
  (Ich bin gesundheitlich überhaupt nicht auf der Höhe. Macht es Ihnen etwas aus, wenn ich für heute Schluß mache?)
  B: Not at all, you go and get a rest.
  (not at all – überhaupt nicht)

* **I think I've got a bad cold coming on.**
  (Ich glaube, bei mir ist eine starke Verkühlung im Anzug.)

* **I've got a temperature. I think I must be going down with the flu.**
  (Ich habe Fieber. Ich glaube, ich habe die Grippe erwischt.)

* **I'm aching all over. I think I must have caught the flu.**
  (Mir tut alles weh. Ich glaube, mich hat die Grippe erwischt.)

* **I've got a cough.**
  (cough – Husten)

* **A: What's the trouble?**
  (Was fehlt Ihnen?)
  B: My back is playing me up again. It aches terribly.
  (Mein Rücken fängt schon wieder an. Er tut fürchterlich weh.)

* **I'm suffering from hay fever.**
  (Ich leide an Heuschnupfen.)

* **My eyes are inflamed.**
  (inflamed – entzündet)

* **I'm allergic to pollen – my eyes and throat are very itchy.**
  (Ich bin allergisch auf Blütenstaub – meine Augen und mein Hals jucken sehr.)

* **My feet are killing me.**
  (kill – umbringen)

* **I'm fit to drop.**
  (Ich krieche bereits auf dem Zahnfleisch daher.)

* **A: I'm absolutely exhausted.**
  (Ich bin völlig erschöpft.)
  B: You need to put your feet up for a while.
  (Sie müssen sich eine Weile ausrasten.)

* **A: What's up, Bill?**
  (Was hast du denn, … ?)
  B: Oh nothing much, I've just got pins and needles in my leg.
  (… , mir ist nur mein Fuß eingeschlafen.)

* **I'm feeling rather faint.**
  (Ich fühle mich ziemlich schwach | matt.)

* **I feel dizzy.**
  (dizzy – schwindlig)

* **I've got a sore throat.**
  (Ich habe Halsweh.)

* **I've got terrible toothache.**

* **I think I must have picked up that virus that's going round.**
  (pick up virus – Virus erwischen)

* **A: I'm having trouble sleeping. I think I'll have to get some sleeping tablets.**
  (Ich schlafe zur Zeit schlecht. Ich glaube, ich muß mir irgendwelche Schlaftabletten besorgen.)
  B: Why don't you try an alternative remedy. Drink a cup of hot milk with some honey in it.
  (remedy – Mittel)

* **I had terrible indigestion all night and I couldn't sleep a wink.**
  (Ich hatte die ganze Nacht fürchterliche Verdauungsstörungen und konnte kein Auge zutun.)

* **I've got an upset stomach – that Chinese food didn't agree with me at all.**
  (Ich habe mir den Magen verdorben – dieses chinesische Essen ist mir überhaupt nicht bekommen.)

* **I feel sick.**
  (Mir ist schlecht.)

* **I've just been sick. I think I'd better go home.**
(Ich habe gerade gebrochen. Ich glaube, ich sollte lieber nach Hause gehen.)

* **I've hurt my leg.**
(hurt – verletzen)

* **I've got stitch.**
(Ich habe Seitenstechen.)

* **My eyes are hurting.**
(Meine Augen tun mir weh.)

* **I've lost my appetite.**
(Ich habe keinen Appetit.)

AT THE CHEMIST'S
In der Apotheke

* **Could you help me, please? I'm trying to find my way to the nearest chemist's.**
(chemist's – Apotheke)

* **Have you got something for a sunburn, please?**
(something for – etwas gegen; ein Mittel gegen / sunburn – Sonnenbrand)

* **Can you give me something for a common cold, please?**
(common cold – Erkältung, Schnupfen)

* **Have you got anything for indigestion?**
(Haben Sie irgend etwas gegen Verdauungsstörungen?)

* **What have you got for headaches?**

* **Do you have anything for the flu?**

* **I'd like something for insect bites, please.**
(insect bite – Insektenstich)

* **Could you recommend something for diarrhoea?**
(recommend – empfehlen / diarrhoea – Durchfall)

* **Could you give me some headache pills, please?**

* **I'd like some pain-killers, please.**
(pain-killer – schmerzstillende Tablette)

* **Do you have homoeopathic medicines here?**
(homoeopathic medicines – homöopathische Mittel)

* **A: What could you give me for a sore throat?**
B: Here, suck one of these lozenges after each meal.
(suck – lutschen / lozenge – Lutschtablette)

* **I need some laxatives, please.**
(laxative – Abführmittel)

* **I've been stung. Do you have any ointment for wasp stings?**
(Mich hat eine Wespe gestochen, haben Sie irgendeine Salbe dagegen?)

* **Do I need a prescription for the medicine?**
(prescription – Rezept)

* **When can I pick it up, please?**
(pick up – abholen)

* **A: How many times a day do I have to take these tablets?**
(how many times – wie oft)
B: Take two three times a day and dissolve them in water.
(dissolve – auflösen)

AT THE DOCTOR'S
Beim Arzt

* **A: I would like to make an appointment, please.**
(make appointment – Termin vereinbaren)
B: Would this afternoon suit you?
(suit – passen)
A: Yes, that would be fine, thank you.

* **I've got acute pains in my chest.**
(Ich habe akute Schmerzen in meiner Brust.)

* **I've got earache.**
  (Ich habe Ohrenweh.)

* **I've got an irritating cough.**
  (Ich habe einen Reizhusten.)

* **I'm suffering from catarrh.**

* **I'm having difficulty breathing.**
  (Ich habe Atembeschwerden.)

* **My glands are swollen.**
  (Meine Drüsen sind geschwollen.)

* **I've had this rash all over my body for two days now.**
  (Ich habe diesen Hautausschlag am ganzen Körper nun schon seit zwei Tagen.)

* **It hurts when I breathe in deeply.**

* **Would you please examine my throat?**
  (examine – anschauen)

* **Should I get undressed?**
  (Soll ich mich ausziehen?)

* **A: Are you being treated at home?**
  (treat – behandeln)
  B: No, I've never had any treatment for it.

* **Do you think it's anything serious?**
  (anything serious – etwas Ernstes)

AT THE DENTIST'S
Beim Zahnarzt

* **I've had terrible toothache for the past three days.**
  (Ich habe schon seit drei Tagen fürchterliche Zahnschmerzen.)

* **It hurts here.**

* **This filling fell out during a meal.**
  (filling – Füllung, Plombe)

* **My crown broke off while I was eating.**
  (crown – Krone / break off – ausbrechen)

* **Will I have to pay for the treatment?**

* **Could you just do a temporary job?**
  (do a temporary job – den Zahn provisorisch behandeln)

* **Before you fill it, could I have an injection, please?**
  (fill – plombieren)

* **May I rinse my mouth out now?**
  (rinse out – ausspülen)

* **A: I'll have to extract it.**
  (extract – ziehen)
  B: Does it really have to come out?

* **How long should I go without eating?**
  (Wie lange darf ich nichts essen?)

* **Do you want to see me again?**
  (Muß ich nochmals kommen?)

EMERGENCIES

Notfälle

LOST PROPERTY

Verlust von Sachen

* A: **Excuse me, I wonder if you could help me. I've lost my wallet.**
(… , vielleicht können Sie mir helfen. Ich habe meine Brieftasche verloren.)
B: **You'll have to inquire at the lost-property office.**
(Sie müssen sich im Fundbüro erkundigen.)

* **I've lost my passport, can you tell me what to do about it?**

* **Have any car keys been handed in by any chance?**
(Sind zufällig irgendwelche Autoschlüssel abgegeben worden?)

* **All my personal effects have been stolen. Could you call the Austrian Embassy, please?**
(personal effects – persönliche Habe / embassy – Botschaft)

* A: **I seem to have mislaid my passport. What can I do?**
(seem – scheinen / mislay – verlegen)
B: **You'll have to report it to the Austrian Consulate.**
(report – melden)

* **I'll need a receipt for my insurance company.**
(receipt – Bestätigung / insurance company – Versicherung, Versicherungsgesellschaft)

* **I'd like to inform you that my credit cards have gone missing.**
(go missing – verlorengehen)

IN HOSPITAL
Im Krankenhaus

* **Nurse, would you get in touch with my family, please. Here's my phone number.**
  (Schwester, verständigen Sie bitte meine Familie. … .)

* **Could you please inform my boss that I'm in hospital.**

* **I'm allergic to plaster and penicillin.**
  (plaster – Gips)

* **Does it have to be X-rayed?**
  (X-ray – röntgen)

* **Do you think a local anaesthetic is sufficient?**
  (Glauben Sie, daß eine örtliche Betäubung ausreicht?)

* **How long will I have to stay here?**
  (stay – bleiben)

* **I'll need a certificate confirming how long I stayed in hospital together with a complete diagnosis.**
  (certificate – Bescheinigung / confirm – bestätigen)

ACCIDENTS
Unfälle

* **Please get a doctor quickly!**
(get – holen)

* **Where is the nearest hospital?**

* **Can you give the kiss of life?**
(kiss of life – Mund-zu-Mund-Beatmung)

* **Do you have a first-aid kit?**
(Haben Sie einen Erste-Hilfe-Koffer?)

* **Call an ambulance!**
(ambulance – Krankenwagen)

* **We need some bandages.**
(bandages – Verbandszeug)

CAR ACCIDENTS
Autounfälle

* **Is anybody hurt?**
(Ist irgend jemand verletzt?)

* **Where's the damage?**
(damage – Schaden)

* **A: Is there any serious damage?**
(serious – ernst)
B: No, it seems to be only slightly damaged.
(Nein, es scheint nur leicht beschädigt zu sein.)

* **You've dented the wing.**
(dent – verbeulen / wing – Kotflügel)

* **It's a write-off.**
(write-off – Wrack)

* **You went through a red light.**

* **You were driving too fast! You were doing 50 in a 30 miles-per-hour limit.**
(limit – Geschwindigkeitsbeschränkung)

* **It was your fault. You didn't observe the right of way.**
(Es war Ihre Schuld. Sie haben den Vorrang nicht beachtet.)

* **It was my right of way.**
(Ich hatte Vorrang.)

* **Could I see your driving-licence?**
(driving-licence – Führerschein)

* **I need particulars of your insurance.**
(particulars – Einzelheiten)

* **We'll have to call the police so that I can claim on my insurance.**
(claim on insurance – einen Anspruch bei einer Versicherung geltend machen)

* **Would you act as a witness, please?**
(witness – Zeuge)

TIME

Zeit und Zeitangaben

APPOINTMENTS

Terminvereinbarungen und Verabredungen

* **A: Hello. Can I make an appointment to see Sandra Henderson, please?**
(make appointment – Termin vereinbaren / see sbdy. – jemanden sprechen)
B: What day would you like to come?
A: Thursday, if possible. Do you think she would be free in the afternoon?

* **I'd like to fix an appointment.**
(fix – vereinbaren)

* **A: I'd need to talk to Mr. Clemence, your Materials Manager. Could you arrange an appointment for me?**
(Ich müßte mit Herrn Clemence, dem Leiter der Materialwirtschaft, sprechen. Könnten Sie einen Termin für mich fixieren?)
B: Yes, would tomorrow three o'clock suit you?
(suit – passen; recht sein)
A: Yes, three o'clock would be perfect. I have another appointment at two just round the corner.
(just round the corner – gleich um die Ecke)

* **Yes, three o'clock would suit me very well.**

* **Couldn't you make it half past three? I've got another appointment at two and I'm not sure how long it will take.**
(take – dauern)

* **A: When would it be convenient for you?**
(be convenient – passen)
B: Well, next Tuesday afternoon would be all right.

* **A: What time does it suit you?**

B: Can we make it quarter past five?
(quarter past five – Viertel nach fünf)
A: Yes, that would be fine by me.

* **A: Would twelve thirty be any good?**
(Würde 12.30 Uhr gehen?)
B: No, that wouldn't do because I have to chair a meeting at our branch at twelve.
(Nein, das würde nicht gehen, weil ich um zwölf eine Sitzung in unserer Zweiganstalt leiten muß.)

* **A: How about Tuesday evening?**
(Wie wär's mit Dienstag abend?)
B: Would it be possible on Friday instead?
(instead – statt dessen)

* **A: Could you manage Tuesday, at about six? Or would you prefer to come a bit later?**
(Geht es Ihnen am Dienstag aus, so um sechs herum? / prefer to come – lieber kommen)
B: No, six o'clock suits me fine.
(suit fine – ausgezeichnet passen)

* **A: I think I could fit you in at around five.**
(fit in – einschieben)
B: I'll just check my diary. Sorry, I've got something scheduled then.
(Ich schau' nur rasch in meinem Terminkalender nach. Leider habe ich zu dieser Zeit schon etwas.)

* **A: Do you think Mr. Thompson would be able to see me this morning?**
B: You'd better see his secretary about an appointment.
(Wegen eines Termins sollten Sie lieber zu seiner Sekretärin gehen.)

* **A: Could you suggest a time for an appointment? Early next week, say?**
(suggest – vorschlagen / . . . . Wie wär's mit Anfang nächster Woche?)
B: Sorry, but Dr. Evans is fully booked until Wednesday, the earliest possible time he could see you is Wednesday afternoon.

* **What time should I come?**

* **A: Could I come and see you on Wednesday?**
(Kann ich Sie am Mittwoch sprechen? | Kann ich am Mittwoch zu Ihnen kommen?)
B: Check with my secretary whether Wednesday at nine is O.K.. She's got a list of all my appointments.
(whether – ob)

* **Could you spare me a minute, please?**
(Hätten Sie bitte einen Augenblick für mich Zeit?)

* **A: Good morning. We have an appointment with Mr. Dobson. It's Mr. Schmidt and Mr. Weber of IBM Austria.**
(appointment – Termin, Verabredung)
B: Yes, he's expecting you, go straight in.
(expect – erwarten / straight – gleich)

* **A: Good morning, my name is Frank Holzer. I have an appointment to see Mr. Glover, the Sales Manager, at eleven fourty-five. My secretary rang you last week about it.**
(Sales Manager – Verkaufsleiter / ring about – anrufen wegen)
B: Yes, he'll be here shortly.
(shortly – gleich)

* **Sorry to be late! How long have you been waiting for me?**
(.... Wie lange warten Sie schon auf mich?)

* **Sorry to have kept you waiting, Mr. Thorpe, but somebody from Headquarters was on the phone and I just couldn't ring off.**
(keep waiting – warten lassen / Headquarters – Konzernzentrale / ring off – auflegen)

* **A: There is a Mr. Martin here in the office. He says he has an appointment with you. But I can't find anything in the appointment book.**
(appointment book – Terminkalender)
B: Sorry, I forgot to tell you that I had promised to see him at four. It's all right. Show him in.
(promise – versprechen / show in – hereinführen)

* **I'm just ringing to inform you that the meeting is now scheduled for tomorrow, at the same time.**
(meeting – Sitzung / schedule – ansetzen)

* **A: What time is the board meeting?**
(board – Verwaltungsrat; Führungsgremium einer britischen/ amerikanischen Kapitalgesellschaft)
B: Well, we've arranged it for four o'clock this afternoon.
(arrange – festsetzen)

* **A: When am I to see the Managing Director?**
(Wann soll ich mich beim Generaldirektor melden?)
B: He suggests a meeting on Friday at eight o'clock or at the weekend. Please phone him as soon as possible.
(meeting – Treffen)

* **Would it suit you if we met at quarter to one at the Ship Restaurant? Then we could discuss things over a meal.**
(meet – sich treffen / at quarter to one – um Viertel vor eins / over a meal – bei einem Essen)

* **A: Let's meet about two o'clock, shall we?**
(Treffen wir uns also um ca. 2 Uhr.)
B: Right then, two o'clock on Monday the twenty-third. Goodbye.

* **A: Can we meet Thursday night or Friday morning?**
B: I'm tied up all week I'm afraid.
(Ich bin leider die ganze Woche voll.)

* **I'm afraid I'm not free this week. Perhaps another time.**
(... . Vielleicht ein andermal.)

* **I'm meeting Jane for lunch in an hour's time.**
(meet sbdy. – jemanden treffen / in an hour's time – in einer Stunde)

* **I'll meet you in about ten minutes under the station clock, O.K.?**
(about – etwa / station clock – Bahnhofsuhr)

* **I'll pick you up at the hotel at around seven, then.**
(pick up – abholen / at around seven – gegen sieben)

* **I'll call for you at three tomorrow.**
(call for – abholen)

* **I'm afraid I'll be late.**
(Tut mir leid, ich werde zu spät kommen.)

* **I'll look forward to meeting you in London this evening.**
(look forward to – sich freuen auf)

——— ❖ ———

* **I'd just like to ask if we can meet an hour earlier next week.**

* **Could you possibly bring our appointment forward by one and a half hours?**
(bring forward – vorverlegen)

* **Would it be possible to postpone the meeting?**
(postpone – verschieben, aufschieben)

* **It seems I won't be able to attend the meeting tomorrow.**
(Es sieht eher danach aus, daß ich an der morgigen Sitzung nicht teilnehmen kann.)

* **It looks as if I won't be able to keep my appointment on Friday.**
(won't – will not / keep – einhalten)

* **I'm calling about my appointment tomorrow morning with Mr. Bennet, your Marketing Manager. I'm afraid I won't be able to come because I've gone down with the flu.**
(call about – anrufen wegen / go down with the flu – die Grippe erwischen)

* **I'm ringing from the airport. Unfortunately, I have to cancel my appointment with Mr. Charlton, your Product Manager.**
(unfortunately – leider / cancel – stornieren, absagen)

* **A: I'm afraid I can't manage tomorrow evening.**
(Ich kann leider morgen abend nicht.)
B: Let's fix another date, then.
(date – Termin)

* **I'm afraid I can't make it on Sunday. I hope it won't mess up your arrangements.**
(make – schaffen / mess up arrangements – alles durcheinanderbringen)

DEADLINES

Termine und Fristen

* **We must finish this by four o'clock at the latest.**
  (Wir müssen das bis spätestens vier Uhr fertig haben.)

* **They need to know by the end of the week.**

* **I don't think we can promise to do it by the thirty-first. It'll be two weeks at least.**
  (promise – versprechen / .... Es wird mindestens zwei Wochen dauern.)

* **I'm afraid it won't be ready till tomorrow.**
  (won't – will not / ready – fertig)

* **The suits will certainly be ready in March.**
  (suit – Anzug / certainly – sicher)

* **It won't be ready in time.**
  (in time – rechtzeitig)

* **They've always delivered on time.**
  (Sie haben immer pünktlich geliefert.)

* **Make sure you're on time.**
  (Sei ja pünktlich!)

* **I'd like you to have them ready on Friday so that I can look at them over the weekend.**

* **The ticket must be collected not later than eleven fifteen.**
  (collect – abholen)

* **We would like to receive your proposals within the next two months.**
  (Würden Sie uns bitte Ihre Vorschläge innerhalb der nächsten zwei Monate unterbreiten.)

* **Could you have a quick look at this questionnaire before tomorrow morning?**
  (questionnaire – Fragebogen)

* **They'll let us know before the end of the month.**

* **A: Have you finished that report for me yet?**
(report – Bericht / yet – schon)
B: Yes, but I haven't had time to prepare the sales figures yet, I'm afraid.
(not ... yet – noch nicht / prepare – zusammenstellen / sales figures – Umsatzzahlen)

* **Oh damn! We missed the deadline again.**
(miss deadline – Termin verpassen)

* **They've set us the deadline for next Monday, but to be honest I don't think we'll meet it.**
(set – setzen / honest – ehrlich / meet – einhalten)

PRESSED FOR TIME
Unter Zeitdruck

* **A: Can I see you for a minute, please?**
(Kann ich Sie kurz sprechen?)
B: I'm afraid I haven't got time just now. Would you mind waiting for a few minutes?
(Leider habe ich jetzt gerade keine Zeit. Würde es Ihnen etwas ausmachen, ein paar Minuten zu warten?)

* **I'm terribly sorry, but I'm pressed for time at the moment.**
(terrible – schrecklich / be pressed for time – unter Zeitdruck sein)

* **I've only got ten minutes to spare. Is it urgent?**
(Ich habe nur zehn Minuten Zeit. Ist es dringend?)

* **He's no time to spare.**
(Er hat im Augenblick keine Zeit.)

* **Listen, I'm a bit busy at the moment. Could you call back later? Say, in half an hour?**
(Du, ich bin im Augenblick etwas unter Zeitdruck. ... . / call back – nochmals anrufen)

* **We're very busy at the moment. Can you come back again on the twenty-fourth?**
(busy – beschäftigt)

* **We can't do this before tomorrow, I'm afraid. We've got a lot of work on at the moment.**

* **I have to hurry up. I'm leaving for Brussels in a few minutes.**
(hurry up – sich beeilen / leave for Brussels – nach Brüssel fahren)

* **Sorry, I can't stay. I must dash – I'm meeting someone at nine.**
(dash – sausen)

* **I really should be going, David. I've got an appointment at two thirty.**

* **I'm afraid I must be going soon.**

* **It's high time we went home.**
(Es ist höchste Zeit, daß wir nach Hause gehen.)

* **Oh! It's five to twelve! You'd better leave now!**
(Es ist fünf vor zwölf. Sie sollten jetzt lieber gehen.)

* **A: Come on! Let's get going now!**
B: Just a moment. I haven't finished yet. I won't be long.
(Einen Augenblick noch! Ich bin noch nicht fertig. Ich bin gleich soweit.)

* **Just look at the time! Twenty past three! The banks shut at half past.**
(shut – schließen)

* **A: How about another cup of tea?**
(Wollen Sie nicht noch eine Tasse Tee?)
B: Oh, do you think we have time?

TIME OF DAY

Tageszeitangaben

(see also "Time: Appointments")

* **A: Could you tell me the time, please?**
  B: I make it about ten to eight.
  (Bei mir ist es ca. zehn vor acht.)

* **A: What time is it?**
  B: I still make it ten o'clock – my watch must have stopped.
  (still – noch immer / watch – Uhr)

* **A: Excuse me, my watch has stopped. Can you tell me the time?**
  B: By my watch it's just gone half past three, but it's a bit fast.
  (Auf meiner Uhr ist es knapp nach halb vier, aber sie geht etwas vor.)

* **My watch is five minutes slow.**
  (Meine Uhr geht fünf Minuten nach.)

* **A: What time is it by your watch?**
  B: It's exactly twenty minutes past eleven.

* **A: What's the time, please?**
  B: It's five thirty on the dot.
  (on the dot – genau)

* **Good heavens, it's three o'clock in the morning.**
  (good heavens – oh du meine Güte)

* **I wonder if you could tell me what time the shops close here?**
  (Können Sie mir bitte sagen, um welche Zeit hier die Geschäfte schließen?)

* **What time does it start?**

* **Is this clock right? It says twenty-five to five.**

* **My watch keeps good time.**
  (Meine Uhr geht genau.)

* **The first bus leaves at nine a.m. and the second at three p.m..**
(Der erste Bus fährt um 9 und der zweite um 15 Uhr. / a.m. – ante meridiem | before noon | vor Mittag / p.m. – post meridiem | after noon | nach Mittag)

* **We have flexi-time, actually, so I can start work any time between seven and nine o'clock.**
(flexi-time – Gleitzeit)

* **A: When do you think he'll be back?**
B: He'll be home by sixish.
(by sixish – so um sechs)

* **I'll be there at six sharp.**
(sharp – genau)

* **I'll see him at twelve noon.**
(noon – Mittag)

* **My plane leaves at eighteen hundred hours.**
(Meine Maschine geht um 18 Uhr.)

* **What were you doing at ten o'clock at night yesterday?**

OTHER EXPRESSIONS INDICATING TIME

Sonstige Zeitangaben

* **A: What's the date today, please?**
(date – Datum)
B: It's October the third.

* **Have you got any plans for the day after tomorrow?**

* **Where were you the day before yesterday?**

* **That was a good party last night, wasn't it?**
(wasn't it? – nicht wahr?)

* **I was there last month, so I'm not going this time.**

* **I'm going to Toronto tonight.**
(tonight – heute abend)

* **I talked to him the other day and he said that I should arrange things with you.**
(the other day – neulich)

* **He came back the next morning.**

* **We are not planning to launch a modified version in the near future, not before 1993.**
(launch – auf den Markt bringen / future – Zukunft)

* **It must have been shortly after seven.**
(shortly – kurz)

* **What are you doing at Easter?**

* **You can call me at any time during the day.**

* **Mrs. Vernon called just a couple of minutes ago.**
(Frau Vernon hat gerade vor ein paar Minuten angerufen.)

* **Some years ago I did a six-month training course.**

* **I was Marketing Manager for Casinos Austria until about three years ago.**

* **I've been working as export manager since the beginning of last year.**
(Ich bin seit Beginn letzten Jahres als Exportleiter tätig.)

* **I've been here since the first of May 1990. How time flies!**
(Ich bin nun schon seit dem 1. Mai 1990 hier. Wie die Zeit vergeht!)

* **I've known her for more than two years.**
(Ich kenne sie schon seit mehr als zwei Jahren.)

* **We haven't heard from him for some time.**
(Er läßt schon seit einiger Zeit nichts mehr von sich hören.)

* **A: How long did the interview take?**
(take – dauern)
B: It took about three quarters of an hour.

* **A: How long is this going to take?**
B: It won't take more than fifty minutes.
(won't – will not)

* **A: How long is it going to take you to obtain the necessary data?**
(Wie lange werden Sie brauchen/benötigen, um die notwendigen Daten zu beschaffen?)
B: A week, I suppose.
(suppose – annehmen)

* **The meeting started late in the afternoon and lasted five and a half hours.**
(last – dauern)

* **Some banks are open on Saturdays from nine to twelve.**

* **From October 1971 until March 1976 I studied at the University of Economics and Business Administration in Vienna.**
(... Wirtschaftsuniversität Wien.)

* **A fortnight today we'll be in Sydney.**
(Heute in 14 Tagen ... .)

* **A: How long will you be staying?**
B: I'll be in London for several days, until the end of next week. My flight's on Saturday morning.
(several – einige)

* **A: What's Scotland like in summer?**
B: Well, I went there in the summer of 1979 and it was unusually hot.

* **Our sales are usually higher in the winter months.**
(sales – Umsatz)

* **I have a dental appointment in three days' time.**
(dental appointment – Termin beim Zahnarzt)

* **He did it in no time.**
(in no time – sehr schnell)

* **Have you been to Manchester recently?**
  (recently – in der letzten Zeit)

* **Have you done anything special lately?**
  (lately – in der letzten Zeit)

* **Have you ever been to London?**

* **Have you been to Vienna yet?**
  (yet – schon einmal)

* **Have you been to Berlin before?**

* **There's a train every hour, on the hour.**
  (Es geht ein Zug zu jeder vollen Stunde.)

* **I catch the seven fifty-eight train every day.**
  (catch – nehmen)

* **I play squash every second day.**

* **There's a bus every twenty minutes.**
  (every – alle)

* **We get together annually.**
  (Wir treffen uns jedes Jahr.)

* **We see each other twice a month.**
  (twice – zweimal)

* **Could you wait a moment, please?**

* **I play golf from time to time.**

* **I have to work in this building temporarily while my office is being renovated.**
  (building – Gebäude / temporarily – vorübergehend)

* **Have we had any complaints so far?**
  (complaint – Beschwerde, Reklamation / so far – bis jetzt)

* **I hear you've just been to Jamaica. Is it worth a visit?**
  (just – gerade / worth – wert)

* **In the past few months, we have received a large number of inquiries concerning our new telephone answering machine.**
(in the past few months – in den letzten Monaten / receive – erhalten / inquiry – Anfrage / concerning – betreffend)

* **During the past five years, we have been able to increase our exports constantly.**
(Wir waren in der Lage, in den letzten 5 Jahren unseren Export ständig zu steigern.)

* **Sales fell during the first half of 1989. They then increased steadily over the next twelve months until the middle of 1990.**
(during – während / increase steadily – ständig steigen / over – während)

* **In Europe as a whole, our market share has increased over the past two and a half years from four per cent at the beginning of 1989 to twelve per cent in mid-91.**
(market share – Marktanteil)

AGE

Altersangaben

* **A: May I ask you how old you are actually?**
B: I'll be thirty next year.

* **I turned twenty-eight last month.**
(turn – werden)

* **A: How old are you?**
B: I'm on the wrong side of forty.
(... leider schon über 40.)

* **I was born on the eleventh of August nineteen sixty-two.**

* **I was born in Vienna in 1959.**

* **My birthday's on the thirtieth of January.**

* **You don't look your age.**
(Sie schauen jünger aus, als Sie sind.)

* **You look much younger.**

* **At the age of nineteen I went to live in New York.**
(age – Alter)

* **All our executives are under forty.**
(executive – Manager)

* **They say you shouldn't rush around at my age!**
(... , man sollte in meinem Alter etwas leisertreten.)

* **A: What's your star sign?**
(star sign – Sternzeichen)
B: I'm Sagittarius.
(Sagittarius – Schütze)

* **A: What sign of the zodiac are you?**
(sign of the zodiac – Sternzeichen)
B: I'm Capricorn. What about you?
(Capricorn – Steinbock)

MISCELLANEOUS
Sonstiges

* **We have plenty of time.**
(Wir haben viel Zeit.)

* **It's getting late.**
(Es wird schon spät.)

* **You can save so much time by using a computer.**

* **We're going through hard times in our company.**
(company – Firma, Gesellschaft)

* **A: I'll be going back to Austria on Friday.**
B: Really? Time's flying, isn't it?
(... . Na, wie die Zeit vergeht!)

* **Take your time.**
(Lassen Sie sich Zeit!)

* **Time's up.**
  (Die Zeit ist um!)

* **Better late than never.**
  (Besser spät als gar nicht.)

* **It's a race against time.**
  (… ein Wettlauf mit der Zeit.)

ASKING THE WAY AND PUBLIC TRANSPORT

Erkundigung nach dem Weg und öffentliche Transportmittel

ASKING THE WAY – GENERAL

Erkundigung nach dem Weg – allgemein

* **A: Where is the International Trading Centre, please?**
B: You see that high building there? That's the International Trading Centre.
(building – Gebäude)

* **A: Excuse me, could you tell me where the police station is?**
B: Walk along this street and it's on the left next to the cinema.
(Gehen Sie diese Straße entlang, und es ist auf der linken Seite neben dem Kino.)

* **A: Excuse me. Can you tell me where Perth Road is, please?**
B: Carry on up this road, and it's the third road on the right, I think.
(Gehen Sie weiter diese Straße entlang, ...)

* **A: Could you tell me where the Palladium Theatre is, please?**
B: Yes, go straight on and turn left at the traffic lights, and you'll see it a little way along, on the right-hand side of the road.
(straight on – geradeaus / turn left – nach links abbiegen I gehen / traffic lights – Verkehrsampel)

* **A: Excuse me. Can you tell me where the Conference Centre is?**
B: You're going in the wrong direction. It's the other way. Cross the bridge and it's just on the other side of the river.
(direction – Richtung / cross bridge – über Brücke gehen / just – direkt / river – Fluß)

* **A: Excuse me, please. Could you tell me the way to the ABC cinema?**
B: Yes, certainly. Go along this street until you come to a set of traffic lights. Then turn right into Shaftesbury Avenue. Then take the first turning on the left and it's at the end of that road.
(first turning on the left – erste Straße | Abzweigung links)

* **A: Excuse me, could you tell me the way to the station? It should be somewhere around here.**
(somewhere around here – irgendwo hier in der Nähe)
B: Yes, it's not far from here. Go straight down there, and take the first turning to your right.

* **A: Excuse me, but could you tell me the way to the British Museum, please?**
B: Actually, you have been walking away from it. Turn round, walk back up the road as far as the traffic lights. It's just around the corner.
(turn round – umdrehen, kehrtmachen / as far as – bis zu / just around the corner – gleich um die Ecke)

* **A: Excuse me. Can you tell me the way to Victoria Street?**
B: Let me see. Go straight along this road until you come to a zebra crossing. Then turn to the left and keep straight on as far as the bus stop. Then take the next turning to the right, cross the square and you'll be on Victoria Street.
(zebra crossing – Zebrastreifen / bus stop – Bushaltestelle / square – Platz)

* **A: Could you tell me how to get to Leicester Square, please?**
(Könnten Sie mir bitte sagen, wie ich zum Leicester Square komme?)
B: I'm afraid I can't help you.
(Tut mir leid, ich kann Ihnen nicht helfen.)

* **A: Excuse me, please. Could you tell me how to get to the Bank of England?**
B: First right, second left. You can't miss it.
(miss – verfehlen)

* **A: Excuse me, is there a bank near here?**
  B: Yes, there is one on the opposite side of the road, only about five minutes from here.
  (opposite – gegenüberliegend)

* **A: Excuse me please, I'm a stranger here. Is this the right way to Trafalgar Square?**
  (I'm a stranger here – ich bin hier fremd)
  B: Sorry, I don't know, I am a stranger here myself.

* **A: Which is the shortest way to Paddington Station, please?**
  B: Let me show you on your map.
  (map – Stadtplan)

* **A: Could I get there by bus?**
  B: Yes, but in that case you'll have to go back a little way. Keep on this side of the road until you come to the bus stop. All the buses from there pass the station.
  (pass the station – zum Bahnhof fahren)

* **A: Can you tell me which way Soho is, please?**
  B: It's rather complicated. You'd better ask again when you get to the Telecom Tower.
  (Das ist ziemlich kompliziert. Sie sollten lieber nochmals fragen, sobald Sie beim Telecom Tower sind.)

* **A: Excuse me. The National Gallery – it's near Trafalgar Square, isn't it?**
  (isn't it? – oder?)
  B: Yes, that's right, it's actually in Trafalgar Square.

* **A: Where can I get a taxi, please?**
  B: There's a taxi rank just round the corner.
  (taxi rank – Taxistand)

* **A: Excuse me. Can you show me where the Apollo Theatre is?**
  B: Well, that's quite easy. You are right in front of it.
  (.... Sie stehen direkt davor.)

* **A: Excuse me, how far away is Radford Street?**
  B: Not very far. It's the first turning on the right.

* **A: Is it very far from here?**
  B: No, not really. It's about a ten-minute walk I'd say.

* **A: Is it too far to walk?**
  B: No, it's only about five minutes from here.

* **A: Should I take a taxi?**
  B: No, it's not very far. You can walk it in less than ten minutes.

* **A: Excuse me. Where is room 405, please?**
  B: Come out of the lift on the fourth floor and take the corridor on the right. Room 405 is on the left.
  (floor – Stock)

* **Sorry, I'm new here.**

* **A: Excuse me. Where is the canteen, please?**
  B: It's downstairs in the basement.
  (basement – Kellergeschoß)

UNDERGROUND

U-Bahn

* **A: Can you tell me the best way to get to Wimbledon, please?**
  B: Well, you can go by tube, by bus or by mainline train. I reckon the tube's best.
  (tube – U-Bahn / mainline train – Eisenbahn / reckon – schätzen)

* **A: I wonder if you could tell me where the nearest tube station is?**
  (Könnten Sie mir bitte sagen, wo die nächste U-Bahn-Station ist?)
  B: Sorry, I've no idea.

* **A: Excuse me, could you tell me how to get to Gatwick Airport from here?**
  B: You can take the underground. The station ist just round the corner. Take the District Line as far as Victoria, and from here take a train to Gatwick. There's one every 20 minutes.
  (underground – U-Bahn / station – U-Bahn-Station)

* **A: Excuse me. Do you know how I can get to Victoria from here?**
  B: I think the best way is to take the Piccadilly Line to Green Park, and then change to the Victoria Line.
  (change – umsteigen)

* **A: How do I get to Bank station, please?**
  B: Take the Northern Line to Tottenham Court Road, then catch the Central Line eastbound.
  (catch – nehmen / eastbound – Richtung Osten)

* **A: Which underground line goes to Wimbledon, please?**
  B: I don't know, let's have a look at the underground map.
  (underground map – U-Bahn-Plan)

* **A: Excuse me, where can I get tickets for the underground?**
  B: If you've got some change you can get them from the ticket-machines, otherwise you'll have to queue at the ticket-office over there.
  (change – Kleingeld / ticket-machine – Fahrkartenautomat / queue – sich anstellen / ticket-office – Fahrkartenschalter / over there – dort drüben)

* **How much is the fare to Tottenham Court Road, please?**
  (fare – Fahrpreis)

* **Two to Marble Arch, please.**

* **A: Where's the Northern Line, please?**
  B: Go down that escalator over there and then if you're going north follow the signs to Platform 3, southbound you need Platform 6.
  (escalator – Rolltreppe / follow signs – Schildern folgen / platform – Bahnsteig / southbound – Richtung Süden)

* **A: Which direction do I have to go?**
  (direction – Richtung)
  B: You need the eastbound train.

* **Where do I have to change for Elephant & Castle, please?**

* **Knightsbridge is four stops from here, isn't it?**
  (stop – Haltestelle / isn't it – nicht wahr?)

* **Mind the gap!**
  (Vorsicht beim Ein- und Aussteigen!)

* **Where's the way out, please?**
  (Wo ist der Ausgang, bitte?)

BUS/COACH
Bus/Überlandbus

* **A: Excuse me, where's the nearest bus stop, please?**
  B: It's just down this road opposite the police station.
  (opposite – gegenüber)

* **A: How do I get to the air terminal from here, please?**
  B: Well, actually the best way is by bus.
  (by bus – mit dem Bus)
  A: I see. How long does it take?
  (.... Wie lange braucht man?)
  B: About twenty minutes – maybe more in the rush hour.
  (rush hour – Stoßzeit)

* **A: Excuse me, how far is it to the airport from here?**
  B: It's rather a long way. I'd take the bus to Merton Road and then ask again.
  (rather – ziemlich)

* **A: Is there a bus or underground to the Royal Exhibition Centre?**
  B: Yes, you should take a Greenline bus – a number three, I think – and get off at the third stop.
  (get off – aussteigen)

* **A: Does the number 52 go down Shooters Hill Road?**
  B: Yes, it goes past the Sun in the Sands, then round the roundabout and then it turns left down Shooters Hill Road to the station.
  (go past – vorbeifahren an / roundabout – Kreisverkehr)

* **A: I have to go for an interview. I wonder if you could tell me how to get there? The address is 23 Ridgeway Avenue.**
B: Oh, yes, that's not very far from here. You can take a number 12 bus and ask the conductor to put you off at Ridgeway Cemetery. It's a ten-minute ride I'd say.
(conductor – Schaffner / put sbdy. off – jemanden aussteigen lassen / cemetery – Friedhof / ride – Fahrt)

* **A: Excuse me, I'd like to go to Heathrow Airport. Can I take a bus?**
B: You can take the bus from Victoria to Heathrow. But I'd take the underground if I were you. The Piccadilly Line takes you right to the airport.

* **Shall I find out when the coaches leave for Stratford?**
(coach – Bus, Überlandbus / leave for – abfahren nach)

* **Where does the airport coach leave from, please?**

* **A: These coaches are very comfortable and almost as fast as a train.**
(almost – fast, beinahe)
B: I'm not so sure.

* **How often do the buses run to Brighton Beach?**
(run – fahren)

* **Do you happen to know if there are any night buses to Croydon?**
(Wissen Sie zufällig, ob ... .)

* **Does this bus go to the Royal Exchange, please?**
(Royal Exchange – Börse in London)

* **A: Excuse me, is this the right bus for Marylebone?**
B: No, you're going the wrong way. You want the 134 from Victoria.
(want – brauchen)

* **A: Excuse me, how long does it take to get to Hyde Park Corner by bus?**
  B: It won't take you long to get there, it's not far from here at all.
  (won't – will not / at all – überhaupt)

* **Do you want to sit upstairs on the top deck or shall we stay down here?**
  (top deck – Oberdeck)

* **A: Excuse me, how many stops is it to the Royal Pavillion?**
  B: Six, I think, but I'm not quite sure. You'd better ask the driver.
  (.... Sie sollten lieber den Fahrer fragen.)

* **Would you mind telling me when we get there?**
  (Könnten Sie mich bitte aufmerksam machen, wenn wir dort sind?)

* **Could you tell me where to get off for the Royal Festival Hall, please?**

* **A: Well, this is where I get off.**
  (Ich steige hier aus.)
  B: Let me give you a hand with your suitcase.
  (give sbdy. a hand – jemandem helfen / suitcase – Koffer)

* **Could you put me down at the Olympia Fair Building, please?**
  (put sbdy. down – jemanden aussteigen lassen)

* **I've left my umbrella on the bus.**
  (leave – liegenlassen / umbrella – Schirm)

TRAM

Straßenbahn

* **A: How do I get to the soccer stadium, please?**
(soccer stadium – Fußballstadion)
B: Go straight ahead, cross the road at the traffic lights and take a number four tram.
(straight ahead – geradeaus / tram – Straßenbahn)

* **A: Excuse me, do you happen to know where the number one tram stop is, please?**
(do you happen to know – wissen Sie zufällig)
B: Sorry, I haven't a clue. Ask the policeman over there.
(clue – Ahnung)

* **I'm sorry, I haven't the slightest idea.**
(slightest idea – geringste Ahnung)

* **What number tram should I take?**

* **Is this the stop for the World Trade Centre, please?**

AIR TRAVEL

Mit dem Flugzeug

BOOKINGS AND OTHER ARRANGEMENTS

Buchungen und alles, was dazugehört

* **Could you tell me how much a first-class ticket to Edinburgh costs?**

* **What is the fare for a return flight to Sydney, please?**
(fare – Flugpreis / return flight – Hin- und Rückflug)

* **When is the next plane to Boston, please?**
(plane – Maschine, Flugzeug)

* **What's the flying time, please?**
(flying time – Flugzeit)

* **A: What time does the last flight to Düsseldorf leave?**
(Wann geht der letzte Flug nach Düsseldorf?)
B: There's a flight leaving London Heathrow at 18.10 and arriving in Düsseldorf at 20.45 local time.
(arrive – ankommen)

* **A: Could you please tell me the time of the first morning plane to Frankfurt?**
B: Yes. The first plane leaves at 8.15.
A: Thanks. And can you tell me when it arrives so that I can let my secretary know?

* **What are the times of the flights after the 12.45?**

∗ **A: Do you happen to know the time of the last plane this evening?**
(Wissen Sie zufällig … ?)
B: Well, there is one at 11.15 but it's fully booked I'm afraid.
(I'm afraid – leider)
A: Oh. Well, I wonder if you'd let me know at my hotel if there's any cancellation on that flight. I'd be very grateful.
(cancellation – Stornierung / grateful – dankbar)

∗ **I wonder if you'd let me know if there is a seat available on the 9.30 flight?**
(Könnten Sie mir bitte sagen, ob in der Maschine um 9.30 Uhr noch ein Platz frei ist?)

∗ **Are there any seats left on the early morning flight to Vienna?**
(left – frei)

∗ **A: Is there a connecting flight to Vienna?**
(Gibt es einen Anschlußflug nach Wien?)
B: Of course, and you can transfer to a connecting flight without reclaiming your luggage.
(Selbstverständlich, und Sie können umsteigen, ohne das Gepäck neu einchecken zu müssen.)

∗ **Is it a scheduled or a charter flight?**
(scheduled flight – Linienflug)

∗ **Is there a direct flight from Brussels? I'd have to be in Dublin by Friday afternoon.**

∗ **Is there a stopover in Singapore?**
(stopover – Zwischenaufenthalt)

∗ **A: Do you make reservations for Lauda Air flights?**
B: Yes, we do.
A: Well, I'd like to book a return flight to Vienna, please.

∗ **A: I'd like to book an open return to New York on flight PA 104 leaving this Thursday, please.**
(open return – Hinflug mit offenem Rückflug)
B: First class or economy?
A: Oh, first class, please.

B: There are no first-class seats available on that flight, I'm afraid. Would you mind travelling economy class?
(would you mind – würde es Ihnen etwas ausmachen)

* **I want to get to Glasgow on Tuesday afternoon. Could I book a one-way flight?**
(one-way flight – Einfachflug)

* **I wonder if you'd tell me which airport the plane leaves from?**
(Könnten Sie mir bitte sagen, von welchem Flughafen die Maschine abfliegt?)

* **I'd like to book a seat on flight number BA 706 to London on Monday.**

* **A: I'd like two reservations from London to Alicante, if possible this evening, please.**
B: I'm afraid there are no direct flights. You'll have to fly to Madrid and then take a domestic flight to Alicante.
(I'm afraid – tut mir leid / domestic flight – Inlandsflug)

* **I see you don't have a service from Paris to Munich on Mondays. Could you book me on a direct flight on a different airline, preferably a late evening flight, on the 19th?**
(service – Flug, Flugverbindung / preferably – am liebsten wäre mir)

* **Please make sure you book me on a non-stop flight.**
(Bitte buchen Sie mich aber ja sicher auf einen Nonstopflug.)

* **Can you get me on the afternoon flight from Gatwick to Dublin?**
(get on – unterbringen auf)

* **A: The tickets should be collected from our reservations desk at the airport at least forty-five minutes before departure this evening, madam.**
(collect – abholen / reservations desk – Buchungsschalter / departure – Abflug)
B: All right. Thank you very much.

* **How long will it take to confirm my booking?**
(take – brauchen / confirm booking – Buchung bestätigen)

* **I'm flying to Washington, D.C. tomorrow. Could you tell me if I have to change at J.F.K.?**
(change – umsteigen / J.F.K. – John F. Kennedy Airport in New York)

* **My conference is ending sooner than I expected and I'd like to take an earlier flight back, would that be possible?**
(expect – erwarten)

* **I'm booked on flight number 567 to Vienna this Thursday at 13.40 and I'd like to change my booking.**

* **A: Could we change our flight booking here?**
B: Certainly. May I have your tickets, please? Thank you.
(certainly – selbstverständlich)
A: Can we make it two weeks earlier?

* **A: I need to change my flight back to San Francisco. I won't be able to catch the plane at 6.30. Do you think you could arrange that for me?**
(need – müssen / won't – will not / catch – erwischen)
B: Certainly. I'll see what I can do.

* **A: I have a reservation on flight BE 344 to Paris, leaving London tonight at eight ten. I'm afraid it'll be difficult for me to make it at that time. Is there a later flight this evening?**
(make – schaffen)
B: There's another flight at ten to twelve tonight.
A: Can you change the reservation, then, please?

* **Thank you for changing the flights. I'm sorry it was so complicated.**

* **Unfortunately, I have to cancel my flight. What is the cancellation fee, please?**
(unfortunately – leider / cancellation fee – Stornogebühr)

* **What time do I have to check in?**

* **A: Check-in time is about an hour before departure, is that right?**
(check-in – Abfertigung)

B: Yes, you should go to the Austrian Airlines check-in desk at the airport at least 60 minutes before departure.
(desk – Schalter)

* **What is the free-luggage allowance?**
(Wieviel Freigepäck darf man mitnehmen?)

* **What is the charge for excess baggage?**
(charge – Zuschlag / excess baggage – Übergepäck)

* **Could you arrange for someone to meet me at the airport? I'm due to arrive at Shannon Airport at 17.15 on flight BA 121.**
(arrange for – veranlassen / meet – abholen / I'm due to arrive – laut Flugplan komme ich an)

* **A: What time are you arriving?**
B: Well, my flight leaves just after two. I should be in around 3.30 your time.
(just – knapp / be in – ankommen)

CHECK-IN

Einchecken

* **I think I'd better check in right away. I don't want to have to rush.**
(Ich glaube, ich sollte lieber sofort einchecken. .... / rush – sich beeilen; hasten)

* **A: Where is the information desk, please?**
B: It's just over there on the other side of the hall, sir.
(just over there – gleich dort drüben)

* **Where is the Lufthansa counter, please?**
(counter – Schalter)

* **Are there any luggage trolleys around here?**
(luggage trolley – Gepäckswagen)

* **Is this the queue for flight OS 456 to Vienna?**
(Stellen Sie sich hier für ... an?)

* **Is this where I have to check in for the Austrian Airlines flight to Salzburg?**

* **Put your luggage on the scales, please.**
(scales – Waage)

* **A: I'm afraid there'll be an excess baggage charge on this.**
(excess baggage charge – Übergepäckszuschlag)
B: Are you sure it's overweight?

* **A: Your luggage doesn't seem to be labelled, sir. Could you pop one of those sticky labels on it for now?**
(seem – scheinen / label – beschriften / pop – kleben / sticky label – Pickerl / for now – vorläufig einmal)
B: No problem, but could you lend me something to write with, please?
(lend – borgen)

* **Can I take this as hand luggage?**

* **A: Can you give me a window-seat?**
B: Smoking or non-smoking?
A: Non-smoking, please.

* **I'd like a seat next to the window.**

* **Is the plane going to be late?**
(Hat die Maschine Verspätung?)

* **Is the plane going to be delayed because of the fog?**
(delayed – verspätet / fog – Nebel)

* **A: Can I have my boarding card?**
(boarding card – Einsteigkarte)
B: Here it is. Go to Gate 23 at least half an hour before the expected departure.
(gate – Flugsteig, Ausgang)

BETWEEN CHECK-IN AND DEPARTURE

Zwischen Einchecken und Abflug

* **I hope you have a pleasant flight back.**
  (pleasant – angenehm)

* **Have a good flight!**

* **Could you tell me where the duty-free shop is, please?**

* **I'll go to the duty-free until my flight is called.**
  (call – aufrufen)

* **What is the duty-free allowance for non-EC countries?**
  (duty-free allowance – Zollfreigrenze / EC – Europäische Gemeinschaft)

* **I seem to have mislaid my boarding card.**
  (mislay – verlegen)

* **Could you page a Ms. Sue Trim for me?**
  (page sbdy. – jemanden durch den Lautsprecher ausrufen lassen)

* **Sorry, I didn't quite catch the announcement over the public-address system. Did they say that Austrian Airlines flight 342 had to be diverted to Manchester because of the fog?**
  (quite – ganz / catch announcement – Durchsage verstehen / public-address system – Lautsprecheranlage / divert – umleiten)

* **A: Excuse me, do you know if flight ST 109 will be leaving on time?**
  (on time – pünktlich)
  B: No, I'm afraid it's going to be twenty minutes late.

* **Sorry to trouble you, but is flight BH 105 on schedule?**
  (trouble – belästigen / on schedule – pünktlich)

* **A: Can you tell me why there's a delay on the flight to Chicago?**
(delay – Verspätung)
B: Due to unforeseen circumstances, we have had to change the aircraft. It'll leave at quarter past five.
(Infolge unvorhergesehener Umstände mußten wir das Flugzeug wechseln. … .)

* **A: Can you tell me where gate 58 is, please?**
B: Straight ahead, then it's on your left.
(straight ahead – geradeaus)

* **Did they say the 11.40 flight to Vienna is now boarding?**
(… , daß die Passagiere für den 11.40-Uhr-Flug nach Wien jetzt an Bord gehen können?)

* **I really must be going. They're calling my flight.**

* **Was that the last call for flight LH 890 to Frankfurt?**
(call – Aufruf)

ON BOARD THE AIRCRAFT
Im Flugzeug

* **A: Is it O.K. to put this piece of hand luggage in the overhead locker, or is it too heavy?**
(piece – Stück / overhead locker – Handgepäcksfach / heavy – schwer)
B: It's rather bulky, sir, you'll have to put it under the seat in front of you.
(rather bulky – ziemlich groß / in front of – vor)

* **I think you must be in the wrong seat. I have row 15, seat B. Look, it says it on the boarding card.**
(row – Reihe)

* **When are we due to take off?**
(Wann starten wir laut Flugplan?)

* **What time do we arrive?**

* **When are we due in London?**

* **A: I don't feel well.**
B: Would you like a travel-sickness pill?
(travel-sickness – Reisekrankheit)
A: Yes, please.

* **I feel sick.**
(Mir ist schlecht.)

* **A: The seats are a bit narrow, aren't they?**
(narrow – eng / aren't they? – nicht wahr?)
B: Next time I'll book a seat in the business class.

* **A: Do you have to pay extra for drinks?**
B: Only for spirits. Beer, wine and soft drinks are free of charge.
(Nur für Spirituosen. Bier, Wein und alkoholfreie Getränke sind gratis.)

* **Can I pay in Austrian schillings?**

* **I ordered a vegetarian dish – I don't eat meat.**
(order – bestellen / dish – Essen)

* **Could I have a towlette, please?**
(towlette – Erfrischungstuch)

* **Excuse me, I don't seem to have a pillow or a blanket. Could you get me them, please?**
(pillow – Polster / blanket – Decke)

* **Can we get duty-frees on this flight, do you know?**

* **A: Excuse me, these headphones don't work. Could you get me another pair?**
(headphones – Kopfhörer)
B: Certainly, I'll exchange them straight away.
(exchange – austauschen / straight away – sofort)

* **If the weather is fine, one gets such a marvellous view from up here, cruising at 30,000 feet.**
(marvellous view – herrliche Aussicht / cruise – fliegen)

* **Did he say we would be passing through some turbulence?**
(pass through – durchfliegen / turbulence – Turbulenzen)

* **It's getting rather bumpy, I think I'll fasten my seat-belt again.**
(bumpy – unruhig / fasten one's seat-belt – sich anschnallen)

* **A: Have we already started our descent into London?**
(descent – Landeanflug)
B: Yes, we will be landing in 15 minutes from now.

POST FLIGHT
Nach dem Flug

* **Where can I claim my luggage?**
(claim – abholen, bekommen)

* **Where does the luggage arrive?**

* **Could you tell me where I can find a baggage trolley?**

* **A: Shall I get a porter?**
(porter – Gepäcksträger)
B: No thanks. I've only got this hand luggage.

* **My suitcase is damaged.**
(Mein Koffer ist beschädigt.)

* **My luggage has been lost. Where can I report it?**
(report – melden)

* **A: I'm afraid my luggage has not arrived, what can I do?**
B: We will do our best to trace it for you.
(trace – ausfindig machen)
A: Here, the number of the baggage check is UI 45621.
(baggage check – Gepäckschein)

* **Which way do I go if I have goods to declare?**
(declare – verzollen)

* **How much is the duty on this?**
(duty – Zoll)

* **A: Where did Dr. Grey say he would meet us?**
(meet sbdy. – auf jemanden warten)

B: Just outside the baggage reclaim.
(just – gleich / baggage reclaim – Gepäcksausgabe)

* **Where does the air terminal bus leave?**
(leave – abfahren)

* **A: What is the best way to get to Victoria Station? I've booked a room in a hotel near there.**
B: Take a train. They go every 20 minutes.

* **Has the plane from Vienna landed yet?**
(yet – schon)

* **I hope you had a good flight.**

* **Did you have a good flight?**

* **A: How was your flight?**
B: The flight was quite good, a bit bumpy on the way down, but not too bad.

* **There was fog at the airport, but our plane landed safely.**
(safe – sicher)

* **We had to make an emergency landing in Frankfurt. – It was pretty hair-raising!**
(emergency landing – Notlandung / .... Das hat mir einen ganz schönen Schrecken eingejagt.)

* **A: How did you get from London to Vienna?**
B: I flew from Gatwick.

* **Did the plane leave on time?**

* **Did the plane arrive on time?**

* **I'm suffering from jet lag. Do you have any good remedies?**
(suffer from – leiden an / remedy – Mittel)

RAIL TRAVEL

Mit der Eisenbahn

INQUIRIES AND TICKETS

Auskünfte und Fahrkarten

* **Can I get to Wimbledon on British Rail or do I have to go by tube?**
(tube – U-Bahn)

* **Which station do trains to Manchester go from?**

* **A: I'm going to Brighton. Let me see – the right station for Brighton's Waterloo, isn't it?**
(isn't it? – nicht wahr?)
B: No, it isn't, actually. You'll have to go to Victoria.

* **A: Good morning. Do you sell rail tickets here?**
(rail ticket – Bahnfahrkarte)
B: No, I'm afraid not. You'll have to get them at the British Rail desk or at the ticket-office at the station.
(I'm afraid not – leider nicht / desk – Schalter / ticket-office – Fahrkartenschalter)

* **Sorry to bother you, but could you tell me the way to the station?**
(bother – belästigen)

* **Where is the timetable?**
(timetable – Fahrplan)

* **Can you give me details of the trains to Edinburgh, please?**

* **A: Do I have to change?**
(Muß ich umsteigen?)
B: Yes, at Birmingham New Street.

* **Is there a good connection at Birmingham New Street?**
(connection – Anschluß)

* **What time is there a connecting train to Burnley?**
(Wann habe ich Anschluß nach Burnley?)

* **A: Excuse me, what time does the next train to Coventry leave, please?**
(leave – abfahren)
B: At six fifty-one. Platform 5.
(platform – Gleis)

* **A: When's the last train back to Victoria?**
B: It leaves here at 23.35.
A: And when does it get in?
(get in – ankommen)
B: At two minutes to midnight.

* **Is there an express to Brighton before ten o'clock?**
(express – Schnellzug)

* **Is there a fast train that gets me into Watford Junction by 9.00?**
(fast train – Eilzug)

* **A: When does the 9.45 get to Milton Keynes Central?**
(get to – ankommen in)
B: It's due in at 10.44.
(Laut Fahrplan kommt er um 10.44 Uhr an.)

* **How long does it take to get from Euston to Manchester Piccadilly?**
(Wie lange braucht man von .... .)

* **Is there a motorail service to Inverness?**
(motorail service – Autoreisezug)

* **Are there any sleepers on the 22.40?**
(sleeper – Schlafwagen)

* **Where's the ticket-office, please?**

* **A: I'd like to reserve a seat on the 8 o'clock train to Glasgow, please.**
B: A window-seat?
A: Yes, facing the engine please in a non-smoking compartment.
(Ja, bitte in Fahrtrichtung in einem Nichtraucherabteil.)

* **Do I have to buy a supplementary ticket for the Intercity?**
(supplementary ticket - Zusatzkarte)

* **A: How much is the fare?**
(fare - Fahrpreis)
B: It depends if you go during peak hours or off-peak after 9.30.
(Es hängt davon ab, ob Sie während der Verkehrsspitze oder später nach 9.30 Uhr fahren.)

* **A: Two first class returns to Brighton, please.**
(Zweimal 1. Klasse retour nach Brighton, bitte.)
B: That'll be £48.90, please.

* **A: Does the train stop anywhere?**
B: No, it goes to Brighton non-stop.

* **How long is the ticket valid?**
(valid - gültig)

* **One day return to Oxford, please.**
(day return - Tagesrückfahrkarte)

* **A second class single to Liverpool, please.**
(Einmal 2. Klasse einfach nach .... .)

* **A: I'd like a ticket to Milton Keynes Central, please. Is it cheaper to get two singles or a return?**
(single - einfache Fahrkarte / return - Rückfahrkarte)
B: When are you coming back?
A: In a week's time - next Friday.
B: In that case there's no difference.

* **Can I break my journey with this ticket?**
(break journey - Fahrt unterbrechen)

* **Could I check my luggage through to Vienna, please?**
  (Kann ich bitte mein Gepäck als Reisegepäck nach Wien aufgeben?)

AT THE STATION

Auf dem Bahnhof

* **Could you tell me where the left-luggage office is, please?**
  (left-luggage office – Gepäcksaufbewahrung)

* **I'd like to leave these two cases here until this evening, please.**
  (leave – lassen / case – Koffer)

* **Are there any luggage lockers at this station?**
  (luggage locker – Gepäckschließfach)

* **I really must be going or I won't catch my train.**
  (won't – will not / catch – erwischen)

* **I don't want to miss my train.**
  (miss – versäumen)

* **Where's platform 6, please?**

* **Which platform is it for the Watford Junction train?**
  (Auf welchem Gleis fährt der Zug nach Watford Junction ab?)

* **Which platform does the night train to Aberdeen leave from?**

* **Does this train go to Dover?**

* **A: Has the train to Bath left yet?**
  (yet – bereits)
  B: No, it's still standing at platform 11, if you hurry you will catch it.

* **I was told I could put my bike in the guard's carriage, is that right?**
  (bike – Fahrrad / guard's carriage – Zugsbegleiterwagen)

* **What platform does the train from Canterbury arrive at?**
(arrive – ankommen)

* **A: Is the train from Bristol running late?**
(run late – Verspätung haben)
B: Yes, I'm afraid it is 20 minutes late.
(I'm afraid – leider)

* **A: Excuse me, has the 8.15 from Cambridge arrived yet?**
B: Yes, madam. It came in five minutes ago. Platform 11, over there.
(come in – einfahren / over there – dort drüben)

* **A platform ticket, please.**
(Eine Bahnsteigkarte, bitte!)

* **A: Let me get you a porter.**
(porter – Gepäcksträger)
B: No, that's all right I can manage, thanks.
(manage – zurechtkommen)

IN THE TRAIN
Im Zug

* **A: Excuse me, is this seat free?**
B: No, I'm afraid it's taken.

* **Excuse me, that's my seat. I have a reservation.**

* **Excuse me, but is this a smoker?**
(smoker – Raucherabteil)

* **Could you give me a hand with this suitcase, please? I can't reach the rack.**
(give sbdy. a hand – jemandem helfen / suitcase – Koffer / rack – Gepäcksnetz)

* **Do you want to sit by the window?**

* **Could we change places? I don't like travelling with my back to the engine.**

(Könnten wir Platz tauschen? Ich sitze nicht gerne gegen die Fahrtrichtung.)

* **A: Do you mind if I shut the window? It's a bit draughty.**
(Haben Sie etwas dagegen, wenn ich das Fenster schließe? Es zieht ein wenig.)
B: Not at all.
(Überhaupt nicht.)

* **Mind if I read your paper?**
(paper – Zeitung)

* **Is this the through carriage to Plymouth?**
(through carriage – Kurswagen)

* **Does this train stop in Norwich?**

* **A: Is there a dining car on this train?**
(dining car – Speisewagen)
B: Yes, it's at the rear.
(Ja, am Ende des Zuges.)

* **Do you happen to know when dinner is being served?**
(Wissen Sie zufällig, wann das Abendessen serviert wird?)

* **Would you mind watching my bag for a moment? I'll be back in a minute.**
(watch – aufpassen auf)

* **When do we arrive in Exeter?**

* **How long are we stopping in York?**

* **A: Will we be arriving on time, do you know?**
(on time – pünktlich)
B: No, I'm afraid we'll be ten minutes late.

* **Doesn't a ticket collector come round and check the tickets?**
(ticket collector – Schaffner / check – kontrollieren)

* **I'm sorry, I seem to have mislaid my ticket.**
(seem – scheinen / mislay – verlegen)

* **Where do I have to get off for the National Exhibition Centre, please?**
(get off – aussteigen / exhibition – Ausstellung)

* **The attendant said he would wake us up 20 minutes before our stop.**
(attendant – Schlafwagenschaffner)

GENERAL
Allgemeines

* **A: Shall we take the train, then?**
B: It's much more convenient going by train. If you count getting to and from the airport, it's actually faster than going by plane.
(convenient – bequem / count – einrechnen / plane – Flugzeug)

* **Throughout Europe they are trying to make the railways more efficient. The TGV in France is already a definite alternative to travelling by air.**

* **From an environmental point of view, trains are much better than either cars or planes.**
(environmental point of view – Umweltstandpunkt)

MOTORING

Mit dem Auto unterwegs

CAR RENTAL

Autovermietung

* **A: I'd like to hire a car, please.**
  (hire – mieten)
  B: Would you like a small, medium or large car? We have several different models to choose from.
  (medium – mittelgroß / several – einige / choose – auswählen, wählen)

* **May I see your price-list, please?**

* **How much does it cost to rent a car?**
  (rent – mieten)

* **A: I need a large car for three days. What's the rate for an Audi 100?**
  (rate – Miete, Tarif)
  B: The daily rate is £58.50 including insurance and with 100 miles free mileage per day. If you exceed the 100 miles it'll cost 15 pence per mile extra.
  (insurance – Versicherung / exceed – mehr fahren als)

* **Could you tell me, is there an additional mileage charge? It does say in the leaflet that on some models there is unlimited mileage.**
  (additional mileage charge – Mehrkilometergebühr / leaflet – Prospekt / unlimited mileage – unbegrenzte Kilometer)

* A: **Could you tell me the weekly rate for a compact car including insurance, please?**
(compact car – Kompaktwagen)
B: **For a Vauxhall Astra it's £310 a week including liability insurance, Collision Damage Waiver, and tax.**
(liability insurance – Haftpflichtversicherung / Collision Damage Waiver – Haftungsausschluß für Unfallschäden am Mietwagen / tax – Steuer)

* **I'd like to rent an estate car for a week. What makes do you have?**
(estate car – Kombi / make – Marke)

* **I'd like a car with a large boot because I've got quite a lot of luggage.**
(boot – Kofferraum / quite a lot of luggage – ziemlich viel Gepäck)

* **What convertibles do you have?**
(convertible – Kabrio)

* **I'd like a car with manual transmission.**
(manual transmission – Handschaltung)

* **Do you have any cars with automatic transmission?**
(automatic transmission – Automatik)

* **Have you got any cars with telephones?**

* **Can you show me how to operate the telephone, please?**
(operate – bedienen)

* A: **Do I have to bring the car back here or can I leave it in Dover?**
(leave – lassen)
B: **You can take it back to any of our offices throughout the UK, but we do charge a drop-off fee of £100 for this.**
(charge – verrechnen / drop-off fee – Rückholgebühr)

* **Do I have to pay a deposit?**
(pay deposit – Kaution hinterlegen)

* **Do you accept credit cards?**

* **I have a few questions because I haven't driven a Ford Escort before.**
  (drive – fahren mit)

* **What happens if the car breaks down?**
  (break down – Panne haben)

* **Do we have to wear the safety-belts?**
  (Müssen wir uns anschnallen?)

* **A: Is there any petrol left in the tank?**
  (Ist noch Benzin im Tank?)
  B: It's full up but you'll have to return it with a full tank of petrol, otherwise we'll charge you for filling it up.
  (return – zurückbringen / otherwise – sonst)

* **Will there be somebody there when I return the car? It might be rather late.**
  (rather – ziemlich)

* **A: Now I need to see your driving licence … Thank you. Will there be an additional driver?**
  (need – müssen / driving licence – Führerschein / additional driver – zusätzlicher Fahrer)
  B: No, just me.
  (just – nur)

* **Could you bring the car round to my hotel, please?**

ASKING THE WAY

Erkundigung nach dem Weg

* **A: We seem to have been going round in circles for ages. Where on earth are we?**
  (Es scheint, daß wir schon seit einer Ewigkeit im Kreis fahren. Wo um Himmels willen sind wir denn?)
  B: Don't ask me! I haven't the foggiest.
  (.... Ich habe nicht den blassesten Schimmer.)
  A: I really think we'd better ask or we're going to be terribly late.
  (Ich glaube wirklich, wir sollten lieber fragen, oder wir werden viel zu spät kommen.)

* **Excuse me, where does this road go?**
  (road – Straße)

* **A: How long will it take me to get to Bath?**
  (Wie lange brauche ich nach Bath?)
  B: I've no idea, I'm afraid. I've never driven there myself.
  (I'm afraid – leider / drive – fahren)

* **I wonder if you could tell me how many miles it is to the nearest town?**
  (Könnten Sie mir bitte sagen, ... ?)

* **A: Excuse me, is this the road to Swindon?**
  B: No, I'm afraid you're on the wrong road. Let me think, you'll have to turn round here, go back down to the crossroads and turn right. Just after the zebra crossing there's a mini-roundabout. Go straight over it and then you're on the Swindon road.
  (turn round – umdrehen / back down to the crossroads – bis zur Kreuzung zurück / turn right – nach rechts abbiegen / fahren / just – gleich / zebra crossing – Zebrastreifen / roundabout – Kreisverkehr / go straight over it – fahren Sie gerade weiter)

* **A: How do I get to Junction 12 of the M1 from here, please?**
  (get – kommen / junction – Autobahnauffahrt / M1 – Autobahnbezeichnung)
  B: I'll show you on the map.
  (map – Karte)

* **A: Excuse me, how do I get to the sea front, please?**
(sea front – "Meer"; ans Meer angrenzender Stadtteil)
B: Just go straight up to the T-junction and turn left. Follow that road right round, go over the level crossing and then you'll see it straight ahead.
(straight – gerade / up to the T-junction – bis dorthin, wo die Straße einmündet / … . Fahren Sie nur immer auf dieser Straße weiter, überqueren Sie den Bahnübergang und dann sehen Sie es direkt vor sich.)

* **A: Excuse me, I've lost my way, I must have taken a wrong turning. Can you tell me how to get to the conference centre, please?**
(lose one's way – sich verfahren / turning – Abzweigung)
B: Yes, certainly. Go straight over the first set of lights to the roundabout, then take the second exit. Then take the first left, drive down there for about 500 yards and then you'll see a sign to the right for the conference centre.
(certainly – gern / set of lights – Ampel / exit – Ausfahrt / first left – erste Straße links / down – entlang / yard – 0,914 Meter / sign – Schild, Tafel)

* **A: Excuse me, how do I get to that factory over there? That's a one-way street.**
(factory – Fabrik / over there – dort drüben / one-way street – Einbahnstraße)
B: Ah yes, you'll have to go round the block.

AT THE PETROL STATION

An der Tankstelle

* **Where's the nearest petrol station, please?**
(petrol station – Tankstelle)

* **I've rented this car. Do I need regular or super?**
(rent – mieten / regular – Normalbenzin)

* **A: How much is diesel, please?**
B: It's 52 pence a litre.

* **A: Four gallons of super, please.**
  (gallon – Gallone | U.K.: 4,54 l | U.S.: 3,78 l)
  B: Leaded or unleaded?
  (unleaded – bleifrei, unverbleit)
  A: Unleaded, please.

* **How much is that?**

* **Twenty-five pounds worth of super, please.**
  (Um 25 Pfund Super, bitte!)

* **Fill it up, please.**
  (Volltanken, bitte!)

* **Would you clean the windscreen and the windows, please?**
  (clean – putzen / windscreen – Windschutzscheibe)

* **Please check the oil, the water and the tyre pressure.**
  (check – kontrollieren / water – Kühlwasser / tyre pressure – Reifendruck)

* **A pint of oil, please.**
  (pint – U.K.: 0,568 l | U.S.: 0,473 l)

* **Top up the oil, please.**
  (top up – nachfüllen)

* **Will you check the brake fluid, please?**
  (Bitte kontrollieren Sie die Bremsflüssigkeit.)

* **A: Shall I check the tyres?**
  B: No thanks, I'm in a bit of a hurry.
  (… , ich bin etwas in Eile.)

* **Do you have a car wash here?**
  (car wash – Autowaschanlage)

* **I'd like a road map of this area, please.**
  (road map – Straßenkarte / area – Gegend)

* **Where is the toilet, please?**

BREAKDOWNS AND MINOR REPAIRS

Pannen und kleinere Reparaturen

* **We've run out of petrol and there's no petrol can.**
(Uns ist das Benzin ausgegangen, und wir haben keinen Benzinkanister mit.)

* **My car won't start. Could you give me a push, please?**
(Mein Auto springt nicht an. Könnten Sie mich bitte anschieben?)

* **Where is there a service garage, please?**
(service garage – Reparaturwerkstatt)

* A: **My car has broken down. Could I use your phone to call the breakdown service, please?**
(call – anrufen / breakdown service – Pannendienst)
B: **Do you want the AA or the RAC?**
(AA – Automobile Association / RAC – Royal Automobile Club)
A: **Well, actually I don't belong to either so it doesn't matter.**
(I don't belong to either – ich bin von keinem dieser beiden Mitglied / it doesn't matter – es ist egal)

* **I'm on the M1 and my car has just boiled over, the fan belt doesn't seem to be working properly. Could you come and fetch me, please?**
(Ich bin auf der M1, und der Kühler kocht; der Keilriemen scheint nicht in Ordnung zu sein. Könnten Sie mich bitte holen?)

* **I've got a flat tyre. I can't change it myself as there's no jack in the boot. Could you send a breakdown truck, please? My car is a red Mercedes and I'm on the A5 just outside Milton Keynes, my registration number is G456 RCP.**
(flat tyre – Patschen, Reifendefekt / change tyre – Reifen wechseln / jack – Wagenheber / boot – Kofferraum / breakdown truck – Pannenwagen / just – knapp / registration number – Autonummer)

* **Excuse me, can you help me? My car's broken down and I need to push it off the road.**
(push off – wegschieben von)

* **It might be the engine. Would you be so kind as to tow me to the nearest garage?**
(engine – Motor / kind – freundlich / tow – abschleppen / garage – Werkstatt)

* **Could I speak to one of your mechanics, please?**
(mechanic – Mechaniker)

* **Should I open up the bonnet?**
(bonnet – Motorhaube)

* **Have you got any spare parts for Ford cars, please?**
(spare part – Ersatzteil)

* **I need a new wing mirror, please.**
(wing mirror – Außenspiegel)

* **I've lost a hub-cap.**
(hub-cap – Radkappe)

* **The battery is flat. Can you recharge it, please?**
(flat – leer / recharge – aufladen)

* **There's something wrong with the clutch. Could you have a look, please?**
(Mit der Kupplung stimmt etwas nicht. Könnten Sie bitte mal nachsehen?)

* **The exhaust seems to be making a really loud noise.**
(exhaust – Auspuff / noise – Lärm)

* **Something keeps rattling every time I accelerate.**
(keep rattling – andauernd klappern / accelerate – beschleunigen)

* **It's very difficult to change gear.**
(change gear – schalten)

* **I can't get into second gear.**
(Ich bringe den zweiten Gang nicht hinein.)

* **The windscreen wipers and the indicators don't work.**
(Die Scheibenwischer und Blinker funktionieren nicht.)

* **I think the spark-plugs need changing.**
(Ich glaube, die Zündkerzen müssen ausgewechselt werden.)

* **Would you check the brakes and the shock absorbers, please?**
(check – kontrollieren / brake – Bremse / shock absorber – Stoßdämpfer)

* **My windscreen's shattered. Could you replace it immediately, please?**
(windscreen – Windschutzscheibe / shatter – zerbrechen / replace – auswechseln / immediately – gleich)

* **Would you repair the left headlight and the bumper, please?**
(left headlight – linker Scheinwerfer / bumper – Stoßstange)

* **How long will it take?**
(take – dauern)

* **When will the car be ready?**
(ready – fertig)

* **Could you have it ready tomorrow at ten?**

* **Could you give me a rough estimate of the cost?**
(rough estimate – ungefähre Schätzung; ungefährer Kostenvoranschlag)

* **Here is my key.**
(key – Schlüssel)

PARKING

Parken

* **A: Can I park my car here?**
B: No, you can't park here, there are double yellow lines.
(... , hier ist Parkverbot.)

* **You can't park here, you'll get clamped.**
(... , sonst hängt man Ihnen Sperrklammern auf das Auto.)

* **It says no parking on that sign over there.**
  (sign – Schild, Tafel / over there – dort drüben)

* **I've got my car in front of the hotel, do you have a car-park?**
  (in front of – vor / car-park – Parkplatz, Parkgarage)

* **A: Can you tell me where the nearest car-park is, please?**
  B: There's a multi-storey just around the corner on the left-hand side.
  (multi-storey – Parkhaus / just around the corner – gleich um die Ecke)

* **Is it open all night?**

* **Excuse me, my car's parked in a No Parking area. How do I get to the hotel car-park, please?**
  (... , mein Auto steht im Parkverbot. ... .)

* **A: It looks like I may have got a parking-ticket.**
  (parking-ticket – Strafzettel wegen Falschparkens)
  B: It's OK, it's only an advert.
  (advert – Reklame)

* **Do you think you could move your car, please? I can't get mine out.**
  (move car – mit dem Auto etwas wegfahren)

* **Could you push back a little, please?**
  (push back – zurückschieben)

* **Where can I pay for the car-park, please?**
  (car-park – Parkplatz, Parkgarage, Parkhaus)

* **Could I have a receipt, please?**
  (receipt – Quittung)

* **I seem to have mislaid my car-park ticket.**
  (seem – scheinen / mislay – verlegen / car-park ticket – Parkschein)

* **I parked my car on the fifth floor.**
  (floor – Etage)

* **Sorry, I'm late. I couldn't find a parking-space.**
(parking-space – Parkplatz, Einzelparkplatz)

* **When is the next lay-by?**
(lay-by – Rastplatz)

CAR FERRY
Autofähre

* **How often does the car ferry to Cork run, please?**
(car ferry – Autofähre / run – gehen)

* **When does the next ferry leave for Calais, please?**
(leave for – abfahren nach)

* **What time is the next sailing, please?**
(sailing – Abfahrt)

* **A: How long does the crossing take, please?**
(crossing – Überfahrt)
B: It's 75 minutes by ferry, but only 30 minutes on the hovercraft.
(hovercraft – Luftkissenboot)

* **Where does the ferry to Dunkirk dock, please?**
(dock – anlegen)

* **Do I have to apply the hand-brake?**
(apply hand-brake – Handbremse anziehen)

* **Could you tell me the way down to the car deck, please?**

* **Do you ever get seasick, Maggy?**
(seasick – seekrank)

MISCELLANEOUS
Sonstiges

* **Finally I'm getting used to driving on the left!**
(finally – endlich / get used to – sich gewöhnen an)

* **I've never driven a right-hand drive before.**
(right-hand drive – rechtsgelenktes Fahrzeug)

* **What are the speed limits in Britain?**
(speed limit – Geschwindigkeitsbegrenzung)

* **I got stopped for speeding on the way over.**
(speeding – Schnellfahren / on the way over – auf der Fahrt hierher)

* **I was just overtaking a tractor and suddenly it was so slippery that I came off the road.**
(Ich überholte gerade einen Traktor, und plötzlich war es so rutschig, daß ich von der Straße abkam.)

* **A: Was the traffic bad this morning?**
(traffic – Verkehr)
B: It was really heavy. There were serious congestions on the motorway.
(heavy – sehr stark / serious – beträchtlich / congestion – Stau / motorway – Autobahn)

* **The traffic wasn't moving at all and I sat in a traffic jam for over half an hour.**
(Der Verkehr kam völlig zum Erliegen, und ich saß mehr als eine halbe Stunde in einem Stau fest.)

* **There are so many road-works on the M25, the tail-backs are worse than ever.**
(road-works – Baustellen / tail-back – Rückstau / worse than ever – schlimmer als je zuvor)

* **They said on the radio that there are long hold-ups on the M45.**
(hold-up – Stau)

* **Here's my car. Let me give you a lift.**
(give sbdy. a lift – jemanden mit dem Auto mitnehmen)

* **A: Where can I drop you off?**
(Wo kann ich Sie aussteigen lassen?)
B: You can drop me right here, that'll do fine.
(... , das paßt schon.)

* **A: Any chance of a lift?**
B: I'd like to, but I'm not going that way today, sorry.

* **Can I give you a lift to the station? It's on my way home.**

* **If I can just ask you to wait here, I'll bring the car round. I won't be a minute.**
(.... Ich bin gleich wieder hier.)

* **Would you like to go for a drive this evening? I could show you a bit of the countryside around here and then we could go to a country pub.**
(go for a drive – eine Spazierfahrt machen / countryside – Gegend)

* **I can pick you up at the office.**
(pick up – abholen)

TAXI

Taxi

* **We'd better take a taxi. The train leaves in twenty minutes.**
(Wir sollten lieber ein Taxi nehmen. .... / leave – abfahren)

* **A: Would you like me to call you a taxi?**
B: Thank you, but really don't bother. It's not far and I'd like to stretch my legs a bit anyway.
(Danke, aber es ist wirklich nicht notwendig. Es ist nicht weit, und ich würde mir ohnehin gerne meine Füße etwas vertreten.)

* **How are you getting back to town? Shall I get you a taxi?**
(get back – zurückkommen / get – besorgen)

* **Good evening, I'd like a taxi for 125 London Road, please.**

* **Where's the nearest taxi rank, please?**
(taxi rank – Taxistand)

* **Would you hail a taxi, please?**
(hail – anhalten, rufen)

* **To the station, please.**
(Zum Bahnhof, bitte!)

* **Will you take me to the airport, please?**
(Bringen Sie mich bitte zum Flughafen.)

* **Do you think you can get me to Victoria Station by 3.30?**
(get – bringen)

* **Do you think we'll make it?**
(make – schaffen)

* **Would you stop here for a minute, please?**

* **What's the fare?**
(fare – Fahrpreis)

* **That's for you.**

HOTEL

Hotel

INQUIRIES, RESERVATIONS, ETC.

Anfragen, Zimmerreservierungen usw.

* **A: I need your advice. Which hotel in Oxford would you recommend?**
(advice – Rat / recommend – empfehlen)
B: I'd recommend the Punting Lodge Hotel.
A: Is it central?
(central – zentral gelegen)

* **A: Listen, do you know a decent hotel in Cardiff?**
(Du, kennst du ein anständiges Hotel … ?)
B: What about the "Western View"?
(Wie wär's mit … ?)
A: What's it like?
(Wie ist es?)

* **What are the prices like?**
(Wie sind die Preise dort?)

* **I've heard the Central Hotel is five minutes from the centre of town, next to the railway station, and is therefore very convenient for people arriving or leaving by train.**
(railway station – Bahnhof / convenient – praktisch / arrive – ankommen / leave – abfahren)

* **Do you think that the Hilton is very full just at present?**
(just at present – zur Zeit; im Augenblick)

* **A: Shall we make a hotel reservation for you?**
B: Yes, that would be a good idea. It would be rather a nuisance for me to do this from London.
(be rather a nuisance – ziemlich umständlich sein)

* **Book me into my usual hotel, would you?**
(would you? – bitte)

* **Could you book me a single room for tonight, please. At the Grand Hotel if possible.**
(single room – Einzelzimmer / for tonight – für die Nacht von heute auf morgen)

* **Cath, would you reserve me a hotel room for Tuesday night?**

* **Sally, have you booked a room for me?**

* **If you can't get me into a hotel in Bristol you could try to find some private accommodation.**
(get into – unterbringen in / accommodation – Unterkunft)

* **I'll be arriving on a late flight from Vienna, so could you book me into a hotel near the airport and arrange dinner?**
(arrange dinner – Essen vorbestellen)

* **I wish to make a reservation. Would you put me through to the reception desk, please.**
(put through to – verbinden mit / reception desk – Rezeption)

* **I'd like to book a single room with bathroom for three nights from the night of Wednesday, February the twenty-second. The reservation is for our Managing Director, Mr. Sepp Volter.**
(Managing Director – Generaldirektor)

* **Could you let me have written confirmation that the reservation has been made.**
(confirmation – Bestätigung)

* **Is that Advance Reservations? I'd like to reserve a single room with shower for four nights, half board, please. I'll be arriving Tuesday afternoon.**
(Advance Reservations – Zimmerreservierung / shower – Dusche / half board – Halbpension)

* **I'd like to reserve a double room with full board for five nights, starting next Saturday.**
(double room – Doppelzimmer / full board – Vollpension)

* **Could you let me have your accommodation charges so that I can prepare an estimate of expenses.**

(accommodation charges – Zimmerpreise / prepare – erstellen / estimate of expenses – Spesenvoranschlag)

* **Could you arrange for someone to meet me at the airport, please?**
(Könnten Sie bitte veranlassen, daß mich jemand vom Flughafen abholt?)

* **My secretary has booked a room for me for tomorrow. It's in the name of Stefan Berger. I'll be checking in rather late, I'm afraid. At about midnight. Would you please hold the room for me?**
(.... Ich fürchte, ich werde ziemlich spät ankommen. So gegen Mitternacht. Würden Sie bitte das Zimmer für mich freihalten?)

* **A: I've made a reservation for the fifteenth and now I'm afraid I'll have to cancel it. The conference in London has been called off.**
(I'm afraid – leider / cancel – stornieren / call off – absagen)
B: What name was the room booked under?
A: It was booked in the name of Dr. Richard Lackner.

* **Good evening. I want a single room, please.**

* **I'd like two double rooms, please.**

* **A: I'm afraid we're full up.**
(Wir sind leider voll.)
B: Could you ring another hotel for me and ask if they have any vacancies?
(ring – anrufen / vacancy – freies Zimmer)

* **A: Have you got any vacancies for tonight?**
B: We have one double room on the second floor.
(floor – Stock)

* **A: How much is this room?**
B: £65 a night including breakfast.
(... inklusive Frühstück.)
A: What about the other meals?
(Und was ist mit den anderen Mahlzeiten?)
B: They are charged for separately.
(Für die muß man extra zahlen.)

* **How much do you charge per night?**
(charge – verlangen)

* **What's the surcharge for a single room?**
(surcharge – Zuschlag)

* **Is there an additional service charge or is service included in your rates?**
(additional service charge – Bedienungszuschlag / rate – Preis)

* **Have you got a room free on the top floor?**
(on the top floor – im obersten Stock)

* **Do you have a quiet room at the back?**
(quiet – ruhig / at the back – nach hinten hinaus)

* **Has the room got a view of the park?**
(view – Blick, Aussicht)

* **Is it a room with a view of the sea?**
(... mit Blick aufs Meer?)

* **Have you got a twin room?**
(Haben Sie ein Doppelzimmer mit Einzelbetten?)

* **I'd like one with a double bed.**

* **I'd like to have a look at it, please.**

* **I'd rather have a room with a bath than one with a shower, if possible.**
(rather – lieber)

* **A: Is this room big enough for you, sir?**
(enough – genug)
B: I suppose you haven't anything a little larger, have you?
(suppose – annehmen / have you? – oder?)

* **All I want is a quiet room away from the noise of the traffic. I don't sleep very well.**
(noise – Lärm / traffic – Verkehr)

* **I'll take it.**

* **I want to stay at least a week.**
(at least – zumindest)

* **Do you want me to fill in this registration form right away?**
(Soll ich dieses Anmeldeformular jetzt gleich ausfüllen?)

* **My company has been in touch with me this morning. They'd like me to stay on for two more days. I wonder if it's possible to extend my stay here until the sixth?**
(Meine Firma hat mich heute morgen kontaktiert. . . . . / stay – bleiben / . . . . Wäre es möglich, bis zum 6. zu verlängern?)

AT THE RECEPTION

Am Empfang

* **Good evening, I've reserved a room. It's a double room with private bath. My name is Kreuz.**
(private bath – eigenes Bad)

* **A: Good afternoon. I believe you have two rooms booked for us: Dr. Baker and Dr. Schrempf.**
(believe – glauben)
B: Ah, yes. Rooms 225 and 226 on the second floor. Shall I call the porter?
(porter – Träger)
A: No, thank you, we've only got this hand luggage.
(hand luggage – Handgepäck)
B: And would you like newspapers in the morning?
A: Yes, we'd both like the Financial Times, please.

* **A: My name is Rolf Peterson, I've had a room booked for me from today for a week.**
(have room booked – Zimmer buchen lassen)
B: Yes, Mr. Peterson. It's Room 345 on the third floor. We'll have your luggage brought up immediately. Would you fill in the registration form, please.
(. . . . Wir werden Ihr Gepäck sofort hinaufbringen lassen. . . . .)
A: What do I fill in here?
B: I just need your signature and your passport number and we'll take care of the rest.
(just – nur / signature – Unterschrift / take care of – erledigen)

* **What do you mean you haven't got a room left? I booked four weeks in advance and I have your confirmation. Here it is.**
(what do you mean – was soll das heißen / left – frei / in advance – im voraus)

* **A: Excuse me, where's room 543, please?**
B: Come out of the lift on the fifth floor and turn down the corridor on the right. Room 543 is on the left.
(... und gehen Sie nach rechts den Gang entlang. ... .)

* **Please have the luggage taken up to my room.**
(Bitte lassen Sie das Gepäck in mein Zimmer hinaufbringen.)

* **Would it be possible for the porter to show me to my room?**
(show – bringen)

* **Can you arrange for my luggage to be collected, please? It is still at the airport.**
(Können Sie bitte veranlassen, daß mein Gepäck abgeholt wird? ... . / still – noch immer)

* **A: Is your room all right?**
B: Yes, it's fine, thanks.

* **Could you tell me whether Mr. Bright has already checked in?**
(whether – ob)

* **Could you tell Mr. Bright when he checks in that I'll be waiting for him in the coffee lounge.**

* **Could you tell me what the voltage in the rooms is, please?**
(voltage – Stromspannung)

* **Do you have an adapter which I can use for my shaver?**
(adapter – Zwischenstecker / shaver – Rasierapparat)

* **Could you cash this traveller's cheque for me, please?**
(cash traveller's cheque – Reisescheck einlösen)

* **Could you look after these valuables for me, please?**
(Könnten Sie bitte diese Wertgegenstände für mich aufbewahren?)

* **Where can I deposit my valuables?**
(deposit – hinterlegen, aufbewahren)

* **Where can I post this letter?**
(post – aufgeben)

* **I'd like to book a table in the hotel restaurant for three at eight.**

* **Where is the dining room, please?**
(dining room – Speisesaal)

* **I'm expecting a long-distance call from Vienna. I'll be in the bar for an hour or so before I go up to my room.**
(expect – erwarten / long-distance call – Ferngespräch)

* **A: Can I make an international call from my room?**
B: Yes, you can, but don't forget to dial 010 before the code of the country you're calling.
(dial – wählen / code – Vorwahl)

* **What is the country code for Austria for calls dialled from here?**
(country code – Landeskennzahl)

* **How do I get an outside line, please?**
(Wie kann ich bitte hinauswählen?)

* **I'd like an early morning call tomorrow at six thirty.**
(early morning call – Weckruf)

*

I'd like to be woken up in the morning at eight o'clock.

* **I'd like to remind you to call me at seven tomorrow morning.**
(remind – erinnern)

* **I need a taxi tomorrow at nine thirty. Could you arrange that for me, please?**

* **I'd like to rent a car. Can you recommend where to go?**
(rent – mieten)

* **Could you call me a taxi, please?**

* A: **I'm staying at the hotel. I'd like to know where the car-park is, please.**
(car-park – Parkplatz, Parkgarage)
B: **It's behind the hotel, sir. You go round to the left.**
(behind – hinter)

* **Key to room 752, please. Is there any message for me?**
(key – Schlüssel / message – Nachricht)

* **Did anyone ask for me?**

* **Are there any letters for me?**
(Ist Post für mich da?)

* A: **I wonder if you'd be prepared to change rooms with another guest, sir? We appear to have made an error.**
(Wären Sie bitte bereit, mit einem anderen Gast Zimmer zu tauschen? Es scheint uns da ein Fehler unterlaufen zu sein.)
B: **I see no objection, provided that the room is of the same standard as my present one.**
(objection – Einwand / provided – vorausgesetzt / present – jetzig)

* A: **Would you object to Room 34, sir? It's very comfortable.**
(object to – etwas haben gegen)
B: **Well, I don't really want to change rooms. I asked for that room in particular.**
(in particular – speziell)

HOTEL SERVICES

* A: **I'd like to know something about the facilities that your hotel has to offer.**
(Könnten Sie mir bitte sagen, was das Hotel alles zu bieten hat?)
B: **We have two restaurants, a sauna, a heated swimming-pool, coffee shop and bar, and we offer free transport to the airport, exchange facilities, same-day laundry service, a hairdresser, souvenir shop, disco and cocktail bar.**
(exchange facilities – Möglichkeit, Geld zu wechseln / laundry – Wäscherei / hairdresser – Frisiersalon)

* **A: What facilities are there in the rooms?**
(facilities – [zusätzliche] Ausstattung)
B: Each room has a mini-bar, colour television, separate WC, shower and bath.
(separate – eigen)

* **Do all the rooms have air-conditioning and central heating?**

* **And what about evening entertainment?**
(evening entertainment – Abendunterhaltung)

* **How about restaurant facilities?**
(Welche Möglichkeiten gibt es hier zu essen?)

* **Do you have a swimming-pool or a sauna?**

* **Is there a fitness room?**

* **A: Do you have an in-house laundry service?**
B: Yes. And an eight-hour dry-cleaning service.
(dry cleaning – chemische Reinigung)

* **A: Where can I watch television?**
B: In the lounge straight over there.
(Im Aufenthaltsraum gleich dort drüben.)

* **Does anyone mind if I switch the TV on?**
(Stört es jemanden, wenn ich den Fernseher einschalte?)

* **Can you tell me where the gents is, please?**
(gents – Herrentoilette)

* **Where's the ladies, please?**
(ladies – Damentoilette)

* **Room Service, please. Could you send up a bottle of champagne and two glasses to room 432? And a small bottle of Perrier, please.**
(bottle – Flasche)

* **Room Service, please. I know it's pretty late, but would it still be possible to have a couple of sandwiches and a bottle of beer?**
(pretty late – ziemlich spät / still – noch / a couple of – ein paar)

* **Could you arrange to have these things washed for me, please?**
(Könnten Sie bitte diese Sachen für mich waschen lassen?)

* **I'd like to have my suits ironed before ten o'clock tomorrow.**
(Würden Sie bitte dafür sorgen, daß meine Anzüge … gebügelt werden.)

* **How long will it take to have my shirts pressed?**
(take – dauern / press shirt – Hemd bügeln)

BREAKFAST
Frühstück

* **What time do you serve breakfast?**
(breakfast – Frühstück)

* **I'd like breakfast in my room at eight thirty, continental breakfast, that is.**
(that is – und zwar)

* **Could you tell me where the breakfast buffet is, please?**

* **Where is the breakfast room, please?**

* **A: What would you like? Coffee or tea?**
B: I'd prefer tea, please.
(Ich möchte lieber Tee, bitte.)

* **A: How do you like your coffee?**
B: White, no sugar please.
(white – mit Milch)

* **Black with two sugars, please.**

* **A: Could I have scrambled eggs, please?**
(scrambled eggs – Rühreier, Eierspeise)
B: And two fried eggs for me, please.
(fried eggs – Spiegeleier)

* **Would you pass me the marmalade, please?**
(Würden Sie mir bitte die Orangenmarmelade geben?)

COMPLAINTS

Beschwerden

* **I'd like to see the manager, please.**
(see sbdy. – jemanden sprechen)

* **I'd like to lodge a complaint.**
(Ich möchte mich beschweren.)

* **A: What seems to be the troube, sir?**
(Worum handelt es sich denn?)
B: I'm not at all satisfied with the service in this hotel.
(satisfied – zufrieden)

* **I wish to complain in the strongest terms about the service in this hotel.**
(Ich möchte mich ganz energisch ... beschweren.)

* **I'm afraid I don't like my room. There's too much noise from the traffic outside. Could you find me a room that is a bit quieter, please?**
(I'm afraid – tut mir leid)

* **I'm not happy with my room. I didn't sleep at all last night.**
(not ... at all – überhaupt nicht)

* **I'm afraid to have to report that I didn't get my early morning call and subsequently was late for a very important meeting.**
(report – mitteilen / subsequently – in der Folge / be late – zu spät kommen / meeting – Sitzung)

* **I'm sorry to say this, but the porter was rather rude to me just now.**
(rather rude – ziemlich unhöflich)

* **This key doesn't fit properly.**
(... paßt nicht genau.)

* **The room hasn't been cleaned.)**
(clean – reinigen)

* **The bed isn't made.**

* **There aren't any towels in my room.**
(towel – Handtuch)

* **The window doesn't shut properly.**
(Das Fenster schließt nicht ordentlich.)

* **The window doesn't open at all.**
(... geht überhaupt nicht auf.)

* **The toilet won't flush.**
(Die Spülung geht nicht.)

* **The light beside the bed doesn't work.**
(beside – neben / work – funktionieren)

* **The tap drips.**
(Der Wasserhahn tropft.)

* **There doesn't seem to be any hot water in my room.**
(Soweit ich das feststellen kann, gibt es kein Warmwasser in meinem Zimmer.)

* **The radio doesn't work.**

* **I can't seem to get the TV to work.**
(Irgendwie schaffe ich es nicht, den Fernseher einzuschalten.)

CHECKING OUT
Abreise

* **By what time do I have to check out?**
(Bis wann muß ich das Zimmer geräumt haben?)

* **When's check-out time?**

* **What time do we have to vacate the rooms?**
(vacate – räumen)

* **I'd like to check out, please.**
(Ich möchte bitte abreisen.)

* **I'm leaving tomorrow. Could you please have my bill ready?**
(Ich reise morgen ab. Könnten Sie bitte meine Rechnung fertig machen.)

* **Could you make up my bill, please. I'm leaving in an hour.**
(make up – fertig machen)

* A: **Would you prefer me to settle my bill now or after breakfast?**
(Möchten Sie lieber, daß ich meine Rechnung jetzt sofort oder nach dem Frühstück begleiche?)
B: **You can settle it right away, I have it ready. The rates include tax and service charge.**
(right away – jetzt gleich / tax – Steuer)

* **There must be a mistake. I didn't make that many telephone calls!**
(mistake – Irrtum)

* **Do you accept Eurocheques?**

* **Can I pay by Visa?**

* **I have to catch my plane to New York at five p.m. at Heathrow. Could you tell me the best way to get there in time?**
(catch plane – Maschine erwischen / five p.m. – 17 Uhr / in time – rechtzeitig)

* **Could you arrange for my luggage to be taken to the airport, please?**
(Könnten Sie bitte veranlassen, daß mein Gepäck zum Flughafen gebracht wird?)

* **Can I leave my things here until I get back?**
(leave – lassen)

BUSINESS FACILITIES

Leistungsangebot für Geschäftsleute

* **I'd need a bilingual secretary for some correspondence tomorrow afternoon. Could that be arranged?**
  (bilingual – zweisprachig)

* **Do you have a copying service? I'd need fifteen copies tomorrow at nine. It is confidential, I might add.**
  (confidential – vertraulich / add – hinzufügen)

* **Do you have an in-house translation service?**
  (translation – Übersetzung)

* **I'd need a room for a meeting tomorrow at two p.m. The group will include about ten people.**

* **What are the dimensions of the room?**
  (dimension – Ausmaß)

* **Does the room have a white board with markers?**
  (board – Tafel / marker – Schreibstift)

* **Could you arrange a flip chart and markers for Room 305 at two p.m., please?**

* **I was wondering if our name cards and holders were ready yet?**
  (Ich möchte bitte wissen, ob unsere Namensschilder schon fertig sind.)

* **We need five rooms seating up to forty people each.**
  (seat – Platz bieten)

* **What is the capacity of your Royal Garden Function Rooms?**
  (capacity – Fassungsvermögen / function room – Veranstaltungsraum)

* **What about office support services? Do you have a fax, photocopiers and secretarial services if necessary?**

* **A: I'd need a fairly large room for a party of about thirty people the day after tomorrow from about seven p.m.. I'd like to show some slides first. Have you got a slide-projector and a screen?**
(fairly – ziemlich / party – Gruppe / slide – Dia / screen – Leinwand)
B: Certainly. We can arrange that for you.
(certainly – selbstverständlich)
A: I'd like to try the equipment out tonight to make sure that everything is O.K..
(try out – ausprobieren / equipment – Geräte / tonight – heute abend / make sure – sich vergewissern)

* **We're looking for a hotel where we could hold a conference next March. Could I speak to the Conference and Banqueting Manager, please?**
(look for – suchen)

* **What AV facilities do you offer?**
(AV facilities – audio-visual facilities | audiovisuelle Einrichtungen)

* **A: How are the conference rooms technically equipped?**
(equip – ausstatten)
B: You'll find all the usual audio-visual aids: There are overhead projectors in each room, microphones and PA systems are available in the larger theatres and other facilities like cassette recorders are available on request.
(aids – Einrichtungen, Hilfen / PA system – public-address system | Lautsprecheranlage / be available – zur Verfügung stehen / theatre – Saal / on request – auf Wunsch)

VISITS AND PARTIES

Besuche und Parties

INVITATIONS

Einladungen

(see also "Restaurants, Bars, etc.: Invitations")

* A: **I don't know what your plans are, Brigitte, but would you like to have tea at my place on Bank Holiday Monday?**
(at my place – bei mir zu Hause)
B: **I've got nothing on so far, that'd be lovely. Thank you.**
(Ich habe bisher noch nichts vor, das wäre wirklich sehr nett. … .)

* A: **If you're free on Sunday, I'd like to invite you to have dinner with us at our house.**
(invite sbdy. to have dinner – jemanden zum Essen einladen)
B: **Yes I am free. That's very kind of you. When should I come?**
(kind – freundlich)

* A: **Well, if you're not doing anything on Tuesday evening, I was wondering if you'd perhaps like to join us for a meal?**
(… , möchten Sie vielleicht zu uns zum Essen kommen?)
B: **Thank you very much. I'd love to.**
(… , sehr gerne.)

* A: **Oh, by the way, we're throwing a little party tonight to celebrate Jim's promotion, Brendan. I do hope you can come.**
(by the way – übrigens / throw party – Party geben / veranstalten / celebrate – feiern / promotion – Beförderung / I do hope – ich hoffe sehr)
B: **That's very nice. I'd very much like to.**
A: **We'll be starting at around eight. Drop in any time you feel like it.**
(… . Komm vorbei, wann es dir paßt.)

* **A: Have you got any plans for tomorrow evening?**
B: Nothing in particular, no. Why?
(Nichts Besonderes, … .)
A: Well, I was just wondering if you'd be interested in coming over to my place for supper? It'd give me a chance to repay some of the hospitality you gave us in Vienna last year.
(supper – Abendessen / hospitality – Gastfreundschaft)
B: I'd be delighted, Alan. Thank you very much, I'll look forward to it.
(Sehr gerne, … . / look forward to – sich freuen auf)

* **A: If you've nothing arranged this evening, Mr. Baines, I was wondering if you'd like to come round for a drink?**
(have nothing arranged – nichts vorhaben)
B: Thanks for the invitation, but I really don't think I'll be able to come. I've got so much preparation to do for tomorrow.
(invitation – Einladung / preparation – Vorbereitungen)

* **A: If you're free on Saturday, why not come round for a drink?**
B: Thank you very much, but unfortunately I won't be here at the weekend. What a pity!
(unfortunately – leider / won't – will not / what a pity – wie schade)

* **A: My wife and I thought it would be nice if you could come to lunch on Saturday. Would that suit you?**
(lunch – Mittagessen / suit – passen)
B: I'd really like to, Mr. Appleby, but I'm afraid I've just accepted an invitation to lunch with Chris. Thank you very much all the same.
(I'm afraid – leider / just – gerade / all the same – trotzdem)

* **A: Would you like to come to dinner at my house on Wednesday at around seven thirty?**
B: I'm terribly sorry, but I'm pressed for time at the moment. Perhaps we could make it next week?
(terrible – schrecklich / be pressed for time – unter Zeitdruck sein)

ARRIVAL
Eintreffen

* **A: Good evening, Mr. Baier. I'm so pleased you could come. Do come in.**
(.... Freut mich wirklich, daß Sie kommen konnten. Kommen sie doch herein!)
B: Good evening. Thank you. What a nice place you have here.
(.... Sie haben es aber wirklich nett hier.)

* **A: Please come in.**
B: Thank you.
A: Take a seat wherever you like and make yourself feel at home.

* **A. Hi, Barbara. Brought you some flowers.**
B: Alex, they're gorgeous. I've never seen so many flowers!
(gorgeous – wunderschön)

* **A: Let me take your coat, Bruno.**
(coat – Mantel)
B: That's very kind of you, thanks.

* **A: I hope you found your way here without any trouble.**
B: Yes, no trouble at all, thank you.
(Ja, war überhaupt kein Problem, ...)

* **A: What a charming dress!**
(charming dress – bezauberndes Kleid)
B: Oh, thanks. Do you like it?

DRINKS
Getränke

(see also "Restaurants, Bars, etc.: Pubs/Pub Lunch; At the Bar")

* **A: While we're waiting, can I offer you a drink?**
B: Thanks very much. What have you got?

* **A: Well, what would you like to drink?**
B: Oh, Scotch, please.
A: With ice?
B: With ice please. On the rocks. Yes, that's fine.
(on the rocks – mit Eis)

* **A: Could you give me a whisky, please?**
B: Neat or with water?
(neat – pur)

* **A: Would you care for a drink, Mr. Bammer?**
(care for – mögen, wünschen)
B: That's very kind of you. A glass of Lager, please.
(Lager – Lagerbier)

* **Here's to you!**
(Auf Ihr Wohl!)

* **A: Drink, Bethan?**
B: Yes, an orange juice, please.
C: Same for me, please.

* **A: You look as if you need a drink. What'll you have? Some more wine?**
B: No, thanks. It's very good, but I've had enough.
(enough – genug)

* **A: Let me get you a drink.**
(get – holen, bringen)
B: I'd like a soft drink, please. A coke with ice and lemon'll do fine.
(soft drink – alkoholfreies Getränk / lemon – Zitrone / will do fine – wäre fein)

* **A: May I have a tomato juice, please?**
  B: I'm sorry, we've only got orange or grapefruit.

TEA/COFFEE

(see also "Visits and Parties: Drinks")

* **A: Would you like some tea or coffee?**
  B: I'd prefer tea, please, if you don't mind.
  (Ich möchte lieber Tee, wenn es leicht geht.)

* **A: Can I get you some tea, Bob?**
  B: Only if you're having one.
  (Nur wenn Sie sich auch einen holen.)

* **A: Would you care for a cup of coffee?**
  (Möchten Sie gerne eine Tasse Kaffee?)
  B: Mmm, I'd love a cup.

* **A: How do you like it?**
  B: Black, no sugar, please.

* **White, two sugars, please.**
  (white – mit Milch)

* **A: Ah, here's the coffee …**
  B: Thanks.
  A: Sugar, Bill?
  B: Two please. Thanks.

* **A: Could I have the sugar, please?**
  B: Yes, here you are.
  (… , hier bitte!)
  A: Thank you.

* **A: Please help yourself to coffee.**
  (Bitte nehmen Sie sich Kaffee.)
  B: Thanks, Alois, I will.

* **A: Won't you have another cup of tea, Bob?**
B: No, I'd rather not, thanks.
(Nein, eher nicht, … .)

* **A: Do you want another cup of coffee?**
B: No thanks, I'm fine.
(… , war sehr gut.)

* **A: How about a piece of cake?**
(Möchten Sie ein Stück Kuchen?)
B: Thank you, but no.

AT THE TABLE

Bei Tisch

(see also "Restaurants, Bars, etc.: During the Meal")

* **The food smells nice.**
(Das riecht aber gut.)

* **Doesn't this look lovely?**
(Das schaut aber gut aus.)

* **Do start, don't let it get cold.**
(do start – fangen Sie doch bitte an)

* **Would you mind passing the vinegar, please?**
(Würden Sie mir freundlicherweise den Essig geben?)

* **I wonder, could I have some mayonnaise or mustard, please?**
(Könnte ich bitte etwas Mayonnaise oder Senf haben?)

* **Help yourself to as much as you like, there's plenty more in the kitchen.**
(… , es ist noch genug in der Küche.)

* **A: Have you had any salad?**
B: Yes, thank you.

* **A: Would you care for a bit more fish, Mr. Burrows?**
B: Not for me, thank you.

* **A: Another slice of roast beef?**
(slice – Scheibe)
B: No, thanks, really. It's delicious but I'm on a diet.
(delicious – ausgezeichnet)

* **A: You must have some more chicken.**
(have – nehmen / chicken – Huhn)
B: No, thanks. It tastes very good, but I'm supposed to be slimming.
(.... Es schmeckt sehr gut, aber ich soll eigentlich abnehmen.)
A: Can't I tempt you?
(tempt – verführen)
B: Well, maybe I could manage a very small piece.
(manage – vertragen)

* **A: Do have the rest of the mashed potato.**
(mashed potato – Kartoffelpüree)
B: It's delicious, but I don't think I ought to.
(..., aber ich glaube, ich soll eigentlich nicht mehr.)

* **A: Could I have a second helping, please?**
(helping – Portion)
B: Please help yourself.

* **A: Would you like some fruit salad to finish with?**
(Möchten Sie etwas Fruchtsalat zum Abschluß?)
B: That sounds very nice. Yes please.
(Das hört sich sehr gut an. ....)

* **I'll have to give in. That's too much for me.**
(give in – Handtuch werfen)

* **Can I bring you some coffee and a liqueur, perhaps?**

* **Oh dear, I'm sorry. I've spilt some wine on the table-cloth.**
(spill – verschütten / table-cloth – Tischtuch)

AFTER THE MEAL

Nach dem Essen

(see also "Visits and Parties: Tea/Coffee")

* **Mmm, that was a delicious meal, Glenda.**

* **Oh, that was a lovely meal.**
  (lovely – wunderbar)

* **A: Well, that was delicious! Thank you very much indeed. I didn't know you were such a good cook!**
  B: Thank you. It's very kind of you to say so.
  A: I could do the washing-up, if you like.
  B: No, don't bother. I can put it all in the dishwasher.
  (Nein, bemühen Sie sich nicht. … ./dishwasher – Geschirrspüler)

* **A: Would you care for some brandy?**
  B: That'd be just perfect.
  (Das wäre jetzt genau das Richtige.)

* **A: Mind if I smoke?**
  (Macht es Ihnen etwas aus, wenn ich rauche?)
  B: No, go ahead.
  (Nein, rauchen Sie nur.)

* **Well, actually we'd prefer you not to. You can go out into the garden, though.**
  (Eigentlich wäre es uns lieber, wenn Sie nicht rauchen würden. … ./though – aber)

* **Could I have an ashtray, please?**
  (ashtray – Aschenbecher)

* **A: Would you like a cigarette?**
  B: No thanks, I'm trying to give up.
  (give up – aufhören)

* **A: Could I scrounge a cigarette, please? I seem to have run out.**
  (scrounge – schnorren/… . Ich glaube, ich habe keine mehr.)
  B: Yes, of course. Here you are.

AT A PARTY

(see also "Restaurants, Bars, etc.: Smoking; Out on the Town")

* **A: Nice of you to come. Come in and join the party.**
(join the party – mach mit)
B: I can't stay long, I'm afraid.

* **Is Robin coming to the party?**

* **A: Hello, Brian, it's nice to see you here ... Who are all these people?**
B: Well, you know Sheila and Joy and the girl with the glasses is Louise.
(glasses – Augengläser, Brille)
A: Oh, I know. The receptionist.
(receptionist – Dame aus der Rezeption)

* **Fancy seeing you here! I haven't seen you for ages!**
(Was, du bist auch hier! .... / for ages – ewig)

* **A: Hello, Mr. Batten. I hope you're enjoying the party.**
(.... Ich hoffe, Sie unterhalten sich gut.)
B: Yes, very much.

* **A: Good party!**
B: It's all right.
A: Nice place!

* **A: Would you like a cheese sandwich?**
B: I'd love one, thanks.
C: Not for me, thanks.

* **A: Would you like something to eat?**
B: Yes, I'll have some cheese, please.

* **A: What's in this punch? It's pretty strong.**
(pretty – ziemlich)
B: Well, it's wine and fruit juice, mainly.
A: I feel quite tipsy.
(quite tipsy – ganz schön beschwipst)

* **A: What about trying a Guinness before you go home?**
  (Möchten Sie noch einen Schluck Guinness-Bier, … ?)
  B: Well, if you don't mind, I'd prefer not to have beer. Is there any wine left?
  (… . Ist noch etwas Wein da?)

* **Excuse me, Helen. Have you got a light?**
  (light – Feuer)

* **A: Cigarette?**
  B: Oh yes, I'm dying for one.
  (… , ich bin schon ganz süchtig nach einer.)

LEAVING AND THANKING FOR HOSPITALITY

Verabschiedung und Dank für die Gastfreundschaft

* **A: Thanks very much for the delicious meal, Mrs. Basinger.**
  B: It was a pleasure to have you.
  (Es war wirklich sehr nett, daß Sie uns besucht haben.)

* **A: Thanks for a lovely evening, Martin. It was most kind of you to invite me over.**
  B: Very glad you could come.
  (glad – froh)

* **Thank you so much for a pleasant evening.**
  (pleasant – angenehm)

* **A: It's time we were off.**
  (Es ist Zeit, daß wir gehen.)
  B: What already? Won't you have another coffee?
  A: I'd love to, but I have to be up early tomorrow. Thank you for a most enjoyable evening, though.
  B: Not at all. Thank you for coming.
  (not at all – aber bitte)

* **A: I'm afraid I really must be going now. Thanks for the coffee.**
  B: Don't mention it.
  (Bitte sehr!)

* A: **Thank you very much for organising this evening. I really appreciate your hospitality.**
(.... War wirklich sehr freundlich, daß Sie uns eingeladen haben.)
B: **Not at all. Hope you can come again.**

* A: **Thank you very much for all your hospitality. I really appreciate it.**
B: **I'm glad you enjoyed it.**
(Freut mich, daß es Ihnen gefallen hat.)

* A: **It really was very kind of you to invite me. I hope it hasn't been too much trouble.**
(.... Ich hoffe, es hat Ihnen nicht zu viele Umstände gemacht.)
B: **Not at all. We've really enjoyed having you.**
(Überhaupt nicht. Wir haben uns über Ihren Besuch wirklich sehr gefreut.)

* A: **Thank you very much for everything. It's been a very relaxing few days.**
(relaxing – erholsam)
B: **It's a pity you can't stay longer.**
(it's a pity – es ist schade)

* A: **If you'll excuse me, I really should be off now. Thank you so much for an excellent tea.**
B: **Not at all. I hope you'll come and see us again soon. Drop in any time you feel like it.**
(not at all – bitte sehr / see – besuchen)
A: **Thank you, that's very kind of you.**

* A: **Bobby, thanks very much for a wonderful party.**
B: **Oh, Alison! Do you have to go? The party's just beginning.**
A: **Oh, I'm sorry. I've got to meet someone at the airport.**
(meet – abholen)

RESTAURANTS, BARS, ETC.

Restaurants, Bars usw.

INVITATIONS

Einladungen

(see also "Visits and Parties: Invitations")

* **A: Why don't we discuss this over a meal?**
(over a meal – bei einem Essen)
B: What a good idea.

* **A: I'm feeling rather peckish, shall we go for something to eat?**
(rather peckish – ziemlich hungrig)
B: Sounds like a good idea.
(Ja, das ist eine gute Idee.)

* **A: May I invite you to lunch? We could discuss some of the points over a good meal.**
(invite – einladen / lunch – Mittagessen)
B: Thank you very much. That would be very nice.

* **A: How about something to eat?**
(Gehen wir etwas essen?)
B: Yes, I'm getting really hungry. Let's have a working lunch at The Swan.

* **A: Could we have lunch together tomorrow at the "Plaza"?**
(together – zusammen)
B: That's a good idea. Let's say twelve thirty at the bar?

* **A: I was wondering if you would care to have dinner with me at my hotel tonight, if you've got nothing planned.**
(Hätten Sie Lust, heute abend mit mir in meinem Hotel zu essen, … .)
B: I'd be delighted.
(be delighted – sich sehr freuen)

* **A: What are you doing this evening?**
B: Oh, nothing special.
A: We're going out to a "Heuriger". How about joining us?
(.... Kommen Sie doch mit.)
B: Yes, with pleasure. Thank you for inviting me. What is a "Heuriger", by the way?
(pleasure – Vergnügen / by the way – übrigens)
A: Well, it's a traditional Austrian wine tavern. The emphasis is on local new wines and there's usually a nice selection of food at the buffet.
(emphasis – Betonung / local new wine – Heuriger aus der näheren Umgebung / selection – Auswahl)

* **A: Would you like to come out to dinner with Dr. Venner and me tonight?**
B: Much as I'd like to, I'm afraid I'm already booked up for tonight.
(So gerne ich auch möchte, ich habe leider für heute abend schon etwas vor.)

* **A: To be quite honest I'm getting a bit hungry. We could go over to my hotel and have dinner there. Of course, you'd be my guest.**
(quite honest – ganz ehrlich)
B: Thank you for inviting me, but I'm afraid I can't come. I've already arranged something else.
(.... Ich habe bereits etwas anderes vor.)

* **A: Shall we grab a bite to eat?**
(Gehen wir eine Kleinigkeit essen?)
B: I'm afraid I've already made other arrangements for lunch.

* **A: I was thinking you might care for some lunch tomorrow, unless you're busy.**
(care for – mögen / unless – wenn nicht / busy – beschäftigt)
B: That's very kind of you, Alice, but I don't think I can. It's my last day and I've still got a lot of work to do.
(kind – freundlich / ... und ich habe noch eine Menge Arbeit zu erledigen.)

* **A: Do you know any vegetarian restaurants around here?**
B: Well, there is an Indian restaurant just down the road which has quite a wide range of vegetarian dishes. It's supposed to

be quite good and very reasonable. Shall we give it a try?
(quite a wide range – eine ziemlich große Auswahl / dish – Gericht, Speise / .... Es soll angeblich ganz gut sein und vernünftige Preise haben. .... / give sthg. a try – etwas versuchen)

* **A: Can you recommend a good restaurant near here?**
(recommend – empfehlen)
B: The "La Grotta" is very good. It's an Italian restaurant. The food is excellent.

PUBS/PUB LUNCH

(see also "Visits and Parties: Drinks")

* **A: What are you doing for lunch?**
B: Let's go to the pub around the corner for a couple of sandwiches and a pint, shall we?
(let's go ... , shall we? – gehen wir doch / around the corner – um die Ecke / a couple of – ein paar / pint – Krügel Bier)

* **I'll just have a quick snack in a pub.**
(just – nur)

* **A: Let me get you a pint and a bite to eat down the Red Lion.**
(Ich lade dich auf ein Bier und eine Kleinigkeit zum Essen im Red Lion ein.)
B: You're on.
(Okay, fein.)

* **What about a quick drink in the Cross Keys before we go back?**
(what about – wie wär's mit)

* **A: Let's find a table.**
B: There's nothing free.
A: Oh well, let's just stand at the bar till we find a place.

* **A: What can I get you?**
(get – bestellen)
B: I'd like a pint of bitter please, Adrian.
(bitter – dunkles englisches Bier)

A: What about you, Chris?
(Und dir, ... ?)
C: The same, thanks.
A: Three pints of best, please.
(best – entspricht etwa der Qualität „Bockbier")

* **A: I could use a gin and tonic.**
(use – vertragen)
B: Me too.

* **A whisky would go down well.**
(... wäre das Richtige.)

* **A: I'm just going to the bar, can I get you a refill?**
(just – gerade / bar – Theke / ... , noch einmal dasselbe für Sie?)
B: I think I'll just have a half this time, thanks.
(just – nur)
A: And do you want any crisps?
(crisps – Kartoffelchips)
B: Yes please, get me a packet of cheese and onion, will you?
(Ja bitte, bringen Sie mir bitte ein Packerl Chips mit Käse- und Zwiebelgeschmack.)

* **A: It's my round. What are you having?**
(.... Was nehmen Sie?)
B: A Campari, please.

* **A: Let me buy you a drink, Bob.**
B: No thanks, I've just had one, and I need a clear head this afternoon.

* **A: Do you fancy something to eat?**
(Möchten Sie etwas essen?)
B: Yes, I think I'll have a ploughman's lunch.
(ploughman's lunch – typisch englisches Gericht in einem Pub)
A: I'm going to have a look and see what they've got in the way of bar meals.
(what ... in the way of – was für / bar meal – Essen, das man an der Theke bestellen und abholen muß)

* **Have they already rung for last orders?**
(ring – läuten / last order – letzte Bestellung vor der Sperrstunde)

* **It's closing time.**
  (Es ist Sperrstunde.)

* **Keep the change.**
  (Der Rest ist für Sie. | Stimmt schon.)

BOOKING A TABLE
Tischreservierung

* **A: What about dinner tonight at the Royal Crown?**
  B: Splendid, but don't you think we'd better book a table?
  (Ausgezeichnet, aber glauben Sie nicht, daß wir lieber einen Tisch reservieren sollten?)

* **I'd like to book a table for two for eight thirty tonight, please. My name is Mennel.**

* **Would you reserve us a table for six for this evening, please?**

* **A: I'd like to book a room for lunch next Thursday. I've got some people from head office coming. We'll be nine or ten.**
  (head office – Zentrale)
  B: Certainly. What kind of menu would you like?
  (certainly – gern / menu – Speisenfolge)
  A: Nothing particularly special – what do you suggest?
  (Nichts Besonderes .... / suggest – vorschlagen)
  B: Our regular menu, then – we normally do a starter followed by a main course and salad, cheese and a dessert.
  (regular – üblich / do – servieren / starter – Vorspeise / main course – Hauptgericht / dessert – süße Nachspeise)

* **Could you check with the restaurant whether the table is booked for Wednesday evening?**
  (check with – rückfragen in)

AT THE RECEPTION

* **Is it possible to have something to eat now?**

* **Do you do lunch?**
  (Kann man hier mittagessen?)

* **Is this table free?**

* **A: Would you like this table by the fireplace?**
  (fireplace – Kamin)
  B: That'll be fine, thank you.

* **A: A table for two, please.**
  B: I'm afraid there's nothing free at the moment. But if you care to have a drink at the bar first, I think I can let you have the table by the window in about twenty minutes.
  (I'm afraid – tut mir leid / about – etwa)

* **Let's go over to the bar and have a drink while we wait for our table.**
  (while – während)

* **A: I have booked a table for two people for eight o'clock. My Name is Ammer.**
  B: Ah yes. Your guest hasn't arrived yet. Would you care for a drink at the bar first?
  (.... Ihr Gast ist noch nicht gekommen. Möchten Sie zuerst einen Drink an der Bar?)
  A: Yes. Could you show her over when she comes? Her name is Hutchinson.
  (show over – herführen)

AT THE BAR

(see also "Restaurants, Bars, etc.: Pubs/Pub Lunch" and "Visits and Parties: Drinks")

* **Let's have a drink, shall we?**
  (Wie wär's mit einem Drink?)

* **The usual dry Martini for you, Brigitte?**
  (dry – trocken)

* **The same again, please.**

* **It's on me.**
  (Das zahle ich.|Das geht auf meine Rechnung.)

* **Here's to the export deal. Cheers!**
  (Auf das Exportgeschäft! Zum Wohl!)

ORDERING

Bestellung

* **Waiter, the menu, please.**
  (Herr Ober, die Speisekarte bitte!)

* **A: Do you think you could ask the people at the next table if we could look at their menu?**
  B: Yes, of course. Excuse me, could you possibly let us see your menu?

* **Could I see the wine list, please?**
  (wine list – Weinkarte)

* **A: Would you like an aperitif before you order?**
  (order – bestellen)
  B: Yes, two dry sherries, please.

* **What's on the menu?**

* **A: What can you recommend?**
(recommend – empfehlen)
B: Why don't you try the "Tafelspitz"? It's an Austrian speciality. It's very tender, boiled beef.
(tender – zart / boil – kochen)

* **A: Have you ever tried "Wienerschnitzel"? It's many Austrians' favourite meal – it's veal or pork fried in egg and breadcrumbs, served with chips or rice.**
(favourite meal – Lieblingsgericht / veal – Kalbfleisch / pork – Schweinefleisch / fried in egg and breadcrumbs – paniert / chips – Pommes frites)
B: I'm not sure because of my cholesterol level.
(cholesterol level – Cholesterinspiegel)

* **A: What would you like to start with?**
(Was möchten Sie als erstes?)
B: I think I'll have the prawn cocktail.
(prawn cocktail – Shrimpscocktail)

* **Would you like an hors-d'oeuvre?**
(hors-d'oeuvre – Vorspeise)

* **A: What would you like, Barbara?**
B: I think I'll try the lamb chop. But I'll start off with the soup of the day.
(lamb chop – Lammkotelett)

* **A: What's the soup of the day?**
B: Cream of mushroom. Served with home-made rolls and butter.
(cream of mushroom – Pilzcremesuppe / home-made rolls – selbstgemachte Brötchen)

* **A: What would you like as a main course?**
B: I really don't know whether I fancy meat or fish.
(whether – ob / fancy – nehmen sollen / meat – Fleisch)

* **A: What are you having?**
(Was nehmen Sie?)
B: I'm famished, I think I'll take the mixed grill.
(Ich bin fast am Verhungern, … .)

C: I think I'll just have something light.
(just – nur)

* **A: I really like shellfish. But it's so incredibly expensive here.**
(shellfish – Austern, Hummer, Langusten usw. / incredible – unglaublich / expensive – teuer)
B: Yes, that's the trouble. I think I'll settle for the T-bone steak, myself.
(trouble – Problem / settle for – sich entscheiden für)

* **A: Do you like seafood?**
(seafood – Meeresfrüchte)
B: I'm not overkeen, actually. And in fact I'm a bit allergic to it.
(Eigentlich bin ich nicht allzusehr versessen darauf. ... .)

* **Would you like boiled or fried potatoes?**
(... Salz- oder Bratkartoffeln?)

* **A: Would you like red or white wine?**
B: No wine for me thanks, I'm driving.
(drive – mit dem Auto fahren)

* **A: May I take your order, sir?**
(order – Bestellung)
B: Could you come back in a moment? We haven't made up our minds yet.
(.... Wir haben uns noch nicht entschieden.)

* **A: Are you ready to order now?**
(order – bestellen)
B: Yes, I'll have the roast beef with Yorkshire pudding and peas, please.
(Yorkshire pudding – typisch englische nichtsüße Beilage / peas – Erbsen)

* **A: Would you like to order your wine, sir?**
B: I've already ordered, thank you very much.

* **Can I order now, please?**

* **I'd like to order something to eat.**

* **A: I'll have avocado to start with, followed by a fillet steak.**
B: How would you like your steak?
A: Well done for me.
(well done – gut durch)
C: Medium to rare for me.
(Halb durch bis blutig … .)

* **For starters we'll have two smoked salmon, followed by the pork dish.**
(smoked salmon – Räucherlachs)

* **A: I think I'll have the roast lamb, please.**
(roast lamb – Lammbraten)
B: What vegetables would you like?
(vegetables – Gemüse)
A: What have you got?

* **What vegetables come with the fried plaice?**
(fried plaice – gebratene oder panierte Scholle)

* **Would you kindly tell us what Mexican dressing is?**
(kindly – bitte / dressing – Dressing, Salatsoße)

* **Do you do half portions for children?**
(Haben Sie Kinderportionen?)

* **Do you serve vegetarian food as well?**
(serve – haben)

* **What would you suggest as a sweet?**
(suggest – vorschlagen / sweet – süße Nachspeise)

* **How about freshly-made apple pie with cream?**
(how about – wie wär's mit / cream – Schlagobers)

* **I could recommend the "Milchrahmstrudel" – it's a type of strudle with cream cheese and custard. Delicious!**
(cream cheese – Topfen / custard – Vanillesoße / delicious – schmeckt ausgezeichnet)

* **A: Do you fancy a dessert?**
(fancy – Lust haben auf)
B: I'd love to, but I really feel full!

* **Well – I really shouldn't, but I will.**

* **No, I don't think I could manage one. You go ahead though.**
  (Nein, ich glaub', es geht nicht mehr. Lassen Sie sich aber nicht abhalten.)

* **Could we see the sweet trolley, please?**
  (sweet trolley – Dessertwagerl)

* **For dessert I'll have a piece of Black Forest gateau.**
  (piece – Stück / Black Forest gateau – Schwarzwälder Kirschtorte)

* **I'd like a selection from the cheeseboard, please.**
  (selection from the cheeseboard – verschiedene Käsesorten)

* **Will it take long? We're a bit in a hurry.**
  (take – dauern)

DURING THE MEAL

Während des Essens

(see also "Visits and Parties: At the Table")

* **That's a very nice sherry.**

* **A: How's your meal?**
  B: Fine. The trout is very good.
  (trout – Forelle)

* **The sole is delicious.**
  (sole – Seezunge)

* **What I like about British cooking is the vegetables.**

* **A: A little more wine?**
  B: Just a little. I'm not used to drinking wine at midday.
  (be used to – daran gewöhnt sein)

* **Would you pass me the salt, please?**
  (pass – geben)

* **A: Could I borrow your salt and pepper?**
  (Könnte ich kurz Ihren Salz- und Pfefferstreuer haben?)
  B: Yes, certainly.
  (certainly – gern)

* **Could you try and catch the waiter's eye? I can't see him at all from here.**
  (Könntest du dem Kellner winken? .... / not ... at all – überhaupt nicht)

* **Would you bring us another bottle of wine, please?**

* **A: I'd like to propose a toast to the new project.**
  (propose a toast to – Toast ausbringen auf)
  All: To the new project!

* **A: Is the wine to your liking?**
  (Schmeckt Ihnen der Wein?)
  B: Yes, it's very good.

* **No, I'm afraid it's corked.**
  (... , er hat leider einen Korkengeschmack.)

* **Could we have a little more bread, please?**

* **Can I have a napkin, please?**
  (napkin – Serviette)

* **A: May I take this away now, sir?**
  B: Yes. Please do. My compliments to the chef. The lobster was delicious.
  (chef – Küchenchef / lobster – Hummer)

* **The service is very friendly and efficient, isn't it?**
  (efficient – flott / isn't it? – meinen Sie nicht auch?)

* **What a lovely place for a business lunch. The food is really excellent here. Do you come here often?**
  (business lunch – Geschäftsessen)

SMOKING

* **A: Do you mind if I smoke?**
  (Macht es Ihnen etwas aus, wenn ich rauche?)
  B: I'd rather you didn't. I'm still eating.
  (Es wäre mir lieber, wenn Sie nicht rauchen würden. .... / still – noch)

* **A: Cigarette?**
  B: No, thanks, not at the moment.

* **A: Have a cigarette.**
  B: No, thanks. I've just put one out.
  (put out – ausdämpfen)

* **No thanks. I'm trying to cut down.**
  (.... Ich versuche, weniger zu rauchen.)

* **A: Would you care for a cigarette?**
  B: No, thanks, I don't smoke.

* **Do you have a selection of cigars?**

* **A: Will you have a cigar?**
  (Möchten Sie eine Zigarre?)
  B: That's very kind of you, but I won't.
  (kind – freundlich / won't – will not)

* **Have you got a light, please?**
  (light – Feuer)

COMPLAINTS
Beschwerden

* **We need another fork and two more knives.**
  (Wir brauchen noch eine Gabel und zwei Messer.)

* **A: Is everything all right?**
  B: Not exactly. My steak is underdone. I asked for it medium. And I'm sorry to say this, but it's rather cold.
  (underdone – zu wenig durch / medium – halb durch / rather – ziemlich)

* **Sorry, but we didn't order this.**

* **I'd like to speak to the head waiter, please. This is not the standard I've come to expect here.**
  (head waiter – Oberkellner / expect – erwarten)

THE BILL
Die Rechnung

* **Waiter, the bill, please!**
  (Herr Ober, die Rechnung bitte! | … , zahlen, bitte!)

* **Could I have the bill, please?**

* **Put it on my bill, please. Room 485.**
  (put – setzen)

* **All together, please.**
  (Alles zusammen, … .)

* **It's my treat.**
  (Sie sind mein Gast | meine Gäste.)

* **We'll split the bill next time, but this time it's on us.**
  (split – teilen / … , aber dieses Mal bezahlen wir.)

* **I must insist that I pay for my own meal tonight.**
  (insist that – bestehen darauf, daß)

* **Separate bills, please.**
  (Getrennte Rechnungen, … .)

* **Shall we go Dutch on the bill?**
  (Machen wir getrennte Rechnung?)

* **A: Is it customary to tip the waiter?**
  (Ist es üblich, dem Kellner Trinkgeld zu geben?)
  B: Yes, I think ten per cent of the bill is the normal tip.
  (tip – Trinkgeld)

* **Thank you for this excellent meal. Let me take care of the tip, if you don't mind.**
  (… . Ich erledige das mit dem Trinkgeld, wenn Sie nichts dagegen haben.)

* **Is service included?**

* **I don't think this is quite right. We didn't have any soup.**
  (quite – ganz)

* **There must be a mistake. Could you check my bill again? You seem to have added the figures up wrongly.**
  (mistake – Fehler, Irrtum / check again – nachrechnen / … . Sie dürften sich verrechnet haben.)

* **I'd like to pay by credit card, please.**

* **That's for you.**

AFTER THE MEAL

Nach dem Essen

(see also "Visits and Parties: Leaving and Thanking for Hospitality")

* **It was a good lunch. Thanks for inviting me.**

* **A: I hope you enjoyed your dinner.**
(Ich hoffe, das Essen hat Ihnen geschmeckt.)
B: Yes, I did, thank you. It was delicious.

* **Well, that was really most enjoyable, David. Thank you very much indeed.**

* **A: Thank you for inviting me, Mr. Baxter. I really enjoyed the meal.**
B: Good. I'm glad you liked it.
(be glad – sich freuen)

* **Thanks for asking me out, Jim. I've enjoyed myself a lot.**
(ask out – ausführen, einladen / … . Ich habe mich wirklich gut unterhalten.)

* **Would you like to go on somewhere else for a drink?**
(go on somewhere else – noch irgendwo anders hingehen)

* **A: I was thinking of going on to a jazz club now. Would you like to join me?**
(join sbdy. – mit jemandem mitgehen)
B: I'm rather tired, I think I'll go straight home, actually, we've got a hard day tomorrow.
(straight – gleich)

OUT ON THE TOWN

Nachtleben

(see also "Visits and Parties: At a Party")

* **We're thinking of going to a disco. Will you come with us?**

* **A: I'm really sorry, but I can't make it to the disco tonight.**
(make – schaffen)
B: Oh, that's a real shame.
(Das ist aber wirklich schade.)

* **A: Shall we go to a night club? I know one where the music's really good.**
B: I wouldn't mind going.
(Ja, gern.)

* **We could go dancing somewhere, if you like.**

* **Do we have to pay to get in?**

* **Do you want to dance?**

* **Can I ask you for this dance?**

* **The music's a bit loud, shall we talk outside?**

* **A: I really must be going if I want to catch the last train back.**
(catch – erwischen)
B: I'll give you a lift back to your hotel, don't worry.
(give sbdy. a lift – jemanden mit dem Auto mitnehmen / don't worry – kein Grund zur Eile)
A: That'd be nice, thank you.

* **Can I walk you home?**
(Kann ich Sie nach Hause begleiten?)

* **May I see you home?**
(Darf ich Sie nach Hause bringen?)

* **A: Let me drive you home.**
(Darf ich Sie mit dem Auto nach Hause bringen?)
B: Well, that's very nice of you, but only if it's not inconvenient.
(… , aber nur, wenn es Ihnen keine Umstände macht.)
A: It's no problem. It's on my way.

FORMAL OCCASIONS

Offizielle Anlässe

TOASTS – GENERAL

Allgemeine Toasts

* **A: Your very good health, Mr. Bentley!**
  (Auf Ihr ganz spezielles Wohl, Herr Bentley!)
  B: Thank you. And yours!
  (… und auf das Ihre!)

* **At this point I should like to propose a toast to our good friend David. Here's to you, David!**
  (Hier möchte ich einen Toast auf unseren guten Freund David ausbringen. Auf dein Wohl, David!)

TOASTS – THANKING SOMEBODY

Toasts in Verbindung mit einem Dank

* **At this point I should like to propose a toast to a member of our working group, whom unforeseen circumstances force to leave us earlier than expected. Thank you very much for your valuable contributions Peter, and here's to your very good health!**
  (unforeseen – unvorhergesehen / circumstances – Umstände / force – zwingen / leave – verlassen / expect – erwarten / valuable – wertvoll / contribution – Beitrag)

* **Ladies and gentlemen, may I have your attention please for a moment. I just want to say thank you to all of you for the splendid job you've done in organising the presentation here in Brighton. I hope you will give me a chance to repay your hospitality next year. Here's to you all!**
  (attention – Aufmerksamkeit / splendid job – großartige Arbeit / repay hospitality – Gastfreundschaft erwidern / Here's to you all! – Auf Ihr Wohl)

TOASTS – BEST WISHES FOR THE FUTURE

Toasts in Verbindung mit besten Wünschen für die Zukunft

* **I'm sure that this will be the start of a long period of mutually beneficial co-operation. Let us raise our glasses to Hunter Cement and Brown Construction and to everything the two companies stand for. May the new arrangement have a long and prosperous future!**
(mutually beneficial – für beide Seiten fruchtbringend / raise – erheben / stand for – repräsentieren / arrangement – Abmachung, Vereinbarung / prosperous – nutzbringend / future – Zukunft)

* **Excuse me, ladies and gentlemen. Before we break up I'd just like to say how glad we from Briars Ltd. are that we have finally managed to come to an agreement. Here's to many years of fruitful co-operation between our two companies!**
(break up – auseinandergehen / glad – froh / Ltd. – private limited company | etwa: GmbH in Großbritannien / finally – schließlich / manage – es schaffen / agreement – Abkommen / .... Auf viele Jahre fruchtbarer Zusammenarbeit zwischen unseren beiden Gesellschaften!)

* **A: Ladies and gentlemen, it is with the greatest pleasure that I invite you to raise your glasses to the future health and prosperity of Brown Construction. May the next hundred years be even more successful than the last. Brown Construction!**
(pleasure – Vergnügen / invite – einladen / future – zukünftig / health – Gedeihen / prosperity – wirtschaftlicher Erfolg / even – noch / successful – erfolgreich)
B: Hear, hear!
(Hört, Hört!)

TOASTS – CONGRATULATING PEOPLE
Toasts in Verbindung mit Gratulationen

* **I'd like to propose a toast! We have a lot to celebrate this evening. First, welcome back to Carl, who has just returned from the United States, where he negotiated a very complex information exchange agreement with UNEX Corp. Here's to you, Carl!**
(a lot – viel / celebrate – feiern / return – zurückkehren / negotiate – aushandeln / information exchange – Informationsaustausch / Corp. – corporation | etwa: Aktiengesellschaft in den U.S.A.)

* **Next I'd like to raise my glass to John, who has successfully completed talks with the Science Secretary on a major R&D grant for our company. John!**
(complete – abschließen / Science Secretary – Wissenschaftsminister / major – größer / R & D – research and development | Forschung und Entwicklung / grant – Subvention; staatlicher Zuschuß)

* **A: And finally a toast to Eve, who has just won the company's first order in India. To Eve! Well done!**
(win – gewinnen; an Land ziehen / order – Auftrag)
B: Eve!

ANNOUNCEMENTS
Ankündigungen und Verlautbarungen

* **Ladies and gentlemen, welcome to Lancer Bikes. We have invited you because we want to make an important announcement.**
(invite – einladen / important – wichtig / announcement – Ankündigung, Verlautbarung)

* **Ladies and gentlemen, thank you all for having taken the trouble to come out here to Friars Ltd. in the middle of a busy week. I think the announcement I have to make will be of some interest to financial analysts covering the furniture industry.**
(trouble – Mühe / busy – arbeitsreich / analyst – Analyst, Wertpapierforscher / cover – bearbeiten / furniture – Möbel)

* **Unfortunately it is my sad duty to announce the closure of one of our plants.**
(Leider ist es meine traurige Pflicht, die Schließung eines unserer Werke anzukündigen.)

* **We have just received word from our representative in Cairo that we have been awarded a major government contract for the construction of fifteen truck service garages. The contract is the largest in the history of the company and if everything goes well, will make a major contribution to our profits.**
(receive word – Mitteilung erhalten / representative – Vertreter / be awarded a government contract – den Zuschlag für einen öffentlichen Auftrag erhalten / truck – LKW / service garage – Service-/Reparaturwerkstätte / history – Geschichte / major contribution – wichtiger Beitrag)

* **Ladies and gentlemen, I am pleased to be able to report another successful year for FG plc. We are proud to say that we have managed to increase profits in spite of the downturn in the economy as a whole.**
(report – melden, berichten / plc – public limited company; etwa: Aktiengesellschaft in Großbritannien / proud – stolz / manage – es schaffen / increase – erhöhen / in spite of – trotz / downturn in the economy as a whole – Konjunkturabschwächung)

CELEBRATIONS

Feiern

* **We have come together here today to celebrate the 50th anniversary of Zorko plc, which from very humble beginnings in a small village in Shropshire has grown into a successful international group.**
(celebrate – feiern / anniversary – Jahresfeier, Jahrestag / humble – bescheiden / village – Dorf / grow – wachsen; sich entwickeln / successful – erfolgreich / group – Konzern)

* **I have called this impromptu gathering to tell you that we have just shipped our 5,000th lathe and I think this merits a little celebration.**
(call – einberufen / impromptu gathering – improvisierte Zusammenkunft / ship – ausliefern / lathe – Drehbank / merit – verdienen / celebration – Feier)

WELCOMING PEOPLE

Jemanden begrüßen

* **Ladies and gentlemen, I'd like to welcome you to our annual salesmen's conference, both on behalf of the Marketing Department and the Board of Directors.**
(annual salesmen's conference – Jahresversammlung des Vertriebspersonals / on behalf – im Namen / department – Abteilung / Board of Directors – Verwaltungsrat; Führungsgremium einer britischen / amerikanischen Kapitalgesellschaft)

* **In particular I would like to extend a cordial welcome to our guests of honour, above all to the Mayor of Telford, in whose city the new factory is to be located.**
(particular – besonders / extend cordial welcome to – herzlich begrüßen / guest of honour – Ehrengast / mayor – Bürgermeister / factory – Fabrik / locate – ansiedeln)

* **An especially cordial welcome to the representatives of the Birmingham Chamber of Commerce, who from the very beginning have stood behind our projects and without whose valuable help we probably would not be opening the new plant today.**
(especial – besonders / chamber of commerce – Handelskammer / valuable – wertvoll / probably – wahrscheinlich / plant – Werk)

THANKING FOR INVITATION

Dank für Einladung

I consider it a great honour to have been asked to award the Best Salesman's Trophy for 1991. The Evaluation Committee have nominated Mr. Boll. Mr. Boll, would you like to come up, please.
(consider – betrachten / honour – Ehre / award – verleihen / evaluation – Bewertung, Selektion / come up – herauskommen, heraufkommen)

* **It is a great honour for me to have been invited to address the annual dealers' conference. The subject of my talk will be "Can selling be overdone?"**
(address a conference – das Wort an eine Konferenz richten / dealer – Händler / subject – Thema / overdo – übertreiben)

THANKING PEOPLE

Wie man sich bedankt

* **We are gathered here today to pay tribute to somebody who has given this company 25 years of uninterrupted valuable service, Mr. Grant Bruster, the well-known and well-liked Head of Marketing. Thank you very much, Mr. Bruster!**
(gather – zusammenkommen / pay tribute – Achtung zollen / uninterrupted – ununterbrochen / head – Leiter)

* **Grant, I would like to thank you, both on behalf of myself and of the Board of Directors, for all you have done for our company!**

* **Special thanks also go to Mr. Binner, who volunteered to host this sales conference in spite of the considerable pressure of work that his position involves.**
(special – besondere[r,s] / volunteer – sich freiwillig bereit erklären / host – als Gastgeber für … fungieren / in spite of – trotz / considerable – beträchtlich / pressure – Belastung / position – Stellung / involve – mit sich bringen)

* **Ladies and gentlemen, my colleagues have asked me to say a few words before we break up. I'd just like to say how grateful we are to you for all the help you have given us in the past three weeks. We thoroughly appreciate it.**
(break up – auseinandergehen / grateful – dankbar / in the past three weeks – in den letzten drei Wochen / thoroughly appreciate sthg. – etwas wirklich zu schätzen wissen)

* **Excuse me everyone. I don't want to make a formal speech or anything. But before I leave I'd just like to say how pleasant my stay has been. I hope that I will be able to repay some of your hospitality. Should you ever come to Vienna, don't fail to contact me.**

(speech – Rede / anything – etwas Derartiges / leave – abreisen / pleasant – angenehm / stay – Aufenthalt / ever – jemals / fail – es verabsäumen)

* **I just want to say a few words of thanks before I leave. I really appreciate how everyone has done their best to make me feel at home. I hope to see you all again as soon as I can arrange my next business trip.**
(appreciate – dankbar sein für; zu würdigen wissen / trip – Reise)

TV, RADIO, VIDEO, ETC.

Fernsehen, Radio, Video usw.

* **A: What do you do in your spare time?**
(spare time – Freizeit)
B: Oh, nothing special. I watch TV or listen to the radio.
(watch TV – fernsehen / listen to the radio – Radio hören)

* **A: Do you watch much TV?**
B: Not really. I do always watch the news, though.
(Eigentlich nicht. Ich schaue mir aber immer die Nachrichten an.)

* **A: Do you enjoy watching TV?**
(Sehen Sie gerne fern?)
B: From time to time – it depends what's on. I like watching documentaries and nature programmes.
(Gelegentlich – es hängt davon ab, was auf dem Programm ist. ….)

* **A: Do you like to watch TV?**
B: We haven't got a TV – we think it's a bad influence on the kids.
(influence – Einfluß / kid – Kind)

* **Do you ever watch telly?**
(ever – jemals / watch telly – fernsehen)

* **A: Is there anything interesting on the radio now?**
B: I don't know, Adrian; here, have a look in the newspaper.

* **A: What's on the radio this evening?**
B: I think there's a concert being broadcast live from Vienna, if you like that kind of thing.
(broadcast – übertragen, senden)

* **What wavelength is the BBC World Service on?**
(wavelength – Wellenlänge)

* **What's on TV tonight?**

* **A: Is there anything worth watching on TV tonight?**
(anything worth watching – irgend etwas Sehenswertes)
B: I think there's a film with Paul Newman on BBC 2. The write-up in the paper was excellent.
(write-up – Kritik, Besprechung / paper – Zeitung)
A: Sounds good. Let's watch it.
(sound – klingen)

* **There's an excellent quiz programme on tonight – you mustn't miss it.**
(… – das dürfen Sie nicht verpassen.)

* **A: What's on TV this afternoon?**
B: They usually have sport on a Saturday afternoon.

* **A: Would you mind if I don't come along with you to the pub tonight, there's something on TV I'd like to watch.**
B: No, not at all – if it's finished before closing time, why don't you come down and join us for last orders?
(closing time – Sperrstunde / join sbdy. for last orders – mit jemandem vor der Sperrstunde noch rasch etwas trinken)
A: I don't think it finishes before 11 o'clock actually.

* **A: Do you mind if I switch over? The news is on the other channel.**
(Haben Sie etwas dagegen, wenn ich umschalte? … .)
B: Not at all, I'd quite like to see it myself actually.
(not at all – ganz im Gegenteil; überhaupt nicht)

* **A: Do you know what channel the tennis match is on?**
B: I think it's on Channel 4.

* **Don't you want to watch part two of the serial?**
(serial – Serie)

* **Does anyone mind if I watch the rugby?**

* **Would you mind turning it down a bit?**
(turn down – leiser stellen)

* **Could you turn it up a bit, please? I can't hear it properly.**
(turn up – lauter stellen / properly – ordentlich)

* A: **The picture is a bit blurred, isn't it?**
(Das Bild ist ein bißchen verschwommen, nicht wahr?)
B: **Yes, it is, isn't it? I'll try and adjust the aerial.**
(aerial – Antenne)

* **The reception is really bad.**
(reception – Empfang)

* **Can you adjust the colour, please?**
(adjust colour – Farbe einstellen)

* **Have you seen the remote control?**
(remote control – Fernbedienung)

* **I find it very difficult to understand the dialects some of the actors are using.**
(actor – Schauspieler)

* **Do you mind if I switch it off?**
(switch off – abschalten)

* **Don't switch it off. I've been looking forward to this programme all day.**
(look forward to – sich freuen auf)

* **Has this set got teletext?**
(set – Apparat)

* A: **What are the TV programmes like in your country, Brian?**
(Wie sind die Fernsehprogramme … ?)
B: **Not bad – compared with other countries.**
(compare – vergleichen)

* A: **What about TV in your country, Berthold?**
(Wie steht's mit dem Fernsehen … ?)
B: **Well, we've got two channels – unless you've got cable TV, of course, then you can pick up about 15 stations altogether, but you have to pay extra. Many Austrians who live near the border can receive foreign programmes. If you live in Salzburg, for example, you can tune into several West German stations.**

(unless – es sei denn / pick up – empfangen / border – Grenze / receive – empfangen / foreign – ausländisch / tune into – empfangen)

* A: **Don't you have any soap operas on Austrian TV? – Everyone watches Eastenders and Coronation Street here!**
(soap opera – Seifenoper)
B: **Oh, I've never heard of those. We've just some of the American soaps like Dallas, Falcon Crest and Dynasty – I think they're a load of rubbish myself!**
(load of rubbish – kompletter Mist)

* A: **Do you have many adverts on TV in Austria, Boris?**
(advert – Werbespot)
B: **No, not too many – they have certain times during the day where you can advertise on TV, that's all. So none of the programmes are ever interrupted.**
(advertise – werben / interrupt – unterbrechen)
C: **That sounds much better than in England. I think there are more commercial breaks on ITV and Channel 4 than on ordinary TV programmes.**
(commercial break – Programmunterbrechung zu Werbezwecken)

* A: **Have you ever tried TV advertising in your company?**
(advertising – Werbung / company – Firma, Gesellschaft)
B: **We did once, but without the right connections it's impossible to get enough slots to carry out an effective campaign – there are only a limited number available, I'm afraid.**
(once – einmal / connection – Verbindung / slot – Werbezeit / carry out – durchführen / available – verfügbar / I'm afraid – leider)
A: **My company is running two commercials at the moment. It's really expensive – I don't think it's a suitable medium for us, to be honest.**
(run commercial – Werbespot schalten / suitable – passend, geeignet / honest – ehrlich)

* **Have you got cable TV in your country?**

* **Have you seen one of the new digital models? Fantastic, I can tell you.**

* **I've got a fairly good TV set with about 40 channels and teletext. I can also use it as a home-banking terminal.**
(fairly – ziemlich)

* **The commercial stations show too many video clips for my taste.**
(commercial station – Privatsender / taste – Geschmack)

* **A: Have you got a VCR, Bill?**
(VCR – video cassette recorder | Videogerät)
B: Yes, I have. But I've found that although I tape loads of things I'd like to watch, I never get round to watching them!
(although – obwohl / tape – aufnehmen / load – Menge / get round to sthg. – zu etwas kommen)

* **One of the best business programmes is on after midnight, so I usually record it on my VCR.**
(record – aufnehmen)

* **A: Home videos are all the rage here now, you know.**
(home video – Videofilm für zu Hause / be all the rage – in sein)
B: Yes, I've noticed – the video rental business isn't quite as large in Austria. I never rent video films, even though I do have a video recorder.
(notice – bemerken / video rental business – Videoverleih / quite – ganz / rent – ausleihen / even though – obwohl)

* **A: So this is your new CD player – it looks pretty good.**
(CD – compact disc / player – Plattenspieler / ... der schaut aber gut aus.)
B: The quality is excellent – especially for classical music.

* **A: I've just invested in a CD player for my car.**
B: That sounds good, I didn't know you could get them for cars as well.

CINEMA, THEATRE, OPERA, CONCERTS AND MUSEUMS

Kino, Theater, Oper, Konzerte und Museen

CINEMA

* **Is there anything on at the cinema worth seeing this week?**
  (be on – auf dem Programm sein / cinema – Kino / worth seeing – sehenswert)

* **What's on at the cinema this week?**

* **A: There's a very good Jane Fonda film on near here.**
  B: I never have liked Jane Fonda, I'm afraid.
  (I'm afraid – tut mir leid)

* **Are you going to be busy this evening? I was wondering if you might like to come to the cinema with me.**
  (be busy – etwas vorhaben; beschäftigt sein / … . Möchten Sie vielleicht mit mir ins Kino gehen?)

* **A: Would you like to come to the pictures tonight?**
  (pictures – Kino / tonight – heute abend)
  B: I'd love to. What's on?
  (Sehr gerne. … ?)

* **A: Shall we go to the pictures tonight?**
  B: That's a good idea. I haven't been for ages.
  (… . Ich bin schon eine Ewigkeit nicht gewesen.)
  A: Fine. I'll come round and pick you up at your hotel.
  (pick up – abholen)

* **A: What do you fancy seeing?**
  (Was möchten Sie gerne sehen?)
  B: I don't mind really. What film would you like to see?
  (Das ist mir eigentlich gleich. … ?)

* A: **How about going to the cinema?**
(Gehen wir ins Kino?)
B: **Oh, good idea. We could meet at the box-office. At quarter past seven?**
(meet – sich treffen / box-office – Kassa / quarter past seven – Viertel nach sieben)
A: **OK. Let's do that.**

* A: **Could you come to the cinema tonight?**
B: **I wish I could, but I've got this wretched meeting tomorrow.**
(… , aber ich habe blöderweise diese Sitzung morgen.)

* A: **It really is a very good film.**
B: **I'm sorry, it's not possible, maybe another evening?**

* A: **Shall we go and see that new film with Robert de Niro tonight?**
B: **Yes, that's great! Robert de Niro is one of my favourite actors.**
(great – super / favourite actor – Lieblingsschauspieler)

* **When does the film start?**

* **How much are the tickets?**
(Wieviel kosten die Karten?)

* A: **What are you going to see?**
B: **The new Kevin Costner film. Why don't you come as well?**
(… . Kommen Sie doch auch mit.)
A: **Oh, that would be nice, yes! … Oh, … oh dear, I'm busy tonight, I'm afraid. What about tomorrow night? Is that any good to you?**
(… . Geht das bei Ihnen?)
B: **Oh dear, no, I'm afraid I'm busy then myself.**

* A: **Have you seen the new film at the Odeon?**
B: **No, not yet, but I was planning to go this week.**
(not yet – noch nicht)
A: **Why don't we go together, then?**
(Gehen wir doch gemeinsam.)
B: **Fine, how about on Wednesday?**
(how about – wie wär's)
A: **That's fine by me.**

* **Shall I get tickets in advance for the film? They're often sold out.**
(get tickets – Karten besorgen / in advance – im voraus)

* **A: I didn't manage to get tickets. It's sold out.**
(Es ist mir nicht gelungen, Karten zu bekommen. … .)
B: Oh, bad luck.
(So ein Pech!)

* **Is this the queue for "The Godfather III"?**
(queue – Schlange / godfather – Pate)

* **A: Do you like French films?**
B: Yes, though I prefer Italian ones.
(though – obwohl / prefer – lieber haben; bevorzugen)

* **What do you think of German films?**

* **A: What do you think of "Switch"?**
B: I don't know I haven't seen it yet. It's supposed to be fairly good, isn't it?
(not … yet – noch nicht / … . Er soll angeblich recht gut sein, nicht?)
A: Well, it's got good reviews here. And it's directed by Blake Edwards.
(reviews – Kritiken / … . Und Blake Edwards führt Regie.)

* **A: Who's in it?**
(Wer spielt mit?)
B: Oh, Ellen Barkin.
A: Oh, great! I really like her. She's a good actress and she's got lovely legs.
(actress – Schauspielerin / legs – Beine)

* **Who stars in that new Alan Parker film?**
(Wer spielt … die Hauptrolle?)

* **Who plays the main part?**
(Wer spielt die Hauptrolle?)

* **I find Westerns rather boring.**
(rather boring – ziemlich langweilig)

* **I can't stand horror films.**
  (stand – ausstehen)

* **I'm rather keen on comedies.**
  (Ich schaue mir gerne Komödien an.)

* **I'm not overkeen on watching violent films.**
  (Ich bin nicht allzusehr versessen darauf, mir gewalttätige Filme anzuschauen.)

——— ❖ ———

* **A: What did you think of that?**
  B: Well, it was entertaining.
  (entertaining – unterhaltsam)

* **The ending was a bit weak, wasn't it?**
  (Der Schluß war ein bißchen schwach, nicht?)

* **I was expecting a completely different ending.**
  (Ich habe mir ein völlig anderes Ende erwartet.)

* **I thought the story-line was a bit weak, but the photography was excellent.**
  (story-line – Handlung)

* **I thought Jack Nicholson was really overacting, didn't you?**
  (overact – übertrieben spielen / … , meinen Sie nicht auch?)

* **A: Did you like that?**
  B: Well, I thought it wasn't that good, actually.

* **A: Did you enjoy that?**
  (Hat Ihnen der Film gefallen?)
  B: Yes, indeed. I enjoyed it very much, thank you.

* **The film was really exciting.**
  (exciting – aufregend, spannend)

* **It has been nominated for 8 Oscars, you know.**

* **I hate films that are dubbed – I much prefer subtitles.**
  (dub – synchronisieren)

* **I thought it was too confusing with all the flashbacks.**
  (confusing – verwirrend / flashback – Rückblende)

* **A: Do you think it was filmed on location or at the studios?**
  (on location – an den Originalschauplätzen)
  B: Actually it said it was filmed on location.

* **I wonder what the critics will say about it in the papers tomorrow.**
  (wonder – neugierig sein / critic – Kritiker / paper – Zeitung)

THEATRE

* **A: I'm going out to the theatre tonight with some friends. Would you like to join us?**
  (.... Möchten Sie mitkommen?)
  B: I'd love to.

* **A: Should I get some tickets for the theatre?**
  B: Yes, that'd be very kind of you.
  (kind – freundlich, nett)

* **Would you prefer the matinee at 2 o'clock, or the evening performance?**
  (prefer – vorziehen / matinee – Nachmittagsvorstellung / evening performance – Abendvorstellung)

* **A: If you're not doing anything special tonight, I was wondering if you would like to come to the theatre. I have some tickets.**
  B: It's very kind of you to invite me, but I'm afraid I've already got something planned.
  (invite – einladen)

* **A: If you're free tomorrow evening, would you like to go to the theatre? I've got a spare ticket.**
  (.... Ich habe eine Karte übrig.)
  B: Thank you very much. That would be very nice. I'll look forward to it.
  (look forward to – sich freuen auf)

* **A: There's an excellent play on at the theatre. Shall I get some tickets for tomorrow?**
  (play – Stück)
  B: That's very kind of you but I've already made other arrangements.
  (... , aber ich habe bereits etwas anderes vor.)

* **A: Is it still possible to get tickets for tonight?**
  B: Tonight is the premiere, so I doubt very much that there'll be any tickets left.
  (doubt – bezweifeln / there are tickets left – es sind noch Karten zu haben)

* **I'll try and get tickets for a play at the Vienna International Theatre.**

* **Would you be interested in going to an avantgarde theatre?**

* **Would you be interested in going to a typical Viennese cabaret?**

* **A: I'm thinking of going to the theatre while I'm here. Could you ring up and find out what's on?**
  (while – während / ring up – anrufen)
  B: Certainly. I'll give them a ring as soon as I've finished this.
  (Gern. Ich rufe an, sobald ich das hier fertig habe.)

* **Can you recommend a good play?**
  (recommend – empfehlen)

* **The play is really worth seeing.**

* **A: I like Shakespeare's plays.**
  B: Oh, so do I. They're doing Hamlet at the Royal Theatre next week.
  (do – aufführen)
  A: Shall we book some tickets, then?
  (book – vorbestellen)

* **Do you think we ought to book tickets?**
  (Glauben Sie, daß wir Karten vorbestellen sollten?)

* **I'd like to book two tickets for tomorrow, please.**

* **A: Do you have any tickets for tonight's performance, please?**
B: I'm sorry, sir, they're all sold. But there are two cancellations for tomorrow, if you're able to come.
(cancellation – Kartenrückgabe)

* **A: I'd like some tickets for tomorrow night's performance, please.**
B: Sorry, madam, you'll have to go to the advance booking office. It's just opposite.
(advance booking office – Vorverkaufskassa / just opposite – gleich gegenüber)

* **A: Do you have two seats left for tomorrow evening, please?**
(left – noch frei)
B: I've got two together in the dress circle at seven pounds fifty each. Or I've got two stalls at ten pounds.
(two together – zwei nebeneinander / dress circle – erster Rang / stall – Parkettsitz)

* **There's nothing in the front row, is there?**
(In der vordersten Reihe ist nichts mehr frei, oder?)

* **Where are the seats? Could you show me on the plan, please?**
(plan – Sitzplan)

* **I'll have the two in the dress circle, please, in Row G.**

* **A: What time does the performance start?**
B: At seven thirty. The doors open at seven.
(. . . . Einlaß ist um sieben.)

* **How long does the performance last?**
(last – dauern)

* **Would you like me to try and change the tickets?**
(change – umtauschen)

* **A: What should I wear to the theatre?**
(wear – anziehen)
B: Well, it's an avantgarde theatre so you can really wear whatever you like.

* **It doesn't really matter what you wear, but most people do wear a tie.**
(Es ist eigentlich belanglos, .../tie – Krawatte)

* **Where's the cloakroom, please?**
(cloakroom – Garderobe)

* **Where can I buy a programme, please?**

* **Shall we go to the bar and have a drink?**

* **What time is the interval, please?**
(interval – Pause)

——— ❖ ———

* **Where are the ladies, please?**
(ladies – Damentoilette)

* **A: Could you tell me where the gents are, please?**
(gents – Herrentoilette)
B: Down the corridor on the right-hand side.
A: Thank you.

* **I think the scenery is fantastic – it's really impressive.**
(scenery – Bühnenbild, Dekoration / impressive – beeindruckend)

* **The acoustics aren't very good. – I'm finding it quite difficult to follow.**
(quite – ziemlich)

* **Let's hope the second half is better!**

——— ❖ ———

* **A: What did you think of the play last night?**
B: I enjoyed it very much.
(Es hat mir sehr gut gefallen.)

* **I didn't think the acting was all that good myself.**
(acting – schauspielerische Leistung)

* **After all we'd heard about it, we found the play a bit disappointing.**
(disappointing – enttäuschend)

* **I thought the cast were brilliant – especially the leading actor.**
  (cast – Schauspieler / leading actor – Hauptdarsteller)

* **They must have rehearsed it for months.**
  (rehearse – proben)

* **It could have been worse.**
  (Es hätte schlimmer sein können.)

* **Frankly, I wish I'd stayed at home.**
  (Ganz ehrlich, ich hätte besser zu Hause bleiben sollen.)

OPERA

* **I was thinking of going to the opera tonight. Would you like to come?**

* **A: Would you like to go to the opera tomorrow evening?**
  B: Oh, thank you, that would be nice.

* **A: We could try and get tickets for the opera tomorrow.**
  B: What's on?
  (Was ist auf dem Programm?)
  A: Let's check the newspaper. It's The Magic Flute.
  (check – nachschauen in / Magic Flute – Zauberflöte)
  B: Yes, I'd love to see that. It's my favourite opera.
  (favourite opera – Lieblingsoper)

* **A: Do you know if it's possible to get tickets for the opera?**
  B: I'm not sure but I could try to find out for you, if you like.
  A: That's very kind of you.

* **A: They're doing "Carmen" at the Opera House. Does opera interest you at all?**
  (do – spielen)
  B: Oh yes, it does. How can I get a ticket for it?

* **No, actually I don't care much for opera.**
  (... , eigentlich mache ich mir nicht allzuviel aus Opern.)

* **A: What do people wear to the opera?**
(wear – anziehen)
B: People usually dress up for the opera. A dark suit or a dinner-jacket would be suitable.
(dress up – etwas Schönes anziehen / dark suit – dunkler Anzug / dinner-jacket – Smoking / suitable – passend, geeignet)

* **Some ladies wear long dresses, but any smart dress or outfit would be fine.**
(... , aber irgendein anderes elegantes Kleid oder sonst etwas Elegantes zum Anziehen ... .)

* **The first act was magnificent, wasn't it?**
(magnificent – großartig, glänzend / wasn't it? – nicht wahr?)

* **She's got a beautiful voice, hasn't she?**
(voice – Stimme / hasn't she? – nicht wahr?)

* **The conductor isn't much good, is he?**
(conductor – Dirigent / is he? – meinen Sie nicht auch?)

CONCERTS

* **A: By the way, I hear Elton John's coming to London soon.**
(Übrigens, ...)
B: That's right. I saw it advertised last week. I imagine it might be a bit difficult to get to see him.
(advertise – ankündigen / imagine – sich vorstellen)
A: Well, we can always try.
(Wir können es zumindest versuchen.)

* **A: Why don't you go to a show or something tonight?**
B: As a matter of fact, I thought Caroline might like to go to a concert.
A: Let's have a look and see what's on ... You might try the Menuhin concert at the Festival Hall.
B: That sounds interesting.
(sound – klingen)

* **A: Would you be free to come to a concert on Saturday evening?**
B: Thank you, but I'm afraid I've arranged to go out then.

* **A: Could you get me some tickets for the concert tomorrow?**
B: I'm afraid not. It's fully booked.
(Leider nicht. ... .)

* **A: Do you think it'd be possible for you to get some tickets for the concert tomorrow?**
B: Of course, that's no problem.

* **How about going to a musical tonight?**
(Gehen wir heute abend in ein Musical?)

* **A: Would you be interested in going to a piano recital?**
(piano recital – Klavierabend)
B: Oh yes, that'd be great, thanks.
(great – sehr schön)

* **A: Is he a good pianist?**
B: Oh, not bad.

* **A: Shall we try and get tickets for U2? They're on at Wembley Stadium next weekend.**
(be on – auftreten)
B: Yes, that sounds great. Is that an open-air stadium?
(great – super)
A: Yes, so don't forget your umbrella!
(umbrella – Schirm)

* **A: How was the concert last night?**
B: It was great. I thoroughly enjoyed it.
(... . Es hat mir wirklich sehr gut gefallen.)

* **The newspaper reviews of the concert were very good indeed.**
(reviews – Kritiken)

MUSEUMS

* **A: Would you be interested in coming to the National History Museum?**
B: Thank you for the invitation, but I'm not sure if I can.
(invitation – Einladung)

* **A: We want to take you to the British Museum. You haven't been there before, have you?**
(have you? – oder?)
B: No, I haven't. I'd very much like to go.

* **A: I'd quite like to see the Chinese Exhibition while I'm here. Have you seen it yet?**
(quite – ganz / exhibition – Ausstellung / while – während / yet – schon)
B: No, I must admit I just haven't found the time, but I've heard it's well worth seeing.
(admit – zugeben / just – einfach / worth seeing – sehenswert)

* **A: By the way, may I ask you something? What's the National Gallery like? Do you think I ought to go there?**
(by the way – übrigens / . . . . Wie ist die National Gallery? . . . . / I ought to go – ich sollte gehen)
B: Well, there are lots of great paintings there, but I prefer the Tate Gallery myself. It's less like a museum.
(lots of – viele / great – großartig / painting – Gemälde / I prefer the Tate Gallery – mir ist die Tate Gallery lieber)

* **A: Don't you think that's an interesting picture?**
(picture – Bild)
B: Yes, it is, isn't it?

SPORTS AND OTHER LEISURE TIME ACTIVITIES

Sport und andere Freizeitbeschäftigungen

* **A: What are your hobbies?**
  B: I love playing tennis and squash.

* **A: What do you do in your spare time?**
  (spare time – Freizeit)
  B: There's nothing I enjoy more than gardening.
  (Am liebsten arbeite ich im Garten.)

* **A: What's your favourite pastime?**
  (Was machen Sie in Ihrer Freizeit am liebsten?)
  B: My main interest is oil-painting.
  (main – Haupt- / oil-painting – Ölmalerei)

* **A: What do you enjoy doing when you've got a spare moment?**
  (spare moment – freie Minute)
  B: I enjoy fishing.
  (Ich fische gerne.)

* **What I particularly enjoy is going for a jog.**
  (Was ich besonders gerne mache, ist laufen.)

* **A: And what do you do when you're not working?**
  B: I'm very fond of skiing.
  (Ich fahre sehr gern Schi.)

* **A: What are your interests?**
  B: Well, I'm very keen on cooking.
  (Ich koche sehr gerne.)

* **A: What are you interested in?**
  B: I'm a bridge fan.

* **A: Are you interested in riding?**
  B: I've never tried it. But I'd like to have a go at it.
  (.... Aber ich würde es gerne einmal probieren.)

* **A: Are people interested in skiing in England?**
B: Yes, it's becoming quite popular now.
(quite – ziemlich)

* **A: Do you take much interest in ballet?**
(ballet – Ballett)
B: Well, I'm not particularly interested in it actually.
(actually – eigentlich)

* **A: Do you like sport?**
B: Actually I'm not overkeen on it – I much prefer art.
(Eigentlich bin ich nicht allzusehr versessen darauf – da interessiere ich mich wesentlich mehr für Kunst.)

* **A: Do you enjoy playing sports?**
(Betreiben Sie gerne Sport?)
B: As a matter of fact, I'm a very keen golfer and ice-skater.
(Eigentlich schon, ich spiele leidenschaftlich gern Golf und bin ein begeisterter Eisläufer.)

* **A: I'm not very keen on sport, are you?**
(Ich mache mir nicht sehr viel aus Sport, und wie ist es mit Ihnen?)
B: I don't mind watching it, but I'm not really into doing it myself.
(Ich schaue zwar ganz gern zu, aber selbst betreibe ich keinen.)

* **Formula One racing is my favourite spectator sport.**
(Am liebsten schaue ich mir Formel-1-Rennen an.)

* **A: By the way, do you like dancing?**
(by the way – übrigens)
B: Oh yes, I'm very fond of dancing.

* **A: Don't you like jogging?**
B: Actually I prefer swimming.

* **I've always liked cross-country skiing.**
(cross-country skiing – Langlauf)

* **I like to go mountaineering at weekends.**
(go mountaineering – bergsteigen gehen)

* **A: Do you play soccer?**
(Spielen Sie Fußball?)
B: Not any more, but I used to play when I was a student.
(... , aber früher einmal, als ich noch studierte, habe ich gespielt.)

* **Have you ever been water-skiing?**

* **A: Sailing is very enjoyable, don't you think?**
(Segeln ist ein netter Sport, meinen Sie nicht auch?)
B: I've never been sailing actually, but I'd love to give it a try sometime.
(... , aber ich würde es gerne irgendwann einmal versuchen.)

* **A: Which do you prefer, tennis or cycling?**
(prefer – lieber tun / cycle – radfahren)
B: I enjoy tennis more than cycling.

* **A: Do you prefer alpine skiing or cross-country?**
B: I like cross-country better than alpine.

* **A: Can you play any musical instruments?**
B: Well, I can play the piano a bit, but I'm pretty hopeless at it.
(... , aber ich bin ein ziemlich hoffnungsloser Fall.)

* **A: Are you keen on music?**
(Sind Sie sehr an Musik interessiert?)
B: I'm absolutely crazy about jazz.
(Ich bin ganz verrückt nach Jazz.)

* **A: Are you into folk music at all?**
(be into – gern haben; ein Fan sein)
B: Well yes, but I like pop better.

* **A: Do you belong to any clubs or societies?**
(belong to – Mitglied sein von / society – Gesellschaft, Verein)
B: Actually I'm a member of the Lions Club.

* **A: Would you care for a round of golf?**
  (Hätten Sie Lust zu einer Runde Golf?)
  B: Great! But I've only got time for 9 holes, is that O.K.?
  (great – super / hole – Loch)
  A: O.K. by me.

* **Would you be interested in coming sledging with us tomorrow?**
  (sledge – Schlitten fahren)

* **How about going for a cycle?**
  (Wie wär's mit einer Radtour?)

* **What about a game of darts at the pub?**
  (game of darts – Wurfpfeilschießen)

* **It'll be nice on the beach today. I think I'll go swimming.**

* **Let's go swimming.**

* **A: Why don't you join us for a game of tennis.**
  (Gehen Sie doch mit uns Tennis spielen.)
  B: I'd love to, thanks.
  (Gern, danke.)

* **We could go for a walk in the Vienna Woods.**

* **Would you like to go for a good run in the Prater tomorrow?**

* **We could go to a sauna afterwards.**

* **A: What I'd really like is a good swim.**
  B: Great, let's go to the swimming-baths tomorrow. Let's say at 11?
  (swimming-baths – Hallenbad)

* **A: Do you fancy a game of snooker?**
  (fancy – Lust haben auf / snooker – Snooker, eine Art Billard)
  B: Sounds like a great idea!
  (Klingt großartig.)

* **We might go to the races, if you like that kind of thing.**
  (races – Pferderennen)

* **Well, John, perhaps you'd like to join me on Saturday? Spurs are playing Arsenal at home.**
  (join sbdy. - jemanden begleiten; mit jemandem mitgehen / Spurs [Kurzform für Tottenham Hotspurs], Arsenal - zwei berühmte Londoner Fußballvereine)

* **What's the score?**
  (Wieviel steht's? | Wie steht das Spiel?)

* **We could play table tennis or watch the tennis tournament on TV - it's up to you to decide.**
  (Wir könnten Tischtennis spielen oder uns das Tennisturnier im Fernsehen anschauen - was immer Ihnen lieber ist.)

* **A: Which would you prefer: rowing or wind-surfing?**
  (row - rudern)
  B: I'd prefer wind-surfing.

SHOPPING

Einkaufen

* **I was thinking of taking a couple of hours off this afternoon to do some shopping, if you don't mind.**
(take off – sich freinehmen / couple of – ein paar / if you don't mind – wenn es Ihnen nichts ausmacht)

* **I did some window-shopping last night in the High Street and quite a few things caught my eye. I think I'll go shopping on Saturday.**
(do window-shopping – Schaufensterbummel machen / High Street – Haupteinkaufsstraße / quite a few – eine ganze Menge / catch one's eye – jemandem ins Auge springen)

* **A: There are a few odds and ends I'd like to buy before I go back this evening. What time do the shops close?**
(odds and ends – verschiedene Kleinigkeiten / close – schließen)
B: Most shops close at about 6 o'clock, apart from the food shops, which usually stay open longer.
(apart from – außer)

* **What time does the off-licence on the corner shut?**
(off-licence – Getränkehandlung / corner – Ecke / shut – schließen)

* **Can you recommend a good supermarket around here where I can get some food to take back with me?**
(recommend – empfehlen)

* **Do you know a good bookshop where they have a wide selection of marketing literature?**
(bookshop – Buchhandlung / wide selection – große Auswahl)

* **A: Where can I buy the Financial Times?**
B: There's a newsagent's just over the road.
(newsagent's – Zeitschriftenhandlung)

* **Is there a shop that specialises in photographic equipment near here?**
(photographic equipment – Fotoausrüstung)

* **Do you know any good department stores around here?**
(department store – Warenhandlung, Kaufhaus)

——— ❖ ———

* **A: Can I help you?**
B: Yes, I wonder if you could tell me where to find a suit like the one in the window?
(I wonder if you could – könnten Sie bitte / suit – Anzug, Kostüm)

* **A: Are you being served?**
(serve – bedienen)
B: Yes, I'm being served, thank you.

* **I'm just looking, thank you.**

* **A: Could you point me in the right direction of the food department, please?**
(Könnten Sie mir bitte sagen, wie ich in die Lebensmittelabteilung komme?)
B: Go down the escalator over there to the basement, through the kitchenware department and it's straight ahead.
(escalator – Rolltreppe / over there – dort drüben / basement – Kellergeschoß / kitchenware department – Küchenabteilung / straight ahead – geradeaus)

* **Aren't there any baskets or trolleys left?**
(basket – Korb / trolley – Einkaufswagerl)

* **Excuse me, where's the menswear department, please?**
(menswear department – Herrenabteilung)

* **I'm looking for the lingerie department.**
(look for – suchen / lingerie – Damenwäsche)

* **Is the sportswear on this floor?**
(sportswear – Sportbekleidung / floor – Stock)

* **A: Can you help me, please? I'm looking for a pure wool pullover.**
(pure wool pullover – Pullover aus reiner Wolle)
B: What size did you want?
(size – Größe)

A: Well, I'm not quite sure; medium I think.
(quite sure – ganz sicher / medium – mittel)

* **A: Are you looking for anything in particular?**
B: Yes, I'm interested in a silk tie, if you've got any.
(silk tie – Seidenkrawatte)

* **A: I wonder if you can help me. I'm looking for a blouse to match this skirt.**
(.... Ich suche eine Bluse, die zu diesem Rock paßt.)
B: Well, I think something in red would go well with it, don't you?
(go with – passen zu / don't you? – meinen Sie nicht auch?)

* **I'd prefer something with a pattern – either stripes or checked or even spots – and not just a plain one.**
(prefer – bevorzugen / pattern – Muster / stripe – Streifen / checked – kariert / spot – Punkt / plain – ungemustert)

* **I'm looking for a shirt to match this jacket but I'm not sure of my collar size.**
(shirt – Hemd / collar size – Kragenweite)

* **A: I'd like to buy a pair of trousers for myself.**
(pair of trousers – Hose)
B: How much would you like to spend?
(spend – ausgeben)
A: That doesn't really matter, as long as they're not too expensive.
(Das ist eigentlich egal, solange sie nicht zu teuer ist.)

* **The trousers are a bit loose, can they be altered?**
(loose – weit / alter – ändern)

* **I'd like a pair of shoes in size 8 to go with this suit, please.**

* **I take size 38.**
(Ich habe Größe 38.)

* **I'm afraid they're too small. Do you do half sizes?**
(Ich fürchte, sie sind zu klein. Führen Sie Zwischengrößen?)

* **They're not really suitable. Can you show me anything else?**
(suitable – geeignet)

* **Excuse me, how much is this dress?**
  (... , wieviel kostet dieses Kleid?)

* **A: Could I try this on, please?**
  (try on – anprobieren)
  B: Certainly, the changing room is over there.
  (certainly – selbstverständlich / changing room – Umkleidekabine)

* **A: I'm afraid it doesn't fit – it's too tight around the waist. Have you got a bigger size?**
  (fit – passen / tight – eng / waist – Taille)
  B: I'm sorry, that's the last one but we should be getting some more in tomorrow.
  (get in – hereinbekommen)

* **It's not quite what I was looking for.**

* **Do you really think this jacket suits me?**
  (Glauben Sie wirklich, daß mir dieses Sakko steht | paßt?)

* **The sleeves are too long, can they be shortened?**
  (sleeve – Ärmel / shorten – kürzen)

* **Do you have anything in different material? This seems to be a bit thick.**
  (different material – anderer Stoff / seem – scheinen / thick – dick)

* **I'm not too keen on the colour – it's too dark.**
  (keen on – begeistert von)

* **A: It's too big. Could I try the next size down?**
  (next size down – nächstkleinere Größe)
  B: I'm sorry, we're out of stock at the moment.
  (be out of stock – keine haben)
  A: Can you order one?
  (order – bestellen)

* **It's a bit expensive, don't you think?**

* **Have you got anything cheaper?**

* **It fits very well. I'll take it. Do you take credit cards?**

* **What have you got in the way of leather handbags?**
  (Was haben Sie an Lederhandtaschen?)

* **I need some films for my camera, please.**

* **20 Benson and Hedges, please.**

* **I'd like a carton of Rothmans, three packets of Marlboro and a lighter, please.**
  (carton – Stange / packet – Schachtel, Packerl / lighter – Feuerzeug)

* **A: Would you like anything else?**
  B: No, thanks. That'll be all.

* **Have you got a map of the city, please?**
  (map of the city – Stadtplan)

* **Could you make up a nice bunch of flowers for me, please? I need them as a birthday present.**
  (make up – zusammenstellen / bunch of flowers – Blumenstrauß / present – Geschenk)

* **Do you stock health food?**
  (Führen Sie Bio-Lebensmittel / Reformwaren?)

* **A: Do you have any whole-meal bread?**
  (whole-meal bread – Vollkornbrot)
  B: Sure, it's on the shelf over there.
  (shelf – Regal)

* **Would it be possible to taste a small piece?**
  (taste – kosten / piece – Stück)

* **Does the price include VAT?**
  (VAT – value-added tax / Mehrwertsteuer)

* **A: How much does it come to altogether?**
  (Wieviel kostet das alles zusammen?)
  B: It comes to seventy-eight pounds and ninety-seven pence.

* **Where can I pay for these?**

* **Where's the cash desk?**
(cash desk – Kassa)

* **Can I pay at any checkout?**
(checkout – Supermarktkassa)

* **The queues are so long at the checkouts, isn't there an express one for just a few items?**
(queue – Warteschlange / express checkout – Schnellkassa / item – Artikel)

——— ❖ ———

* **A: Cash or charge?**
(Bar oder mit Kreditkarte?)
B: I'd like to charge it. Here's my card.

* **Put it on my credit card, please.**

* **I've got a credit card, would that be all right?**

* **Can I pay by Eurocheque?**

* **A: Would you be prepared to accept a Eurocheque?**
(Nehmen Sie auch Euroschecks?)
B: Yes, if you can show me your cheque card and your passport.

* **I'm willing to pay cash if you can give me a discount.**
(discount – Preisnachlaß)

* **I'm sorry, I've only got a fifty-pound note, can you change it?**
(change a fifty-pound note – auf eine 50-Pfund-Note herausgeben)

* **I'm sorry but I haven't got any change.**
(change – Kleingeld)

* **A: Here's your change – fifty pence.**
(change – Wechselgeld)
B: Sorry, that's not right, I gave you a ten-pound note.
(ten-pound note – 10-Pfund-Note)

* **Would you count the change again, please? You seem to have made a mistake.**
(count again – nachzählen / change – Wechselgeld / . . . . Es dürfte Ihnen da ein Fehler unterlaufen sein.)

* **The bill comes to £6.50, and as I gave you a ten-pound note the change should be £3.50 and not £2.50.**
(come to – ausmachen)

—— ❖ ——

* **A: If it's not right, can I change it?**
(change – umtauschen)
B: Yes, as long as you keep your receipt.
(receipt – Kassenbeleg)

* **Could you gift-wrap it, please?**
(gift-wrap – als Geschenk verpacken)

* **Have you got any carrier-bags, please?**
(carrier-bag – Tragtasche)

* **Could you put it in a paper-bag, please?**

* **A: Would you like us to deliver this afternoon?**
(Möchten Sie, daß wir Ihnen die Sachen heute nachmittag zustellen?)
B: Oh, yes please. That'd be lovely.
(lovely – nett, freundlich)

* **A: I bought this from you yesterday and it's the wrong size. I was wondering if you could change it.**
B: Have you got your receipt?

* **I want to complain about this compact disc. When I got it home I realised I had the wrong disc inside the cover.**
(complain – sich beschweren / realise – bemerken / cover – Hülle)

* **I got a real bargain at the sales last week.**
(bargain – günstiger Kauf; Gelegenheitskauf / sales – Ausverkauf)

* **That was a really good buy. The price was reduced from forty-five to twenty-five pounds.**
(buy – Kauf)

AT THE POST OFFICE

Auf der Post

* **Where is the nearest post office, please?**

* **Could you tell me where the nearest pillar-box is, please?**
(pillar-box – Briefkasten)

* **Excuse me, how much is a letter to Austria?**
(how much is – wieviel kostet)

* **How much does a postcard to Spain cost?**
(postcard – Ansichtskarte)

* **How much do I have to put on a postcard to Scotland?**
(put – kleben, picken)

* **A: I want to send these letters and postcards to the United States. How much will they cost?**
B: 25p for a letter. And 20p for a postcard.
(p – pence)

* **What stamps do I need for an airmail letter to the United States?**
(stamp – Briefmarke / airmail letter – Luftpostbrief)

* **A: What's the postage on these letters to Thailand, please?**
(postage – Porto)
B: I'll have to check. Do you need anything else?
(check – nachschauen)

* **It's 20 pence for an airmail letter to Brazil, isn't it?**
(isn't it? – nicht wahr?)

* **Five twenty pence stamps, please.**
(twenty pence stamp – 20-Pence-Marke)

* **Six stamps for letters and five for postcards, please.**

* **Here's a ten-pound note. I'm sorry I haven't anything smaller.**
(ten-pound note – 10-Pfund-Note)

* **How long does a letter to Vienna take?**
(take – brauchen)

* **Could you weigh this letter, please?**
(weigh – abwägen)

* **Could you tell me the ZIP Code for Chicago, please?**
(ZIP Code – Postleitzahl in den U.S.A.)

* **What's the Postcode, please?**
(Postcode – Postleitzahl im Vereinigten Königreich)

* **I'd like to send this letter by airmail.**

* **I'd like to send this letter Express, please.**
(Als Expressbrief bitte! | Express bitte!)

* **I'd like to send this as a registered letter, please.**
(Eingeschrieben bitte!)

* **I want to send this parcel to Dublin, please.**
(parcel – Paket)

* **A: Would you please tell me how much this parcel to Austria is?**
B: Put it on the scales, please. Hm, that'll be four pounds fifty.
(scales – Waage)

* **Do I need a customs declaration?**
(customs declaration –Zollerklärung)

* **I'd like to send a money order for £100.**
(money order – Geldanweisung)

* **What does it cost to send a fax?**

* **A: I'd like to send a telemessage. Can I have a form, please?**
(telemessage – Telegramm / form – Formular, Vordruck)
B: You'll find one in that box over there.

* **How do I fill this in?**
(fill in sthg. – etwas ausfüllen)

* **Could you help me fill in the form, please?**

* **How much does it cost per word?**

* **Do you think it will get to Vienna before six?**
(get – ankommen)

* **Will it be delivered before five o'clock?**
(deliver – zustellen)

* **A: Where can I post these letters?**
(post letter – Brief aufgeben)
B: There's a letter-box just around the corner.
(letter-box – Briefkasten / just around the corner – gleich um die Ecke)

* **A: Are there any letters for me? My name is Maier. M-A-I-E-R.**
(Ist Post für mich da? . . . .)
B: Yes, there is something for you. Could I see your passport, please?

* **A: Where can I collect a parcel?**
(collect – abholen)
B: Counter four, please.
(counter – Schalter)

* **I'd like to have a post-office box, please.**
(post-office box – Postfach)

* **I would like to have my mail forwarded, please. This is my new address.**
(have mail forwarded – Post nachsenden lassen)

* **A: Where can I make a telephone call, please?**
B: There are a number of call-boxes just outside the post office.
(call-box – Telefonzelle)

——— ❖ ———

* **I'd like to make a call to Vienna.**
(call – Telefongespräch / Es sei darauf hingewiesen, daß in England die Postverwaltung keinen Telefondienst betreibt.)

* **The telephone directory, please.**
(telephone directory – Telefonbuch)

* **How much is a call to Paris, please?**

* **What does a local call cost?**
(local call – Ortsgespräch)

* **What coins do I need?**
(coin – Münze)

* **Can you give me change, please? I need some 10p pieces.**
(Können Sie mir bitte wechseln? Ich brauche ein paar 10-Pence-Stücke.)

TELEPHONING

Telefonieren

ANSWERING THE SWITCHBOARD

Telefonzentrale meldet sich

* **Good morning. Paper Mills plc. Can I help you?**
(plc – public limited company | etwa: Aktiengesellschaft in Großbritannien)

* **Good afternoon. Stiegel Bräu Restaurant. May I help you?**

REQUESTING IDENTITY

Bitte um Namensnennung

PERSON/COMPANY CALLED REQUESTS IDENTITY

Angerufene Person oder Firma bittet um Namensnennung

* **Who is calling, please?**
(Wer spricht bitte?)

* **Who is speaking, please?**

* **May I ask who is calling?**

* **Can I have your name, please?**

PERSON CALLING REQUESTS IDENTITY

Anrufer/in bittet um Namensnennung

* **Hello, is that the Brinely Garage?**

* **Hello, is that 564 321?**

* **Is that you, Mr. Mutter?**

CALLER IDENTIFIES HIMSELF/HERSELF IN REPLY TO A REQUEST FOR IDENTITY

Anrufer/in nennt auf Ersuchen hin seinen/ihren Namen

* **This is Jack Nickolson, of Briers Ltd.**

* **Brown, of Hertz & Co. I'm calling from Vienna about our Order No. 4567.**
  (.... Ich rufe aus Wien an, und zwar wegen unseres Auftrages Nr. 4567.)

* **This is Simone Weller calling from Munich.**

* **Peter Brittle speaking.**

* **Geoffrey Sellers here.**

PERSON CALLED ANSWERS THE PHONE

Angerufener/Angerufene meldet sich

* **Good morning, Peter File here.**
  (Guten Morgen. Peter File am Apparat.)

* **Hello, Ron Myers speaking.**
  (Hallo. Hier spricht Ron Myers.)

* **A: Can I speak to Miss Baxter, please?**
  B: Speaking.
  (Am Apparat!)

* **Good afternoon, Fun Bikes Ltd., John Sage speaking.**
  (Ltd. – private limited company | etwa: GmbH in Großbritannien)

* **Nancy Rhine's office.**

CALLER REQUESTS A PARTICULAR PERSON OR SERVICE

Anrufer/in verlangt eine bestimmte Person oder Abteilung

* **I'd like to speak to Mr. Brown, your export manager, please.**

* **May I speak to someone in the Sales Department, please? I have a complaint to make.**
  (sales department – Verkaufsabteilung / complaint – Beschwerde, Reklamation)

* **Could I have the Research and Development Department, please?**
  (Könnten Sie mir bitte die Forschungs- und Entwicklungsabteilung geben?)

* **Please connect me with the Export Department.**
  (connect – verbinden)

* **Could you put me through to extension 715, please?**
  (Könnten Sie mich bitte mit der Klappe 715 verbinden? / 715 – seven-one-five)

* **Can you put me on to someone in the Sales Department, please? I've got a couple of questions about your new filing system.**
  (Könnten Sie mir jemanden aus der Verkaufsabteilung geben. Ich hab' ein paar Fragen zu Ihrem neuen Ablagesystem.)

* **This is John Weir speaking. Could I speak to Gert Moon on extension 567, please? I dialled his extension direct but there was no reply.**
  (on extension 567 - auf Klappe 567 / dial an extension – direct eine Klappe durchwählen / there was no reply – niemand hat abgehoben)

* **Could you put me through as quickly as possible? I'm calling from Singapore and that's quite expensive.**
  (possible – möglich / quite – ziemlich / expensive – teuer)

REACTION TO CALLER'S REQUEST FOR A PARTICULAR PERSON

Reaktion auf den Wunsch eines Anrufers/einer Anruferin, jemanden bestimmten zu sprechen

* **Hold the line, please. I'm putting you through.**
  (Bleiben Sie am Apparat. Ich verbinde Sie.)

* **Hold on, please.**
  (Bleiben Sie am Apparat, bitte.)

* **One moment, please. She'll be here in a minute.**

* **Hang on for a minute.**
  (Bleiben Sie eine Sekunde dran!)

* **I'll put you through now. In case it shouldn't work, Mr. Sutter's extension is 345. You can dial it direct.**
  (. . . . Falls es nicht funktioniert, die Klappe von Herrn Sutter ist 345. Sie können durchwählen.)

* **Well, normally dialling extensions direct works fine. But hold the line, I'll try to put you through.**

* **A: Mr. Brown's extension is engaged. Will you hold?**
  (engaged – besetzt / . . . . Wollen Sie warten?)
  B: Yes, I'll hold.
  (Ja, ich werde warten. | Ja, ich bleibe dran.)

* **Mr. Leer will be free in a minute. I'm putting you on hold.**
  (. . . . Wenn Sie bitte warten wollen.)

* **I've got Mr. Brown on the line for you.**
  (Ich habe Herrn Brown für Sie in der Leitung.)

* **A: Do you still want to hold?**
  (Wollen Sie noch länger warten?)
  B: Yes, I'm holding.

CALLER STATES HIS/HER BUSINESS

Anrufer/in gibt den Grund für seinen/ihren Anruf an

* **I'm calling about the consignment of electric power drills which you promised us by Thursday.**
(about - wegen / consignment - Sendung / power drill - Bohrmaschine / promise - versprechen / by - bis spätestens / Thursday - Donnerstag)

* **My call is in reference to your stand at the Vienna Fair.**
(Ich rufe im Zusammenhang mit Ihrem Stand auf der Wiener Messe an.)

* **I'm ringing you because we still haven't received any payment on our invoice A-1990 / 5432.**
(ring - anrufen / still - noch / receive - erhalten / payment - Zahlung / on - für; in Zusammenhang mit / invoice - Rechnung)

* **The reason why I'm calling you is that I want to make a change in our last order. I hope it isn't too late.**
(Der Grund, warum ich Sie anrufe, ist, daß ich unseren letzten Auftrag abändern möchte. ... .)

* **I'm calling on behalf of our Export Manager. He would like to know whether the last consignment has arrived in good order.**
(on behalf - für; im Auftrag von / whether - ob / arrive - ankommen / in good order - in gutem Zustand; gut)

* **I'm phoning because I don't think I'll be able to keep our appointment I'm afraid. I've got the flu.**
(keep appointment - Termin einhalten / I'm afraid - leider / flu - Grippe)

* **I'm phoning for some price information on Austrian wines.**

THE PERSON WANTED IS NOT AVAILABLE

Die gewünschte Person ist nicht erreichbar

* **I'm afraid she's not in at the moment. I'm a colleague of hers. Would you like to leave a message?**
(Leider ist sie im Augenblick nicht hier. .... Möchten Sie eine Nachricht hinterlassen?)

* **He's in a meeting with the Managing Director. If it's really important I could ask the operator to ring him there.**
(meeting – Sitzung / Managing Director – Generaldirektor / important – wichtig / operator – Telefonzentrale, Telefonist/in / ring – anrufen)

* **His secretary tells me that he won't be back before three p.m..**
(won't – will not / p.m. – am Nachmittag)

* **Mr. Brinner is away for a few days. He'll be back Friday afternoon. Can I take a message?**
(a few – ein paar)

* **I'm sorry, Ms. Moat has gone to London on business for a few days. Can I give her a message?**
(on business – geschäftlich)

* **Mr. Grout has just left for the factory. You can reach him there on 564 311 in about ten minutes.**
(Herr Grout ist gerade in die Fabrik gefahren. Sie können ihn dort in etwa 10 Minuten unter der Nummer ... erreichen.)

* **Mrs. Ondine is on holiday. Perhaps I can help you.**

* **Mr. Brix is in another office at the moment. I could have the call transferred, if it's urgent.**
(transfer call – ein Gespräch umlegen | umleiten / urgent – dringend)

* **Can you tell me what you are calling about? Maybe I can help you.**
(call about sthg. – wegen etwas anrufen)

* **Would you like him to call you back?**
(Möchten Sie, daß er Sie zurückruft?)

* **Would you like to ring back later?**
(Möchten Sie später noch einmal anrufen?)

* **I'm afraid Mr. Lone is with a client at present.**
(at present - zur Zeit)

REACTING TO UNAVAILABILITY OF PARTY CALLED

Reaktion auf Nichterreichbarkeit des/der Angerufenen

* **Yes. That would be very kind. My number is 4567. The area code for Vienna is 0222. But when calling from England leave off the 0 and dial 222 right after the country code, which is 43.**
(kind - freundlich / area code - Vorwahlnummer, Ortskennzahl / leave off - auslassen / dial - wählen / right after - direkt nach / country code - Landeskennzahl)

* **Would you ask him to call me as soon as possible, please. It's urgent. My number is Norwich 546781 extension 305.**

* **No, thank you. That's not necessary. Tell him that I called and that I'll call again at around four.**
(at around four - um etwa vier Uhr)

* **It's very urgent. Are you sure Mr. Briner is not in the building? Have you tried paging him?**
(building - Gebäude, Haus / page sbdy. - jmdn. anpiepsen; jmdn. mit dem Piepserl rufen; jmdn. ausrufen lassen)

* **When I call back, do I have to go through the operator or can I call straight through to his extension?**
(call back - noch einmal anrufen / go through operator - die Vermittlung benötigen / straight through - direkt)

* **What is his extension?**

* **At what time can I phone him?**

* **When can I reach her?**
(reach - erreichen)

* **Could you ask him to call me on 562 345, please. I'll be on that number until about 6 p.m..**
(on 562 345 – unter der Nummer 562 345)

* **Yes. Could he call me back? I'll be at 876 211 all day.**
(call back – zurückrufen / be at 876 211 – unter der Nummer 876 211 zu erreichen sein)

DIFFICULTIES IN UNDERSTANDING THE OTHER PARTY

Schwierigkeiten, den Gesprächspartner zu verstehen

* **Would you please repeat your name?**
(repeat – wiederholen)

* **Could you spell your name, please?**
(spell – buchstabieren)

* **I didn't catch your name. Would you please spell it?**
(catch – verstehen)

* **Ah, it's you Mr. Buttler. I didn't recognise your voice. The line's pretty bad. Sounds as if you're talking from the other end of the world.**
(recognise – erkennen / voice – Stimme / line – Leitung, Verbindung / pretty – ziemlich / sound – klingen)

* **Sorry, I couldn't hear what you said. Would you mind repeating the fIgure?**
(.... Würden Sie bitte die Zahl wiederholen.)

* **I didn't catch what you said. Could you repeat the last sentence, please?**

* **Could you speak a bit more slowly, please? My English is still a bit rusty.**
(.... Ich bin im Englischen noch etwas aus der Übung.)

* **What was that? Did you really say 500 or have I got it wrong?**
(get sthg. wrong – etwas falsch verstehen)

* **This is a very bad line, I'm afraid. I'll try to ring you again in half an hour.**
(I'm afraid – tut mir leid)

* **Are you still there?**
(Sind Sie noch dran?)

* **Can you hear me?**

SPELLING WORDS, NUMBERS AND OTHER DETAILS

Buchstabieren von Wörtern, Zahlen und anderen Details

* **A: Could you spell the name for me, please?**
B: Yes, certainly. D for Dora, I for Island, double N for Northpole, E for Edward, and R for Richard.
(certainly - gern / D for Dora – D wie Dora)

* **Yes, it's five hundred. 5 double O.**
(O – Null)

* **A: What is the order number?**
(order – Auftrag)
B: The number of the order in question is 5312 / A12. (five – three – one – two – stroke – capital A – one – two)
(order in question – Auftrag, um den es sich handelt / stroke – [britisch] Schrägstrich / capital A – großes A; Großbuchstabe A)

* **A: Is it the number in the bottom line?**
(bottom line – letzte Zeile)
B: No, I mean the code in the top right-hand corner of the document. It should read 82(40)5 / 33.1-g (eight – two – open parenthesis – four – zero – close parenthesis – five – slash – three – three – point – one – hyphen – lower case g)
(top right-hand – rechts oben / corner – Ecke / read – lauten / open parenthesis – [U.S.] Klammer auf / close parenthesis – Klammer zu / slash – [U.S.] Schrägstrich / hyphen – Bindestrich / lower case g – kleines g)

* **The figure I want you to check is in column three, line four.**
(figure – Zahl / check – überprüfen / column – Spalte / line – Zeile)

* **The AWB number which I gave you a couple of hours ago is wrong. The last figure is a six and not – I repeat – and not a nine.**
(AWB – airway bill | Luftfrachtbrief / repeat – wiederholen)

* **The figure in the quantity column should read 2.6 tonnes, not 3.6 tonnes.**
(quantity – Menge / 2.6 – two point six | zwei Komma sechs / tonne – metrische Tonne)

* **The name is Holt & Frier: Capital H – o – l – t ampersand capital F – r – i – e – r.**
(capital H – großes H / ampersand – Et-Zeichen)

* **A: The command you suggested for starting the program does not work.**
(command – Computerbefehl / suggest – vorschlagen / work – funktionieren)
B: That's strange. Are you sure you put in an asterisk?
(strange – seltsam / asterisk – Sternchen)

* **Put in a full stop after "now", a dash between "right" and "Waterfield", a colon after "price", and a semi-colon after "butter".**
(put in – einfügen / full stop – Punkt / dash – Gedankenstrich / colon – Doppelpunkt / semi-colon – Strichpunkt)

RINGING OFF

Beendigung des Telefongesprächs

* **I must ring off now. But I'll get back to you soon.**
(Ich muß jetzt auflegen. Aber ich melde mich bald wieder bei Ihnen.)

* **Thanks a lot. Goodbye.**

* **Sorry, I'll have to ring off now. I've got a call on the other line. Thank you for calling us.**

* **I think that's all. Bye, bye then.**

* **What time would it be convenient for me to call you again?**

(Wann wäre es Ihnen angenehm, daß ich Sie wieder anrufe?)

* **I'll switch on the answering machine before I leave.**
  (switch on – einschalten / answering machine – Telefonanrufbeantworter / leave – weggehen)

* **Kind regards to your wife.**
  (Grüße an Ihre Frau.)

* **Remember me to your girl friend.**
  (Schöne Grüße an deine Freundin.)

TALKING ABOUT THE TELEPHONE

Gespräche rund um das Telefon

* A: **I've heard about these prepaid telephone cards. Since I'll have to make a lot of calls, do you think I should buy one?**
  (prepaid telephone card – Telefonwertkarte / since – da / a lot of – viele; eine Menge)
  B: **Yes, cards are very convenient if you've got to make a lot of calls.**
  (convenient – praktisch)

* A: **How much is a telephone card?**
  B: **You can have one for £10, for £20, or for £50.**

* **Are there enough public telephone boxes that will take a card?**
  (telephone box – Telefonzelle)

* **You couldn't change a five-pound note, could you? I need some 50p coins for a telephone call.**
  (change – wechseln / coin – Münze)

* **You can't use coins in a telephone box, you need special tokens.**
  (token – Jeton, Wertmünze)

* **Can I borrow your telephone directory for a moment, please?**
  (telephone directory – Telefonbuch)

* **He's not in the directory. He must have an unlisted number.**
  (unlisted number / ex-directory number – Geheimnummer)

* **You have to press the button before you lift the receiver.**
(press button – Knopf drücken / lift receiver – Hörer abheben)

* **Dial 0 for external calls.**
(dial – wählen / call – Anruf)

* **Press the black button until you can hear a buzzing sound. Then lift the receiver.**
(buzzing sound – Summton)

* **The new push-button telephones are ever so much more convenient.**
(push-button telephone – Tastentelefon)

* **I've got the latest in telephone technology back home. My phone can store up to 50 numbers. It has an automatic redialling feature as well. Very convenient if the number you're calling is engaged.**
(store – speichern / redialling feature – Wahlwiederholung [-svorrichtung] / engaged – besetzt)

* **No, you can't dial direct to Ghana. You've got to place your call through the international operator.**
(place call through operator – Anruf über die Vermittlung machen)

* **Where is the nearest pay phone, please?**
(pay phone – Telefonzelle, Münztelefon)

* **Could I use your phone for a moment?**

* **Mind if I use your phone to make a call to Germany?**
(Haben Sie etwas dagegen, … ?)

PERSONAL BANKING

Persönliche Bankgeschäfte

OPENING HOURS

Öffnungszeiten

* A: **What are the bank opening hours in this country?**
(opening hours – Öffnungszeiten)
B: **Banks are open from 9 a.m. to three thirty in the afternoon.**

* **When do your banks open?**

* **Some banks are open until twelve on Saturday mornings.**

* A: **What time do the banks close? I need to change some money.**
(close – schließen / need – müssen / change – wechseln, umwechseln)
B: **Banks close at three thirty. But there are quite a few exchange offices that are open much longer. I think there is even one at Victoria Station that's open round the clock.**
(quite a few – eine ganze Reihe von / exchange office – Wechselstube / even – sogar)

TRAVELLERS' CHEQUES

Reiseschecks

* A: **I'm travelling to Malaysia on business next week, what advice could you give me on taking money?**
(travel – reisen / on business – geschäftlich / advice – Rat)
B: **The best idea would be for you to take travellers' cheques denominated in dollars, because they can be cashed everywhere.**
(be denominated in – lauten auf / cash – einlösen / everywhere – überall)
A: **And what happens if I lose them?**

B: You should report the numbers and amounts to the issuing institution without delay. Your money will be reimbursed, providing you haven't countersigned them.
(report – melden / issue – ausstellen / without delay – unverzüglich / reimburse – rückerstatten / providing – vorausgesetzt / countersign – gegenzeichnen)

* **I'd like $1,000 in travellers' cheques, please. What denominations are available?**
(.... In welchen Beträgen sind sie erhältlich?)

* **Where should I put my signature?**
(signature – Unterschrift)

* **I'd like to cash some travellers' cheques, please.**

* **How much is your commission on cashing travellers' cheques, please?**
(commission – Provision)

* **A: Good morning. Can I cash this traveller's cheque here?**
B: Yes, would you take it to the cashier at the foreign counter, please?
(cashier – Schalterbeamter / foreign counter – Auslandsschalter)

* **A: Is it possible to cash travellers' cheques without any means of identification?**
(means of identification – Identitätsnachweis)
B: I'm afraid not, sir. I need to see your passport.
(Leider nein. .... / need – müssen)

* **Where should I countersign?**

EUROCHEQUES

Euroschecks

* **Do you cash Eurocheques?**

* **Would you kindly cash this Eurocheque?**
  (kindly – bitte)

* **What is the maximum amount for one Eurocheque?**
  (amount – Betrag)

* **Do I have to make it out in English or in German?**
  (make out – ausstellen)

* **Should I endorse it?**
  (endorse – auf der Rückseite unterschreiben; girieren)

ORDINARY CHEQUES

* **A: I'd like to cash this cheque, please.**
  B: I'm afraid you can only pay this into an account, sir. It's a crossed cheque. Only open cheques are payable in cash.
  (I'm afraid – tut mir leid / account – Konto / crossed cheque – gekreuzter Scheck; Verrechnungsscheck / open cheque – Barscheck / in cash – in bar)

* **Here is my cheque card.**

* **I'm sorry, I think I've forgotten my signature on the reverse side.**
  (reverse side – Rückseite)

* **Should I sign it on the back?**
  (Soll ich ihn auf der Rückseite unterschreiben?)

* **A: How would you like it, madam?**
  B: Twenty-pound notes will do fine, thank you.
  (Ich möchte gerne 20-Pfund-Noten.)

* **In fifties, please.**

* **Two notes of a hundred, please.**

* **Two twenties, five tens, a five and five one-pound coins, please.**

* **I seem to have mislaid my cheque card. What should I do?**
(Ich dürfte meine Scheckkarte verlegt haben. ... ?)

* **A: Do you have crossed cheques in Austria?**
B: No, not really, but we have something very similar called 'Verrechnungsscheck'.
(similar – ähnlich)

* **A: By the way, you seem to use a lot more cheques than transfers here. And most of them are order cheques, aren't they?**
(Übrigens, es scheint, daß man hier viel mehr Schecks als Überweisungen verwendet. .... / order cheque – Namensscheck, Orderscheck / aren't they? – nicht wahr?)
B: What do you mean order cheques?
A: Well, cheques payable to a particular person, and not to bearer. We in Austria use mostly bearer cheques.
(particular – bestimmt / bearer – Inhaber / bearer cheque – Inhaberscheck)

CHANGING MONEY

Geld wechseln

* **I'd like to change Austrian schillings into pounds, please.**
(change – umwechseln)

* **How many pounds do I get for 2,000 Austrian schillings, please?**

* **Could you change these Dutch guilders for me, please?**
(Dutch guilders – holländische Gulden)

* **A: I've got some German marks. I wonder whether you could change them for me, please?**
(.... Könnten Sie sie mir bitte umwechseln?)
B: Certainly, madam. I'll just check the exchange rates.
(certainly – natürlich / just – nur / check – nachschauen / exchange rate – Wechselkurs)

* **A: Do you change foreign coins?**
(foreign coins – ausländische Münzen)
B: No, I'm afraid we can't take foreign currency in small change.
(foreign currency in small change – ausländisches Kleingeld)

* **Can you give me £100 in German marks, please?**

* **Can you change this fifty-pound note into dollars, please?**

* **A: Could you tell me the current rate of exchange for US dollars, please?**
(current rate of exchange – heutiger Kurs)
B: Would you like to know the buying rate or selling rate?
(buying rate – Geldkurs, Ankaufskurs / selling rate – Briefkurs, Verkaufskurs)
A: Well, I'd like to buy dollars, so that's your selling rate, isn't it?
(isn't it? – nicht wahr?)

* **What's today's rate of exchange?**
(rate of exchange – Wechselkurs)

* **I'd like to know the rate for Swiss francs, please.**

* **A: I need $2,000 to take with me to the US, please.**
B: Would you like it in cash or in cheques?
(in cash – bar)
A: I'll have cash, please.

* **A: How would you like the money?**
B: In hundred-dollar notes, please.

* **Notes only, please.**

* **Some small change, too, please.**
(small change – Kleingeld)

* **I wonder if you could tell me whether there are any restrictions on taking foreign currency into the United States?**
(Könnten Sie mir bitte sagen, ob … / foreign currency – Fremdwährung; ausländisches Geld)

* **Do you think you could change this fifty-pound note for smaller notes, please?**
(change – wechseln)

* **Can you give me change, please?**
(Können Sie mir bitte wechseln?)

OPENING AND CLOSING AN ACCOUNT

Eröffnung und Schließung eines Kontos

* **A: I was thinking of opening an account over here as I'll probably be travelling back and forwards regularly from now on. Which bank could you recommend?**
(probably – wahrscheinlich / back and forwards – hin und her / regularly – regelmäßig / recommend – empfehlen)
B: Well, if you just want a current account with the normal services, there isn't much to choose between the Big Four clearing banks, which are Nat West, Barclays, Lloyds and Midland. If you want to earn interest on your money then you're probably better off with an account at a building society, which can offer you attractive interest-bearing accounts with a cheque book and cash dispenser card, too.
(current account – Kontokorrentkonto, Girokonto, Scheckkonto / there isn't much to choose between – es gibt kaum einen Unterschied zwischen / clearing bank – britische Geschäftsbank / earn interest – Zinsen bekommen / be better off – besser daran sein / building society – Bausparkasse / offer – anbieten / interest-bearing – verzinslich / cash dispenser – Geldausgabeautomat, Bankomat)

* **A: Do current accounts in Britain bear interest?**
(Werden Kontokorrenteinlagen ... verzinst?)
B: Usually only if you're more than £100 in the black.
(Normalerweise nur, wenn Sie mehr als 100 Pfund auf dem Konto haben.)

* **A: I'd like to open a bank account, please.**
B: Certainly. May I ask you what type of account you had in mind?
(Gerne. Darf ich Sie fragen, an welche Art von Konto Sie gedacht haben?)
A: A current account, I think.

B: Well, with our current account you have all the normal services such as free cheques, a £100 cheque guarantee card and cash card, plus a guaranteed overdraft of up to 50% of your salary and 9% interest is paid on every pound in your account.
(cash card – Bezugskarte, Bankomatkarte / overdraft – Überziehungsmöglichkeit / salary – Gehalt / interest – Zinsen)

* **I'd like to open a deposit account, please.**
(deposit account – Sparkonto)

* **I'd like to transfer my account from this branch to your Manchester branch, please.**
(transfer – verlegen / branch – Filiale)

——— ❖ ———

* **I'm going back to Austria next week, so I won't be needing my current account any more. Could you close it and have the balance transferred to my account in Salzburg? Here's my account number.**
(won't – will not / close – schließen / have balance transferred – Überweisung des Guthabens veranlassen)

DEPOSITS

Einzahlungen

* **A: I'd like to pay some money into my account, please.**
B: Certainly, sir. Could I have your account number, please?
A: Yes, here's my cheque card.

* **A: I'd like to pay this crossed cheque in pounds sterling into my wife's account, please.**
B: Do you know the number of her account?
A: Yes, here you are.
(... , hier bitte!)

* **May I have a paying-in slip, please?**
(paying-in slip – Einzahlungsschein)

* **If I deposit this cheque today, when will the amount be credited to my account?**
(deposit – einzahlen / amount – Betrag / credit – gutschreiben)

* **A: By the way, Bill, how much did you pay into our account with Midland Bank?**
B: I deposited £300 two weeks ago. Here's the receipt.
(receipt – Beleg)

WITHDRAWALS

Abhebungen

* **A: I'd like to take £50 out of my current account, please.**
(take out – abheben)
B: Certainly, sir. Just make out a cheque payable to "Self" or "Cash".

* **A: I'd like to withdraw some money from my savings account, please.**
(withdraw – abheben / savings account – Sparkonto)
B: Certainly, how much would you like?
A: Two hundred pounds.
B: Could I have your passbook, please?
(passbook – Sparbuch)

* **A: I'd like to draw some money on my husband's account.**
(Ich möchte Geld vom Konto meines Gatten abheben.)
B: Have you got power of attorney, madam?
(power of attorney – Vollmacht)

* **Where should I sign?**

* **A: Your cash dispenser seems to have broken down. Could I withdraw £20 in cash, please?**
(... scheint kaputt zu sein. ... ?)
B: Certainly. The easiest way is to make out a cheque, madam.

* **A: My cash dispenser card has been swallowed up.**
(swallow up – schlucken)
B: Did you key in the wrong PIN-code?
(key in – eingeben / PIN – Personal Identification Number / Bankomatcode)

TRANSFERS

Überweisungen

* **A: I would like to transfer £25.40 to this account, please.**
(transfer – überweisen)
B: Well, for such a small amount, and as it's a domestic transaction, it'd be much easier and less expensive for you to send a cheque.
(domestic transaction – Inlandstransaktion / expensive – teuer)

* **A: I'd like to pay a bill in Austria for 1,000 schillings. Could I make a transfer?**
(bill – Rechnung / transfer – Überweisung)
B: Well, we could transfer the money for you, but for a small sum like that it's simplier to give you a cheque which you can send direct.

* **A: I'd like to transfer £450 from my current account to my deposit account, please.**
B: Yes, could you sign here, please ... Thank you.

* **Have the amount transferred by a bank.**
(Lassen Sie den Betrag von einer Bank überweisen.)

* **A: I've heard that the best way to transfer money abroad is by SWIFT, is that right?**
(abroad – ins Ausland / SWIFT – SWIFT | Society for Worldwide Interbank Financial Telecommunications)
B: It is the quickest method, and in fact most of our international funds transfers are sent via SWIFT.
(funds – Geld)

* **A: I'd like to transfer £300 to my mother in Innsbruck. Shall I pay cash or can you charge it to my account?**
(charge – anlasten, belasten)
B: We'll make the payment and debit it to your account.
(debit an amount to an account – ein Konto mit einem Betrag belasten)

* **A: Could you transfer £500 from my deposit account to this account in Germany, please?**
  B: Certainly. Would you like us to make the transfer by ordinary mail or by telex?
  (by ordinary mail – brieflich)

* **I'm expecting some money which was transferred to me about a week ago from Vienna. Is it in yet?**
  (expect – erwarten / … . Ist es schon da?)

* **I'd like to arrange for my telephone bills to be paid by direct debit, please.**
  (arrange for – veranlassen / direct debit – Abbuchungsverfahren, Lastschriftverfahren)

* **A: Could you arrange a standing order for £260 per month payable to this account, please?**
  (standing order – Dauerauftrag)
  B: Yes, that should be no problem. Could you just complete this form, please?
  (complete form – Formular ausfüllen)

* **I'd like to transfer £250 on the first of each month, starting next month and until further notice, to my daughter, who's studying in Linz.**
  (until further notice – bis auf Widerruf; bis auf weiteres)

* **Could I cancel a standing order arrangement which I have for my rent? I'm leaving London to go back to Austria at the end of the month.**
  (cancel – stornieren / rent – Miete / … . Ich gehe … nach Österreich zurück.)

OVERDRAFTS

Kontoüberziehungen

* **I wonder if it'd be possible to overdraw my account by up to £500 next month?**
  (Wäre es möglich, daß ich mein Konto nächstes Monat bis zu 500 Pfund überziehe?)

* **A: How much would it cost for an overdraft of five hundred pounds?**
  (overdraft – Überziehungskredit)
  B: First of all there is a small commitment fee and then on top of that you'll have to pay interest.
  (commitment fee – Bereitstellungsprovision / on top of that – zusätzlich)

* **What is the current rate of interest on an overdraft, please?**
  (Wie hoch sind zur Zeit die Zinsen für … ?)

STATEMENTS AND BALANCE OF ACCOUNT

Kontoauszüge und Kontostand

* **Can you give me a statement, please?**
  (statement – Kontoauszug)

* **A: Could you send me a statement at the end of each month?**
  B: Actually, you might find it more convenient to order statements as and when you need them from our ATMs using your cash card.
  (convenient – praktisch / order – abrufen / ATM – automated teller machine | automatischer Bankschalter / cash card – Bezugskarte, Bankomatkarte)

* **A: I'd like to know the balance of my account, please. It's number 4647839.**
  (balance – Saldo, Stand)
  B: Ah, yes, you have a debit balance of £46.97.
  (debit balance – Minus)

* **Your account is overdrawn by £46.97.**

* **A: Could you tell me the balance on my account, please?**
  B: Your account shows a credit of £167.90.
  (credit – Guthaben, Plus)

CREDIT CARDS

Kreditkarten

* **Here is my credit card.**

* **Do you accept Visa credit cards?**

* **Can I withdraw cash with my credit card?**
  (withdraw cash – Geld abheben)

* **I wish to report that I've lost my credit card.**
  (report – melden)

* **Here are my credit card details. ... Should I give you the expiry date, too?**
  (expiry date – Verfallsdatum)

MY JOB

Mein Job

WHAT DO YOU DO FOR A LIVING?

Wie verdienen Sie sich Ihren Lebensunterhalt?

* **What kind of job do you have?**

* **I'm a civil servant, with permanent tenure.**
  (civil servant – Staatsangestellter / permanent tenure – Pragmatisierung; unkündbare Stellung)

* **I work for the subsidiary of an American corporation.**
  (subsidiary – Tochtergesellschaft / corporation – [Kapital-] Gesellschaft, Konzern)

* **I'm a free-lance management consultant.**
  (Ich bin freiberuflicher Betriebsberater.)

* **I work as a software engineer for a large software house.**

* **I'm still a student.**
  (still – noch)

JOINING THE COMPANY

Eintritt in die Firma

* **I joined the company in 1970 as a management trainee.**
  (join company – in Firma | Gesellschaft eintreten / trainee – Praktikant, Trainee)

* **You won't believe it, but I've been with my present company for over 15 years.**
  (Sie werden es nicht glauben, aber ich bin schon seit über 15 Jahren bei meiner jetzigen Firma.)

* **I replied to an advertisement in 1983. They invited me for an interview and I got the job.**
  (reply to – antworten auf / advertisement – Anzeige / invite – einladen)

* **I met my present boss at the tennis club. That's how I got the job.**
  (meet – kennenlernen / present – jetzig, gegenwärtig / that's how – so; auf diese Weise)

* **I knew one of the managers from school.**
  (know – kennen)

* **I've worked for quite a few companies already. I think the one I'm with now is the sixth.**
  (quite a few – einige; nicht wenige / sixth – sechst)

WORKING HOURS AND WORKING CONDITIONS

Arbeitszeit und Arbeitsbedingungen

* **A: When do you start in the morning?**
  B: I have to start at nine.
  A: Nine? Well, that's rather late. In my country we start at eight. Some firms even at seven thirty.
  (rather – ziemlich / even – sogar)

* **It's not a nine-to-five job. As long as I meet my deadlines they don't bother too much about attendance.**
  (nine-to-five job – 08/15-Job / meet deadline – Termin einhalten / bother about – sich kümmern um / attendance – Anwesenheit)

* **I work long hours. And, if I've got a deadline to meet, I sometimes have to take work home with me over the weekend.**
  (work long hours – oft sehr lange arbeiten; oft bis spät in die Nacht hinein arbeiten)

* **The official working week is 40 hours, but my company expect me to work up to 10 hours overtime.**
  (working week – Arbeitszeit / expect – erwarten / overtime – Überstunden)

* **I did a lot of overtime last year.**
(a lot of – eine Menge; viel)

* **We've got a very rigid system. You have to get your card punched whenever you enter or leave the building.**
(rigid – starr / get card punched – [Stech-]Karte lochen l abstempeln lassen / enter – betreten / leave – verlassen / building – Gebäude)

* **We are on flexitime. This means I can start any time between 8 and 11 and leave between 4 and 7 in the afternoon, as long as I do my eight hours.**
(be on flexitime – gleitende Arbeitszeit haben / leave – weggehen)

* **I've got a nice office.**
(office – Büro)

SUPERIORS, SUBORDINATES AND COLLEAGUES

Vorgesetzte, Untergebene und Kollegen

* **My boss is very nice. Very constructive. Never tells you off, even if you've made a mistake.**
(tell sbdy. off – jmdn. heruntermachen / mistake – Fehler)

* **My boss is a woman actually. We've got a fairly large number of female managers.**
(fairly – ziemlich / female – weiblich)

* **A: I've never worked for a woman. What's it like?**
(... . Wie ist das?)
B: Well, at first it was a bit strange. But you get used to it, especially if the woman is a competent manager.
(strange – seltsam / get used to sthg. – sich an etwas gewöhnen / especially – besonders)

* **We've got lots of women managers in our company. It doesn't seem to make any difference.**
(seem – scheinen / difference – Unterschied)

* **My boss is a very difficult person to work with.**

* **He likes to show us who's the boss.**

* **Working under her was not much fun. But I learned a lot.**
(not much fun – nicht gerade lustig)

* **Most of the people in the Marketing Department are quite young and the atmosphere there is very relaxed.**
(quite – ziemlich / atmosphere – Klima / relaxed – locker)

* **Most of my colleagues are very nice people.**

——— ❖ ———

* **I report to the Marketing Manager.**
(report to sbdy. – jmdm. unterstellt sein)

* **I work under the Controller.**

* **My section comes under Materials Management.**
(Mein Referat gehört zur Abteilung Materialwirtschaft.)

* **I'm responsible for a team of about 50 sales reps.**
(responsible – verantwortlich, zuständig / sales rep – Vertreter, Reisender)

JOB DESCRIPTION AND DUTIES
Beschreibung des Arbeitsplatzes und Aufgaben

* **What exactly are your duties?**
(duty – Aufgabe)

* **What does your job involve?**
(Welche Tätigkeiten bringt Ihr Posten mit sich?)

* **I'm a sales engineer.**
(sales engineer – Verkaufsingenieur)

* **I'm responsible for maintaining contact with our advertising agency.**
(maintain – aufrechterhalten, halten / advertising agency – Werbeagentur)

* **I'm in charge of the Personnel Department.**
(Ich leite die Personalabteilung.)

* **I look after our overseas customers.**
(Ich betreue unsere ausländischen Kunden.)

* **I used to work as an account executive but transferred to the Personnel Department when they needed an assistant to the Personnel Manager.**
(Früher einmal habe ich als Kundenbetreuer I Kontakter gearbeitet, aber dann bin ich in die Personalabteilung übersiedelt, als ein Assistent für den Personalchef benötigt wurde.)

* **My main task is negotiating contracts with foreign suppliers.**
(Meine Hauptaufgabe ist es, Verträge mit ausländischen Lieferanten auszuhandeln.)

* **The sales people negotiate the contract in outline. I'm responsible for the legal details.**
(in outline - in groben Zügen; im Umriß / legal - juristisch)

* **My job involves a lot of travelling.**
(Mein Posten ist mit sehr viel Reisen verbunden.)

* **I joined my company as a design engineer but switched to selling after four years.**
(join company - in Firma I Gesellschaft eintreten / design engineer - Konstrukteur / switch - umsteigen)

* **I work in the field, selling specialised software to chemical companies.**
(in the field - im Außendienst)

* **I'm mainly concerned with making insurance claims.**
(Meine Hauptaufgabe ist die Anmeldung von Versicherungsansprüchen I das Melden von Schadensfällen.)

* **Currently I'm helping out in the Auditing Section.**
(Zur Zeit helfe ich in der Innenrevision aus.)

* **I deal with the incoming German correspondence.**
(deal with - bearbeiten)

JOB SATISFACTION
Arbeitszufriedenheit

* **Are you satisfied with your present job?**
  (satisfied – zufrieden / present – gegenwärtig, jetzig)

* **I like my present job.**

  Yes, I enjoy my work, although it is a bit much sometimes.
  (enjoy sthg. – etwas gerne tun | haben / although – obwohl)

* **What I like about my job is that I meet a lot of interesting people.**
  (meet – treffen; zusammenkommen mit)

* **What I particularly like about my job is that it involves a lot of travelling.**
  (particularly – besonders / involve – mit sich bringen / travel – reisen)

* **I don't like my present job.**

* **I hate sitting in the office all day. I'd prefer to travel and meet people.**
  (hate – hassen / all day – den ganzen Tag / prefer – vorziehen)

* **I don't like what I'm doing right now. Too much of a grind.**
  (right now – zur Zeit; gerade jetzt / grind – Mühe, Plackerei)

* **I've a lot of independence.**
  (independence – Unabhängigkeit)

* **What I can't stand is the paperwork.**
  (Was ich nicht leiden kann, ist der Papierkram.)

LEAVING THE COMPANY AND LOOKING FOR A NEW JOB

Ausscheiden aus der Firma und Suche nach einem neuen Arbeitsplatz

* **I'm thinking of leaving the firm.**
(leave firm – aus Firma ausscheiden)

* **I'm planning to move to another company.**
(move to – wechseln zu)

* **Unless I get promotion within the next year or two I might move on.**
(unless – wenn nicht / promotion – Beförderung / move on – weiterziehen; sich beruflich verändern)

* **I'm between jobs. I left the company after a row with my** immediate superior.
(row – Krach / immediate superior – unmittelbare[r] Vorgesetzte[r]

* **I was fired when they found out that I had a second job.**

* **I'm looking for a job.**
(look for – suchen)

* **I've handed in my resignation.**
(Ich habe meinen Rücktritt eingereicht. | Ich habe gekündigt.)

* **I'm still working for them because there is a six-week period of notice in my contract of employment.**
(still – noch immer / period of notice – Kündigungsfrist / contract of employment – Arbeitsvertrag)

* **I'm going to hand in my notice next week.**
(hand in – einreichen / notice – Kündigung)

* **I'm still trying to find something suitable in public relations or advertising.**
(suitable – geeignet, passend / advertising – Werbung)

* **I'm going to retire in three years.**
(retire – in Pension gehen)

* **I'm not what you might call a job-hopper, but I've worked for quite a few companies already. I'm always interested in a new challenge.**
(job-hopper – jemand, der häufig den Job wechselt / quite a few – ziemlich viele / challenge – Herausforderung)

* **No, I wouldn't dream of leaving my firm. I really like it there. It's like a second home to me.**
(Nein, mir würde es nicht im Traume einfallen, ...)

* **A: Ever thought of setting up your own business?**
(Jemals daran gedacht, sich selbständig zu machen?)
B: I briefly toyed with the idea of setting up a partnership or a company with a couple of friends.
(briefly – kurz / toy – spielen / partnership – Personengesellschaft / company – Kapitalgesellschaft / a couple of – ein paar)

* **One of my colleagues left the firm to join a workers' co-operative. Earns much less there but finds it more rewarding to work for an organisation that is owned and controlled by its own workers.**
(join – eintreten in; sich anschließen / workers' co-operative – Betrieb in Arbeiterselbstverwaltung / earn – verdienen / rewarding – lohnend / owned by – im Eigentum von / control – führen)

COMPENSATION

Entlohnung

* **A: How much do you make?**
(make – verdienen)
B: That's a good question.

* **I don't mind telling you how much I earn. But in my country people don't usually talk about their salaries, not even with fairly close friends.**
(Es macht mir nichts aus,.... / salary – Gehalt / not even – nicht einmal / fairly close friends – ziemlich gute Freunde)

* **My basic salary is around £40,000. And then I get about £10,000 in commissions, and the usual benefits of course.**

(basic salary – Grundgehalt / around – ungefähr / commission – Provision / benefits – Nebenleistungen, Sozialleistungen)

* **I make about ATS35,000 a month, that is before tax and national insurance.**
(Ich verdiene rund 35 000 öS im Monat, und zwar vor Abzug der Steuern und Sozialabgaben.)

* **They gave me a company car last year.**
(company car – Firmenauto)

* **To make it comparable with a British salary you would have to multiply that by 14.**
(comparable – vergleichbar)

* **Yes 14. Because we are paid 14 monthly salaries a year. Sounds odd, I know, but makes sense for tax reasons.**
(sound odd – seltsam I komisch klingen / make sense – sinnvoll sein / for tax reasons – aus steuerlichen Gründen)

* **The statutory minimum holiday in Austria is five weeks.**
(Der gesetzlich vorgeschriebene Mindesturlaub in ....)

* **If you want to compare this figure with a British or American salary, you would have to take into account the number of salaries paid per year, the longer paid holidays, the larger number of public holidays and, of course, the higher taxes.**
(compare – vergleichen / figure – Zahl / take into account – berücksichtigen / number – Anzahl / public holiday – Feiertag / tax – Steuer)

* **The gross figure looks quite good. But with all the deductions, take-home pay isn't much to write home about, especially if you consider the high rate of inflation.**
(gross – brutto / quite – ganz / deduction – Abzug / take-home pay – ausbezahlter Betrag / sthg. is not much to write home about – mit etwas ist es nicht weit her / consider – berücksichtigen)

* **The meals in the works cafeteria are subsidised.**
(works cafeteria – Werkskantine / subsidised – subventioniert)

* **A: Do you have a share option scheme for managers in your company?**
(share option scheme – Aktienbezugsrechtsprogramm)
B: Share option schemes for managers are not very common in Austria. But we do have a share-save scheme for ordinary employees.
(common – häufig / share-save scheme – Ansparprogramm für Aktien / employee – Mitarbeiter, Arbeitnehmer)

PROMOTION

Beförderung

* **I'm after the Sales Manager's job.**
(be after – aussein auf)

* **I'm waiting for the Controller to retire. I think I've got a good chance of getting his job.**
(retire – in Pension gehen)

* **I'm in line for the position of Sales Manager.**
(be in line – in Warteposition sein)

* **I was promoted last month.**
(promote – befördern)

* **He is being groomed for moving into the top spot.**
(Er wird auf eine Übersiedlung ins Chefzimmer vorbereitet.)

* **I'm number two now in the Sales Department.**

* **A: I have just been promoted to the position of Office Manager.**
B: Congratulation!

* **They offered me the top spot in the Advertising Department.**
(top spot – Leiterstelle)

* **I was promoted to Procurement Manager last week.**
(Procurement Manager – Leiter des Beschaffungswesens)

* **I was given a job higher up the ladder.**
(ladder – Hierarchie)

* **The pay is lousy, but I've got good career prospects.**
(pay – Bezahlung, Entlohnung / career prospects – Aufstiegschancen)

* **Mine has been a fairly typical career pattern.**
(Ich habe eine ziemlich typische berufliche Laufbahn.)

* **I've been invited to join the Management Board of my company.**
(Man hat mir einen Sitz im Vorstand meiner Gesellschaft angeboten.)

YOUR BUSINESS HERE IN BRITAIN

Zweck Ihres Aufenthaltes in Großbritannien

* **I've come over for a job interview.**
(job interview – Einstellungsgespräch)

* **I'm trying to find a firm to represent my company in England and Wales.**
(represent – vertreten)

* **I'm doing an IBM internship in London.**
(internship – Praktikum)

* **My company has sent me over to attend a language course.**
(attend – besuchen / language course – Sprachkurs)

* **I've been sent over to audit our branch in Brighton.**
(audit – Revision durchführen in / branch – Filiale)

* **My assignment is to call on some of our important customers.**
(Ich habe den Auftrag, einige unserer wichtigen Kunden zu besuchen.)

* **The main purpose of my visit is to inspect the books of our British licensee.**
(main purpose – Hauptzweck / inspect – inspizieren, prüfen / licensee – Lizenznehmer)

* **My mission is to negotiate a licensing agreement with a company in Oxford.**
(mission – Auftrag, Aufgabe / negotiate – aushandeln / licensing agreement – Lizenzabkommen)

EDUCATIONAL BACKGROUND

Bildungsweg

SECONDARY EDUCATION

Höhere Schulen, „Mittelschulen"

* **A: What school did you go to?**
  B: I attended what we call a "Commercial Academy". This is a high school with a strong business element in its curriculum.
  (attend – besuchen / high school – [US] höhere Schule; „Mittelschule" / curriculum – Lehrplan, Studienprogramm)

* **I went to a grammar school with special emphasis on modern languages.**
  (grammar school – [brit.] Gymnasium; allgemeinbildende höhere Schule; „Mittelschule" / emphasis – Betonung / language – Sprache)

* **I did my Matura – approximately equivalent to your A levels – in 1982.**
  (do [exam] – [Prüfung] ablegen / approximately – ungefähr / be equivalent to sthg. – einer Sache entsprechen)

* **After doing my A levels I began my studies at the University of Vienna.**

* **I dropped out of grammar school when I was 15. I simply didn't see any point in going on at that time.**
  (drop out – ausscheiden, austreten / simple – einfach / point – Sinn)

* **I became apprenticed to a bookseller and went back to school when I was 19.**
  (Ich bekam eine Lehrstelle bei einem Buchhändler. . . .)

* **A: Is your school system really all that different from ours?**
(all that – so / different – verschieden)
B: I think the main difference between British grammar schools and our equivalent – called „Gymnasium“ – is that we have a much broader curriculum. There is much less specialisation, particularly in the higher forms.
(main – wichtigst, Haupt... / curriculum – Lehrangebot, Lehrplan / particularly – besonders / form – Klasse)

* **The final exam is also different. Above all it's not a national exam. It is set by your own teachers.**
(final exam – Abschlußprüfung / national exam – einheitliche Prüfung für ein ganzes Land / set exam – Prüfung erstellen)

* **The greatest cultural difference is certainly the students' attitude towards cheating.**
(attitude – Einstellung / cheat – schwindeln)

* **Cribbing and cheating in exams are a national pastime. They are not considered dishonourable.**
(Abschreiben und Schwindeln bei Prüfungen sind ein Volkssport. .... / be considered – gelten als / dishonourable – unehrenhaft)

* **As a matter of fact, you are regarded as a sissy if you don't cheat or help your friends in exams.**
(be regarded as – gehalten werden für / sissy – Seicherl, Schwächling)

ACCESS TO UNIVERSITIES

Zulassung zum Universitätsstudium

* **A: Is it difficult to get into a university in your country?**
B: In my country access to universities is not restricted.
(access – Zutritt / restricted – beschränkt)

* **If you manage to get through secondary school successfully, you are entitled to a place at a university of your choice. They can't turn you down.**
(manage – es schaffen / secondary school – höhere Schule; „Mittelschule“ / successful – erfolgreich / be entitled to – Anspruch haben auf / choice – Wahl / turn down – ablehnen)

* **There are no admission exams, not even interviews.**
(admission exam – Aufnahmsprüfung, Zulassungsprüfung / not even – nicht einmal)

* **Obviously this system creates a lot of problems, like overcrowding and a high drop-out rate.**
(obviously – klarerweise / create – mit sich bringen; führen zu / a lot of – viele; eine Menge / overcrowding – Überfüllung / drop-out rate – Ausfallsquote)

* **There's, however, talk about changing the system.**
(Man diskutiert aber eine Änderung des Systems.)

DEGREES

Akademische Grade

* **What is your academic background?**
(Was haben Sie für eine akademische Ausbildung?)

* **I graduated from the University of Economics and Business Administration in Vienna in 1989.**
(graduate from university – Studium an Universität mit akademischem Grad abschließen / University of Economics and Business Administration – Wirtschaftsuniversität / economics – Volkswirtschaftslehre / business administration – Betriebswirtschaftslehre)

* **I earned a Master's degree in Business Administration. That's not an MBA, because in my country the Master's degree is the first university degree, while the MBA is post-graduate.**
(earn degree – akademischen Grad erwerben / MBA – Master of Business Administration / post-graduate [degree] – zweiter / ranghöherer akademischer Grad)

* **A: What does M.A. on your business card stand for?**
(business card – Visitenkarte / stand for – stehen für)
B: I hold a Master of Arts degree.
(hold degree – akademischen Grad innehaben / Master of Arts – etwa: Magister der Philosophie)

* **Are you a graduate of the London School of Economics?**
(graduate – Absolvent)

* **I majored in Business Administration.**
  (Mein Hauptfach war Betriebswirtschaftslehre.)

* **I did what I think the Americans call a double major. I read Law at the University of Vienna and I did Business Administration at the University of Economics and Business Administration in the same city.**
  (double major – doppeltes Hauptfach; Doppelstudium / read – studieren / law – Rechtswissenschaften, Jus)

* **My brother is a university-trained chemist.**
  (Mein Bruder ist ein akademisch ausgebildeter Chemiker I Diplomchemiker.)

* **Only the big companies have a policy of hiring graduates.**
  (policy – Politik / hire – anstellen, einstellen / graduate – Akademiker)

* **I'm thinking of going back to university and doing a Social Science Doctorate in Operations Research.**
  (social science – Sozialwissenschaft)

STUDIES AND EXAMINATIONS

Studium und Prüfungen

* **We had to attend a number of seminars. In most of them you had to write a fairly long paper and present it either alone or together with some other students.**
  (attend – besuchen / fairly – ziemlich / paper – Referat / present – präsentieren, halten)

* **Maths was my favourite subject, both in high school and at university, but I didn't like Law.**
  (maths – mathematics / favourite subject – Lieblingsgegenstand / both ... and ... – sowohl ... als auch ...)

* **I liked university. Might even have stayed on and gone in for an academic career if a suitable opening had turned up.**
  (even – sogar / stay on – dort bleiben / go in for – sich entscheiden für / suitable opening – geeignete freie Stelle / turn up – sich ergeben)

* **Under the new regime, which was adopted in 1985, languages and Computer Science became much more important.**
(under – im Rahmen / regime – [Studien-]Ordnung / adopt – einführen / language – Sprache)

* **As I enrolled for the Commerce Course I had to do two languages. One in Part I of the Course only and the other both in Part I and in Part II.**
(enrol for – inskribieren; sich anmelden für / Commerce Course – handelswissenschaftliche Studienrichtung / Part I – erster Studienabschnitt)

* **My university offers a number of courses. The most popular one is Business Administration, followed by Commerce. Economics and Business Education are less important.**
(course – Studienrichtung / business administration – Betriebswirtschaftslehre / commerce – Handelswissenschaften / economics – Volkswirtschaftslehre / business education – Wirtschaftspädagogik / important – wichtig)

* **In Part II, I specialised in Materials Management.**
(materials management – Materialwirtschaft)

* **A: When did you take your final exams?**
B: I sat for my finals in 1985.
(sit for an exam – zu einer Prüfung antreten / final – final examination | Abschlußprüfung)

* **The final exams are quite tough. In many subjects you have a four-hour written exam and, if you pass that, a short oral one.**
(quite – ziemlich / tough – streng, schwer / subject – Gegenstand / pass exam – Prüfung bestehen / oral exam – mündliche Prüfung)

* **The course covered a wide range of subjects, some quite irrelevant to what I did later, like Constitutional Law, Commoditology, Financial Accounting and Cost Accounting.**
(Das Programm der Studienrichtung umfaßte eine breite Palette von Gegenständen, wovon einige für das, was ich später machte, ganz irrelevant waren, wie z. B. Verfassungsrecht, Warenkunde, Finanzbuchhaltung und Kostenrechnung.)

* **Some of the teachers were a pain in the neck.**
(pain in the neck – kaum zum Aushalten)

* **I had a couple of very good teachers. One of them even made it internationally.**
(a couple of – ein paar / even – sogar / make it – reüssieren; Erfolg haben)

* **The subject of my master's thesis was "The Property Market in Vienna".**
(subject – Gegenstand / master's thesis – Diplomarbeit / property market – Immobilienmarkt)

* **I developed a model of the car market in Austria as part of my master's thesis. Sold it to a big car dealer after I had graduated.**
(develop – entwickeln, erstellen / sell – verkaufen / car dealer – Autohändler)

FINANCE

Finanzierung des Studiums

* **A: How much does it cost you a year to study at a university?**
B: Well, I couldn't really say. Anyway, tuition is absolutely free in Austria. Only foreign students have to pay a moderate fee.
(anyway – jedenfalls / tuition – Unterricht, Studium / free – kostenlos / foreign – ausländisch / moderate fee – mäßige [Studien-]Gebühr)

* **The other costs – like everywhere – depend a lot on your personal circumstances.**
(depend on – abhängen von / a lot – stark / circumstances – Umstände, Verhältnisse)

* **I managed to get a place in a hall of residence, which was much cheaper than renting private accommodation.**
(manage – es schaffen / hall of residence – Studentenheim / cheap – billig / rent – mieten / accommodation – Unterkunft)

* **I shared a small flat with two friends. That helped to keep down our cost of living.**
(Ich hatte eine kleine Wohnung gemeinsam mit zwei Freunden. … . / keep down – niedrig halten)

* **Since I am from Vienna, I continued to live with my parents when I started university.**
(since – da / continue to live – weiterhin wohnen / parents – Eltern)

* **We have means-tested student grants. That is, you can get a grant if your parents don't earn too much money.**
(means-tested – an einen Bedürftigkeitsnachweis gebunden / grant – Unterhaltsstipendium)

* **Then there are scholarships for which you need a good grade average.**
(scholarship – [Begabten-]Stipendium / grade average – Notendurchschnitt)

* **My parents gave me quite a generous monthly allowance so I didn't have to do any part-time jobs.**
(quite – ziemlich / generous – großzügig / allowance – geldliche Zuwendung / part-time job – Teilzeitbeschäftigung)

* **I had to interrupt my studies because my father died and so I had to earn some money to finish the Course.**
(interrupt – unterbrechen / die – sterben / earn – verdienen / finish – abschließen / course – Studienprogramm [einer bestimmten Studienrichtung])

* **I worked my way through College, doing part-time jobs during the academic year and working full-time in the holidays.**
(Ich war ein Werkstudent, und zwar war ich während des Studienjahres teilzeit- und während der Ferien ganztags beschäftigt.)

* **In Austria, regular full-time students are entitled to a number of benefits, e.g. to free travel in the city where they study.**
(regular full-time student – ordentlicher Hörer / be entitled to - Anspruch haben auf / number – Reihe / benefit – Vergünstigung / e.g. – for example | zum Beispiel / free travel – Freifahrt)

CONDITIONS AT UNIVERSITY

Studienbedingungen

* **A: What was life like at your university?**
  B: Since I went to one of the small universities, conditions were not too bad.
  (since – da / condition – Verhältnis)

* **Some of our universities are grossly overcrowded. Classes are large and the drop-out rate is very high.**
  (grossly overcrowded – krass überbelegt / drop-out rate – Ausfallsquote)

* **Registering for major exams sometimes involved waiting in queues for hours on end.**
  (register – sich anmelden / major – größer / involve – bedeuten, heißen / queue – Schlange / for hours on end – stundenlang)

* **What you learn is how to survive under pressure.**
  (survive – überleben / pressure – Druck)

* **Since there are so many students and not enough teachers, it was very difficult to find a supervisor for my master's thesis.**
  (enough – genug / supervisor for master's thesis – Diplomarbeitsbetreuer)

* **The student-teacher ratio was appalling.**
  (student-teacher ratio – Betreuungsverhältnis / appalling – schrecklich)

STUDY RECORD

Studienergebnisse

* **I had fairly good grades.**
  (fairly – ziemlich / grade – Note)

* **I was among the top two per cent of the class graduating in 1989.**
  (class – Jahrgang)

* **I must admit my marks were not that good.**
(admit – zugeben / mark – [brit.] Note)

* **In Austria, most people don't take the grades they earn at university too seriously.**
(earn – bekommen / serious – ernst)

* **It took me seven years to get my degree. I must admit I didn't work very hard in the first two years. It was so exciting being in Vienna. There were lots of things to do apart from studying.**
(it took me – ich brauchte / exciting – aufregend / lots of – eine Menge / apart from - abgesehen von)

* **You are not thrown out if you fail an exam. You can sit most exams three or four times before you get into trouble.**
(throw out – hinauswerfen / fail exam – bei Prüfung durchfallen / three times – dreimal / trouble – Schwierigkeiten)

STUDYING ABROAD

Studium im Ausland

* **I studied abroad for a year and my university gave me credit for some of the work I had done there.**
(abroad – im Ausland / give credit for sthg. – etwas anrechnen)

* **Unfortunately they did not give me any credit for the courses I completed in the United States. There was some administrative snag I did not understand.**
(unfortunately – leider / complete course – Lehrveranstaltung absolvieren / snag - Haken, Schwierigkeit)

* **I managed to get a scholarship and did a year in France at one of the Grandes Ecoles. That's why my French is much better than my English.**
(manage – es zuwege bringen; es schaffen / scholarship – Stipendium)

EXTRACURRICULAR ACTIVITIES

Außeruniversitäre Aktivitäten

* **I was a representative of the Students' Union and organised a couple of large conventions, one on post-cold-war marketing issues.**
(students' union – Hochschülerschaft / convention – Kongreß / issue – Problem)

* **I edited the students' magazine for two years.**
(edit – herausgeben)

* **I worked part-time at a bank while I was still at the university.**
(work part-time – teilzeitbeschäftigt sein / while – während / still – noch)

* **I attended a Spanish course in 1988.**

* **I did several traineeships during the summer vacations.**
(traineeship – [Ferial-]Praxis / vacations – Ferien)

* **I was lucky to be accepted by IBM Vienna for an internship in the summer before I graduated.**
(be lucky – Glück haben / for an internship – für ein Praktikum; als Praktikant)

POST UNIVERSITY

Nach dem Studienabschluß

* **After I had finished university, I spent a year abroad working for a company in France.**
(finish – beenden / spend – verbringen / company – Gesellschaft)

* **I was hired straight from university.**
(Ich wurde direkt von der Universität weg eingestellt.)

* **I went on a world tour after I had graduated.**

* **Unfortunately I had to do my military service before I could start looking for a job.**
(unfortunately – leider / look for – suchen; sich umsehen um)

* **I dithered around for a time after I had finished. Didn't really know what to do until I got this interesting offer.**
(dither around – unentschlossen sein; zögern / know – wissen / until – bis / offer – Angebot)

MY COMPANY

Meine Firma

TYPE, SIZE, LOCATION, OWNERSHIP, HISTORY, ETC.

Art, Größe, Standort, Eigentumsverhältnisse, Geschichte usw.

* **What kind of company do you work for?**
(kind – Art / company – Gesellschaft)

* **Where is your company based?**
(Wo hat Ihre Gesellschaft ihren Sitz?)

* **I work for a medium-sized steel company based in Vienna.**
(medium-sized – mittelgroß / steel – Stahl)

* **My company is a wholly-owned subsidiary of an American corporation. It is fairly large, at least by Austrian standards.**
(wholly-owned subsidiary – 100%ige Tochter / corporation – [US] Gesellschaft, Kapitalgesellschaft, Konzern / fairly – ziemlich / by – gemessen an / standards – Verhältnisse, Normen)

* **Our Headquarters is in Vienna, but we've got subsidiaries and branches in most European countries.**
(headquarters – [Konzern-]Zentrale / branch – Zweiganstalt, Filiale)

* **We're thinking of opening a representative office in New York.**
(representative office – Repräsentanz)

* **We were taken over by a U.S. corporation last year.**
(take over – übernehmen, aufkaufen)

* **We fought the take-over bid tooth and nail because we thought they would replace the whole management. In the end they allowed us to continue much as before.**
(fight – bekämpfen / take-over bid – Übernahmeangebot / tooth and nail – ganz energisch; mit Klauen und Zähnen / replace – ersetzen / in the end – letzten Endes / continue – weitermachen)

* **We went public last year, because we needed to raise more capital.**
(go public – an die Börse gehen / need – müssen / raise – aufbringen)

* **Most of our shareholders are small private investors.**
(shareholder – Aktionär)

* **A couple of months ago an American corporation acquired a 30 per cent stake in our company.**
(a couple of – ein paar / acquire – erwerben / stake – Beteiligung)

* **There are rumours that the public corporation I work for is going to be privatised next year.**
(rumours – Gerüchte / public corporation – [brit.] verstaatlichte Gesellschaft / privatise – privatisieren, entstaatlichen)

* **Just imagine, our major shareholder is planning to take the company private.**
(imagine [sthg.] – sich [etwas] vorstellen / major shareholder – Hauptaktionär / take private – von der Börse abziehen)

* **We are a fairly small private company.**
(fairly – ziemlich / private company – etwa: GmbH; kleine Familien-AG)

* **Originally the firm was established as a partnership. But when one of the partners died in 1984, we converted into something that corresponds fairly closely to your private limited company.**
(originally – ursprünglich / establish – errichten, gründen / partnership – Personengesellschaft / partner – Teilhaber / die – sterben / convert – sich umwandeln / correspond to – entsprechen / close – genau / private limited company – [brit.] etwa: GmbH)

* **No, an Austrian GmbH is not exactly the same as a private limited company. One important difference is that in Austria there is a fairly high minimum capital requirement.**
(important – wichtig / minimum capital requirement – Mindestkapitalerfordernis)

* **We'll probably make a major acquisition later this year.**
(probably – wahrscheinlich / major – größer / acquisition – Firmenerwerb)

* **We are considering merging with an American chemical firm.**
(consider – in Erwägung ziehen / merge – fusionieren)

* **We've got outlets in all European countries, including Russia.**
(outlet – Laden, Verkaufsgeschäft)

* **Irish tax breaks are so generous that we decided to locate the new facility on an industrial estate near Dublin.**
(tax break – steuerliche Vergünstigung / generous – großzügig / decide – beschließen; sich entscheiden / locate – ansiedeln / facility – Produktionsstätte, -einrichtung / industrial estate – Industriepark, Industriezone)

* **We have done our sums and are relocating to Scotland.**
(Wir haben die Sache durchgerechnet und übersiedeln nach Schottland.)

* **We have one green-field site development going at the moment.**
(green-field site – [Bauplatz] auf der grünen Wiese / development – Bauvorhaben / have sthg. going – etwas laufen haben)

* **Are you an independent company or part of a larger group?**
(independent – unabhängig / group – Konzern)

* **Our parent company keeps us on a fairly short leash.**
(parent company – Muttergesellschaft / keep on a short leash – eng an der Kandare halten)

* **We shall probably need five new distribution depots to serve the new retail outlets.**
(distribution depot – Auslieferungslager / serve – beliefern / retail outlet – Einzelhandelsgeschäft)

PRODUCTS AND ACTIVITIES

Produkte und Tätigkeitsbereiche

* **Our main activity is prospecting for oil.**
(main activity – Hauptgeschäftsbereich / prospect for – suchen; schürfen nach)

* **We are a highly diversified group, a conglomerate in fact.**
(highly diversified – stark diversifiziert / conglomerate – Mischkonzern)

* **Our product range includes machine tools and mini-computers.**
(product range – Sortiment, Produktionsprogramm / machine tool – Werkzeugmaschine)

* **My company has been engaged in manufacturing high-pressure valves since it was founded thirty years ago.**
(be engaged in – sich befassen mit / manufacture – erzeugen / high-pressure valve – Hochdruckventil / found – gründen)

* **We trade in plastic and steel semis.**
(trade in – handeln mit / semis – Halbzeug)

* **We represent several American and Japanese companies in Europe.**
(represent – vertreten)

* **We are subcontractors to two German car manufacturers.**
(subcontractor – Zulieferer / car manufacturer – Autohersteller)

* **We have decided to farm out the manufacture of some key components.**
(decide – beschließen / farm out – an eine andere Firma vergeben / key component – wichtiger Bauteil)

* **My company specialises in buying and selling commercial property.**
(specialise in – spezialisiert sein auf / commercial property – Büro- und Geschäftsimmobilien)

* **More than half of our turnover is achieved abroad.**
(turnover – Umsatz / achieve – erzielen / abroad – im Ausland)

* **Our export ratio has always been very high, around 90 per cent in most years.**
(export ratio – Exportquote / around – rund)

* **Last year exports accounted for 85 per cent of total sales.**
(Voriges Jahr entfielen 85% des Gesamtumsatzes auf Exporte.)

* **At the last board meeting it was decided to commit a large sum to the development of bauxit deposits in Western Australia.**
(board – Verwaltungsrat; Führungsgremium einer brit./US Kapitalgesellschaft / meeting – Sitzung / commit to – verbindlich vorsehen für; binden für / development – Erschließung / deposit – Lagerstätte)

ORGANISATIONAL STRUCTURE AND MANAGEMENT

Organisationsstruktur und Management

* **In Austria we have a two-tier system. This means my company has two separate boards: a supervisory board – similar to your non-executive directors – and a management board.**
(two-tier system – zweistufiges System / board – Führungsgremium / supervisory board – Aufsichtsrat / non-executive director – nichtgeschäftsführendes Mitglied des brit./US [einstufigen] Führungsgremiums / management board – Vorstand)

* **The main difference to your system is that in Austria a director cannot be an executive at the same time. The directors are all non-executive.**
(director – Mitglied des Aufsichtsrates / executive – [hochrangiger] Manager)

* **Yes, the management board are appointed by the directors. But, as I've already said, they are not allowed to appoint one of their own members.**
(appoint – bestellen)

* **Our organisation chart is pretty complicated. But basically we are organised on functional not on divisional lines.**
(Unser Organigramm ist ziemlich kompliziert. Aber im wesentlichen sind wir nach dem funktionalen und nicht nach dem Geschäftsspartenprinzip gegliedert.)

* **Our organisational structure was revamped two years ago. We got rid of a whole layer of middle managers. We are now what Drucker calls a "flat organisation" and much leaner and more efficient.**
(revamp – völlig neu gestalten / get rid of – loswerden / layer – Schichte / flat – flach / lean – mager; ohne unnötiges Fett)

* **A: In my company Production Scheduling comes under Materials Management.**
(In meiner Gesellschaft untersteht die Arbeitsvorbereitung der Materialwirtschaft.)
B: That's interesting. And to whom is the Materials Manager responsible?
(.... Und wem untersteht der Leiter der Materialwirtschaft?)

* **I'm in charge of Personnel and report directly to who you in the States would probably call the President.**
(be in charge of – Leiter sein von; leiten / Personnel – Personalabteilung / report to – unterstehen / president – Verwaltungsratsvorsitzender; Vorstandsvorsitzender [mit gleichzeitiger Aufsichtsratsfunktion] einer US-Kapitalgesellschaft; „Generaldirektor")

* **A: We have a fairly large Market Research Section, which is part of the Marketing Department.**
(market research – Marktforschung / section – Abteilung, Referat)
B: Does this mean that you do most research in-house?
A: Yes, although we do farm out the really large surveys.
(although – obwohl / do farm out – natürlich extern vergeben / survey – Erhebung, Studie)

CURRENT CONDITIONS
Gegenwärtige Lage

ORDERS AND CAPACITY UTILISATION
Aufträge und Kapazitätsauslastung

* **We can't complain. We have a satisfactory order book that will keep us busy for the next three months.**
(Wir können uns nicht beklagen. Wir haben einen zufriedenstellenden Auftragsbestand, der uns für die nächsten drei Monate beschäftigen wird.)

* **Can't grumble. We're working flat out to meet the demand for the new printer.**
(grumble – sich beklagen / work flat out – volles Rohr fahren / meet demand – Nachfrage decken)

* **I'm a bit worried about capacity utilisation. It's been stuck at around 60 per cent and that's just not good enough in the long run.**
(be worried – besorgt sein / capacity utilisation – Kapazitätsauslastung / be stuck – steckenbleiben; hängen / around – ungefähr / in the long run – auf lange Sicht)

* **Orders are down on last year but still at a satisfactory level.**
(order – Auftrag / be down on – niedriger sein als / still – noch immer / satisfactory – zufriedenstellend / level – Höhe, Niveau)

* **I don't think we will be awarded the contract. Our prices are probably too high.**
(Ich glaube nicht, daß wir den Zuschlag bekommen werden. .... / probably – wahrscheinlich)

* **We managed to land a couple of large, profitable contracts.**
(manage – es schaffen / land – an Land ziehen / a couple of – ein paar / contract – Auftrag)

COMPETITION

Konkurrenz

* **We won the tender against keen competition from Japanese firms.**
(Wir haben die Ausschreibung gegen starke Konkurrenz seitens japanischer Firmen gewonnen.)

* **Competition is getting tougher by the hour.**
(Die Konkurrenz wird mit jedem Tag härter.)

* **The Japanese are our keenest competitors. They are difficult to beat because they come up with new products all the time.**
(keenest competitor – härtester Konkurrent / beat – schlagen / come up with – daherkommen mit; sich einfallen lassen / all the time – die ganze Zeit; immer)

* **We've been under a lot of pressure lately from German competitors. Their products are really good and not too expensive.**
(be under a lot of pressure – stark unter Druck stehen / lately – in der letzten Zeit / expensive – teuer)

* **We can handle domestic competition but we simply cannot match the prices of Third World competitors.**
(handle – fertig werden mit / domestic – inländisch / match prices – mit Preisen Schritt halten)

* **We are probably fourth or fifth in our line, in terms of sales, that is.**
(Wir liegen in unserer Branche wahrscheinlich an vierter oder fünfter Stelle, und zwar gemessen am Umsatz.)

* **We used to be number one in banknote printing machines but have now fallen back to third place. Two Dutch companies have overtaken us.**
(Wir waren früher einmal die Nummer eins bei Banknotendruckmaschinen .... / Dutch – holländisch / overtake – überholen)

* **We are number two, breathing down the industry leader's neck.**
  (breathe down sbdy.'s neck – jmdm. dicht auf den Fersen sein / industry leader – Branchenführer)

* **Our industry is dominated by a couple of big firms.We belong to the small fry.**
  (industry – Branche / dominate – beherrschen / a couple of – ein paar / belong to – gehören zu / small fry – Kleingemüse)

* **We are a typical niche operator.**
  (Wir sind ein typisches Beispiel für eine Firma, die sich in einer Marktnische etabliert hat.)

* **We are in a mature market, where you can increase market share only at the expense of competition.**
  (Wir sind auf einem gesättigten Markt, wo man Marktanteile nur auf Kosten der Konkurrenz erhöhen kann.)

* **We managed to obtain a foothold in the market in the teeth of cut-throat competition from a couple of Korean firms.**
  (Es ist uns gelungen, trotz härtester Konkurrenz seitens einiger koreanischer Firmen auf dem Markt Fuß zu fassen.)

* **We are worried about cheap imports.**
  (be worried – sich Sorgen machen / cheap – billig)

* **A competitor managed to lure away two of our key accounts last month.**
  (manage – es zuwege bringen / lure away – weglocken, abwerben / key account – wichtiger Großkunde)

* **We have got a lot of catching up to do.**
  (Wir haben eine Menge aufzuholen.)

* **If prices stay depressed for much longer, we'll have to get out of domestic appliances altogether.**
  (stay depressed – gedrückt bleiben / get out of – aussteigen bei / domestic appliances – Haushaltsgeräte / altogether – gänzlich)

* A: **How much is your market share?**
  (Wie hoch ist Ihr Marktanteil?)
  B: **We have about five per cent of the British soap market.**
  (soap market – Seifenmarkt)

* **Dumping by Japanese firms has hit our sales badly.**
(hit – treffen / badly – hart, stark)

SALES
Umsatz | Absatz

* **Sales have been a bit slack lately. We have commissioned a survey to find out why.**
(slack – flau, lustlos / lately – in der letzten Zeit / commission – in Auftrag geben)

* **Strangely enough, sales are holding up pretty well considering that we are in a recession. It's a bit of a surprise. We didn't expect it.**
(strangely enough – seltsamerweise / hold up – sich halten / pretty – ziemlich / considering – wenn man bedenkt / surprise – Überraschung / expect – erwarten)

* **Our new advertising campaign has really paid off. It's pushed sales up by all of 20 per cent.**
(advertising campaign – Werbekampagne / pay off – sich auszahlen / push up – in die Höhe treiben / by all of 20 per cent – um ganze 20%)

* **We are still relying on a couple of old brands.**
(Wir stützen uns noch immer auf ein paar alte Marken | Markenartikel.)

* **We haven't put anything new on the market for quite a long time. That's bound to hit sales sooner or later.**
(Wir haben schon ziemlich lange nichts mehr Neues auf den Markt gebracht. Das muß sich zwangsläufig früher oder später negativ auf den Umsatz auswirken.)

* **Sales of big-ticket items have been hit hardest.**
(Den Absatz der teuren Artikel hat es besonders hart erwischt.)

* **Exports have not been doing too well lately, mainly because of the lower dollar.**
(do well – gut abschneiden / mainly – hauptsächlich / lower dollar – niedrigerer Dollarkurs)

* **It's becoming increasingly difficult to export to Bulgaria. They are short of foreign exchange and countertrade is very complicated.**
(Es wird immer schwieriger, nach Bulgarien zu exportieren. Es herrscht dort eine Devisenknappheit, und Gegengeschäfte sind sehr kompliziert.)

* **Half our sales come from services.**
(Die Hälfte unseres Umsatzes entfällt auf Dienstleistungen.)

* **Exports have always accounted for more than two thirds of our sales.**
(account for – ausmachen)

* **Last year we actually exceeded our sales target. This year is going to be much more difficult. We'd be glad if we could get anywhere near it.**
(Voriges Jahr haben wir tatsächlich unser Umsatzziel übertroffen. Heuer wird es viel schwerer werden. Wir wären froh, wenn wir irgendwo in die Nähe kommen könnten.)

* **The sales target we set ourselves last year was much too ambitious.**
(set – setzen / too ambitious – zu hoch gegriffen)

* **Our sales were right on target last year.**
(Wir haben im Vorjahr unser Umsatzziel genau erreicht.)

PROFITS AND LOSSES

Gewinn und Verlust

* **We managed to maintain profits in spite of lower sales.**
(Es gelang uns, die Gewinne trotz eines niedrigeren Umsatzes zu halten.)

* **Our profits have been hit by the increase in interest rates.**
(be hit – beeinträchtigt werden / increase – Erhöhung / interest rate – Zinssatz)

* **Last year was really terrible. We lost a packet because the dollar slumped and we hadn't hedged our open currency positions.**

(terrible – schrecklich / lose a packet – einen Haufen Geld verlieren / slump – abstürzen / hedge – absichern / open currency position – offene Währungsposition)

* **We managed to get back into the black in fiscal 1985 by cutting costs wherever possible.**
(get back into the black – zurück in die Gewinnzone kommen / fiscal – Geschäftsjahr / cut – senken / wherever possible – wo immer es möglich war)

* **Our pre-tax profits were higher than last year, but there was also a higher tax charge and so the bottom line was about the same.**
(pre-tax – vor Steuern / tax charge – Steuerbelastung / bottom line – Reingewinn, Endergebnis / about – ungefähr)

* **Our main financial ratios are O.K..**
(Unsere wichtigsten finanzwirtschaftlichen Kennzahlen sind in Ordnung.)

* **I wouldn't really know what our Return on Investment is. I would have to check with our Controller's Department.**
(return on investment – [Gesamt-]Kapitalrentabilität / check with – nachfragen / rückfragen bei)

* **Our profits were caught in a squeeze: labour costs went up and prices fell due to slack demand.**
(Wir gerieten in die Kosten-Preis-Schere: die Lohnkosten stiegen und die Preise fielen aufgrund der flauen Nachfrage.)

* **We have been in the red for far too long.**
(Wir stecken schon viel zu lange in der Verlustzone.)

* **We had a fairly large exchange loss last year.**
(exchange loss – Wechselkursverlust)

* **We now break even at only 40 per cent of capacity.**
(break even – ausgeglichen bilanzieren)

* **We went nearly bust but were bailed out by the government. Couldn't allow us to go under because of the jobs involved.**
(go bust – pleite gehen / bail out – retten / go under – zugrunde gehen / the jobs involved – die Arbeitsplätze, die auf dem Spiel standen)

COSTS
Kosten

* **We have started a cost-cutting drive.**
(Wir haben eine Kostensenkungskampagne gestartet.)

* **Our overheads are much too high. Administration is probably a bit top-heavy.**
(Unsere Gemeinkosten sind viel zu hoch. Wahrscheinlich ist unsere Verwaltung etwas zu kopflastig.)

* **We installed a new cost-control system last year.**
(install – installieren, einführen)

* **The thing is, too much of our capital is tied up in stocks. The interest expense involved takes a big bite out of our profits.**
(Die Sache ist, daß wir zuviel Kapital in den Lagerbeständen gebunden haben. Der damit verbundene Zinsaufwand frißt einen beträchtlichen Teil unseres Gewinnes auf.)

* **We tried JIT in an effort to reduce inventories. Didn't work because our suppliers weren't reliable enough.**
(JIT – just in time / effort – Bemühung / inventory – Lagerbestand / work – funktionieren / supplier – Lieferant / reliable – verläßlich)

* **We are handicapped by some of the highest labour costs in Europe. It's not so much the hourly rates themselves but the high supplementary wage costs, such as paid holidays, national insurance contributions, maternity benefits, etc.**
(Wir sind durch Lohnkosten, die zu den höchsten in Europa zählen, belastet. Dabei sind es nicht so sehr die Stundenlöhne an sich als die hohen Lohnnebenkosten, wie z. B. bezahlter Urlaub, Sozialversicherungsbeiträge, Mutterschaftsgeld usw.)

* **We have decided to partly automate our production line to cut labour costs and increase productivity.**
(automate – automatisieren / production line – Fertigungsstraße / cut – senken / increase – erhöhen)

* **We had to cut back on fringe benefits last year, which were, however, very generous anyway.**
(Wir mußten voriges Jahr die Nebenleistungen | Sozialleistungen kürzen. Die waren aber ohnehin sehr großzügig.)

* **Headquarters put in a new Controller, who cut R&D expenditure drastically to stop the red ink.**
(headquarters – [Konzern-]Zentrale / put in – einsetzen / R&D – Research & Development | Forschung & Entwicklung / expenditure – Aufwand, Ausgaben / red ink – rote Zahlen; Verluste)

* **We have got a fairly high debt-equity ratio, so our profits are very sensitive to changes in interest rates.**
(Wir haben einen ziemlich hohen Verschuldungsgrad, sodaß unser Gewinn sehr empfindlich auf Zinsänderungen reagiert.)

* **Our gearing is much too high. As long as interest rates are as low as they are that's not a problem. But even a moderate increase could wipe out our profits.**
(gearing – Verschuldungsgrad / interest rate – Zinssatz / even – selbst / moderate – mäßig / increase – Erhöhung / wipe out – zum Verschwinden bringen)

FINANCING
Finanzierung

* A: **We have been ploughing back a fairly high percentage of our profits to strengthen our equity position.**
(Wir führen [seit einiger Zeit] einen ziemlich hohen Prozentsatz unseres Gewinnes den Rücklagen zu, um unsere Eigenkapitalbasis zu stärken.)
B: **What do your shareholders say to that?**
(shareholder – Aktionär)
A: **Well, since our share price has risen quite sharply, they don't seem to mind too much.**
(since – da / share price – Aktienkurs / rise – steigen / quite – ziemlich / seem – scheinen / mind – [etwas] dagegen haben)

* **At yesterday's closing price our shares are on a multiple of 25.**
(at – auf der Basis / closing price – Schlußkurs / be on a multiple of ... – ein Kurs-Gewinn-Verhältnis von ... aufweisen)

* **Interest rates are so low at the moment that we've decided to refinance part of our debt.**
(refinance – umschulden / debt – Schulden)

* **We are planning a rights issue for later this year. We will use the money to make a major acquisition.**
(rights issue – Ausgabe von jungen Aktien [auf Bezugsrechtsbasis] / major acquisition – größerer Firmenerwerb)

HUMAN RESOURCES | EMPLOYEES

Personalressourcen | Mitarbeiter

* **We have 600 employees. 200 white-collar, or salaried, employees, and around 400 blue-collar workers.**
(employee – Mitarbeiter, Arbeitnehmer / white-collar employee – Angestellter / blue-collar employee – Arbeiter)

* **A: Unfortunately we had to make 100 people redundant last year as part of a cost-cutting exercise.**
(unfortunately – leider / make redundant – [brit.] abbauen / cost-cutting exercise – Kostensenkungsaktion)
B: Ah, you mean you had to lay them off.
(lay off – [US] abbauen)

* **We have two employee directors on the supervisory board. It's a statutory requirement for large companies.**
(employee director – Arbeitnehmervertreter [im Aufsichtsrat] / statutory requirement – gesetzliches Erfordernis)

* **We are planning to expand our work-force.**
(work-force – Belegschaft)

* **We do our recruiting through a special consulting firm.**
(recruiting – Personalbeschaffung / consulting firm – Beratungsfirma)

* **We have been experimenting with worker participation for a number of years.**

(worker participation – Arbeitnehmermitbestimmung)

* **Employee participation works well on the shop-floor but it's a problem further up, in particular at board level.**
(work – funktionieren / shop-floor – unmittelbarer Produktionsbereich; „Werkbank" / further up – weiter oben / level – Ebene / board – Verwaltungsrat; Führungsgremium einer brit./US-Kapitalgesellschaft)

* **The trade unions are not the main problem. But workers are represented through a second channel, a body called „Betriebsrat".**
(trade union – Gewerkschaft / represent – vertreten / body – Gremium)

* **Generally speaking, we get along quite well with our workers. We've never had a strike and we've always managed to reach a compromise.**
(generally speaking – im allgemeinen / get along – auskommen / manage – es schaffen)

* **I'm glad to say that our labour turnover has always been very low.**
(glad – froh / labour turnover – Mitarbeiterfluktuation)

* **The trade unions are pushing for a shorter working week again.**
(push for – drängen auf / shorter working week – Arbeitszeitverkürzung)

* **What with the fairly long holidays with pay and the large number of public holidays – also with pay -, I don't think that this is really an important issue.**
(what with – angesichts / holidays with pay – bezahlter Urlaub / public holiday – Feiertag / important – wichtig / issue – Problem, Thema)

* **We have a very keen equal opportunities employment policy. As a result, quite a few of our managers are women.**
(keen – engagiert, radikal / equal opportunities employment policy – auf dem Gleichbehandlungsprinzip basierende Personalpolitik / quite a few – ziemlich viele)

PREMISES
Räumlichkeiten, Betriebsstätten

* **A: Would you like me to show you round our premises?**
(Möchten Sie, daß ich Ihnen unsere Räumlichkeiten zeige | Sie durch unsere Räumlichkeiten führe?)
B: Yes, very much so.

* **A: The building seems very new. When was it built?**
(building – Gebäude)
B: Well, this particular office block was put up in 1986. Before that we were in a suburb on the other side of the river.
(office block – Bürogebäude / put up – errichten / suburb – Vorstadt / river – Fluß)

* **We've leased the building from a property company. It's a more flexible arrangement than buying your own property.**
(property company – Immobiliengesellschaft / own – eigen / property – Gebäude, Immobilie, Liegenschaft)

* **A: The warehouse is over there.**
(warehouse – Lagerhaus)
B: Is that where you store the heavy machines?
(store – lagern)

* **A: This is the new machine shop. We put in a flexible manufacturing system two years ago. Would you like to take a look at it?**
(machine shop – Maschinenhalle / manufacturing system – Fertigungssystem / take a look at sthg. – etwas anschauen)
B: Yes. I'd be very interested. We're thinking of switching to FM ourselves.
(switch to – umsteigen auf / FM – flexible manufacturing)

* **The R&D Section is on the third floor. Let's take the lift.**
(R&D – Research and Development | Forschung und Entwicklung | F&E / section – Abteilung, Referat / floor – Stockwerk)

* **A: What you see over there in the far corner is our loading bay. We deliver most of our orders in our own trucks.**
(far corner – Ecke ganz hinten / loading bay – Verladezone / deliver – liefern / truck – Lastwagen)

B: Do you have a big fleet of trucks?
(fleet of trucks – LKW-Fuhrpark, LKW-Flotte)
A: Yes. I wouldn't know the exact number though.
(though – aber, doch)

COMPUTERS

Computer

* **I bought myself a PC before I came over.**
(PC – PC | Personalcomputer / come over – herüberkommen)

* **It's very user-friendly. It didn't take me more than a couple of hours to get the hang of it.**
(Er ist sehr benutzerfreundlich. Ich brauchte nur ein paar Stunden, um zu kapieren, wie er funktioniert.)

* **The manual is terrific. Explains everything step by step. So you can't go wrong.**
(manual – Handbuch / terrific – super / explain – erklären / step by step – Schritt für Schritt / go wrong – sich verirren; Fehler machen)

* **I just use it for word-processing.**
(just – nur / word-processing – Textverarbeitung)

* **A: What application programs do you use?**
(application program – Anwendungsprogramm)
B: Word Perfect 5.0 for word-processing and Lotus 1,2,3 for spreadsheets and that sort of thing.
(spreadsheet – Tabellenkalkulation / that sort of thing – dergleichen)

* **I don't use pirate copies any more. Had a virus once and lost umpteens of important files. It's not worth it.**
(Ich verwende keine Raubkopien von Programmen mehr. Hatte einmal einen Virus und verlor zig wichtige Dateien. Zahlt sich nicht aus.)

* **A: What storage capacity does it have?**
(storage capacity – Speicherkapazität)
B: It's got a floppy with 1.2 megabytes. But I'm thinking of having a hard disk added. I'll need a bit more storage capacity for the applications I have in mind. Also, hard disks are much faster.
(floppy – Diskette / megabyte – Megabyte / hard disk – Festplatte / have sthg. in mind – an etwas denken; etwas im Sinn | Auge haben)

* **I had a head crash last year. Fortunately I had made back-up copies of everything on the hard disk. Otherwise I don't know what I would have done.**
(Voriges Jahr stürzte mir die Festplatte ab. Glücklicherweise hatte ich Back-up-Kopien von allem gemacht, was auf der Festplatte war. Sonst weiß ich nicht, was ich getan hätte.)

* **I'm going to swap my desk-top model for a portable. Portables are much more convenient and the features are the same as on a regular PC.**
(swap – umtauschen, eintauschen / desk-top model – Tischmodell / portable - tragbarer Computer; Portable / convenient – praktisch / feature – Leistungsmerkmal / regular – normal)

* **Don't know what I would do without my computer!**
(Ich weiß nicht, was ich ohne meinen Computer täte.)

* **A: The things are getting cheaper by the day. I think I'll take the plunge and buy one too.**
(cheap – billig / by the day – Tag für Tag / take the plunge – den Sprung wagen)
B: Yes, you can get a very good configuration for under three hundred pounds: computer, operating system, VDU, dot matrix printer, the lot. Most firms throw in a couple of application programs as well.
(configuration – Konfiguration / operating system – Betriebssystem / VDU – visual display unit | Bildschirm | Monitor / dot matrix printer – Nadeldrucker / the lot – einfach alles, was dazugehört / throw in – draufgeben)

* **Macs are fun to use, but compatibility with IBM machines and IBM clones is still a bit of a problem.**
(Mac – Macintosh / fun to use – lustig zu benutzen / compatibility – Kompatibilität / clone – Clone; nachgebautes Gerät)

* **I get a headache if I sit in front of the computer for more than two hours. Don't understand how our VDU workers can stand it.**
(headache – Kopfweh / in front of – vor / VDU worker – Bildschirmarbeiter / stand sthg. – etwas aushalten)

* **I know it sounds odd, but I hate computers. Can't seem to get used to them.**
(Ich weiß, es klingt seltsam, aber ich hasse Computer. Ich kann mich anscheinend nicht daran gewöhnen.)

* **My son sits in front of the computer all day long. He is so interested that he will be an expert by the time he's fifteen.**
(all day long – den ganzen Tag / by the time – wenn)

* **Paperless office, my foot! We have to shuffle more paper than before the introduction of the new system.**
(paperless office – papierloses Büro / my foot – oder sonst noch was / shuffle – herumschieben / introduction – Einführung)

* **We had to call in a consultant to sort out our computer problems.**
(call in – beiziehen / consultant – Beratungsfirma / sort out – lösen; in Ordnung bringen)

* **All of our executives have ATs, and we are planning to link them in a LAN to improve communication between them.**
(executive – Führungskraft / AT – AT-Computer / link – verbinden / LAN – local area network | lokales Datennetz / improve – verbessern)

* **We have decided to install a mainframe. In spite of the latest improvements in micros and minis, they still couldn't handle the vast amounts of data we have to process.**
(decide – sich entschließen / mainframe – Großrechner / in spite of – trotz / micro – Mikrocomputer, PC / mini – Minicomputer / still – noch / handle – verarbeiten, manipulieren / vast amount – ungeheure Menge / process – verarbeiten)

* **Yes, you're right. Computer fraud is a problem. One of our employees nicked our customer file and sold it to a competitor.**
(computer fraud – Computerkriminalität / employee – Mitarbeiter / nick – klauen / customer file – Kundendatei / competitor – Konkurrent)

NEGOTIATING CONTRACTS

Vertragsverhandlungen

CHAT PHASE

Vorgeplänkel

(see also "Weather" and "Meeting People")

* **A: I hope you had a good flight.**
  (flight – Flug)
  B: Yes, the weather was fine and there was no turbulence.

* **A: Is this your first time in England?**
  (Sind Sie zum ersten Mal in England?)
  B: No. I attended a language course in Brighton when I was sixteen. But I've never been here on business before.
  (attend – besuchen / language – Sprache / on business – geschäftlich)

* **A: I hope the hotel room we reserved for you is all right.**
  B: Yes, I've got a very nice and quiet room. And I had a good night's sleep, which means I'm going to be a very tough negotiator today.
  (quiet – ruhig / mean – bedeuten / tough – hart / negotiator – Verhandler)

* **A: Sorry, I'm a bit late, but my taxi got stuck in a traffic jam.**
  (sorry – tut mir leid / get stuck – steckenbleiben / traffic jam – Stau)
  B: I'm sorry to hear that. Must have been something exceptional. The rush-hour is normally over by 10 o'clock.
  (rush-hour – Verkehrsspitze / by – bis [längstens])

* **Would anybody like a cup of coffee before we start?**

* **Would you care for coffee or something else to drink?**
  (care for sthg. – etwas mögen / wollen)

* **I've asked Reception to serve some tea at ten, if that's O.K. with you.**

OPENING THE DISCUSSION

Eröffnung der Diskussion

* **Let's begin, shall we?**
(Fangen wir doch an.)

* **We might as well get down to business.**
(Wir könnten eigentlich anfangen.)

* **If you agree, I'd say let's get straight to the point without wasting any time on preliminaries.**
(agree – zustimmen / get straight to the point – gleich zur Sache kommen / waste – verschwenden / preliminaries – Vorgeplänkel)

* **May I suggest that we first discuss the less controversial points and leave the thorny knots, like price, for tomorrow?**
(suggest – vorschlagen / controversial – kontroversiell, umstritten / leave – lassen / thorny knot – kniffliger Punkt)

* **I think you will have received and read my proposals.**
(receive – erhalten / proposal – Vorschlag)

* **May I suggest a procedure for this first meeting?**
(procedure – Vorgangsweise / meeting – Sitzung)

* **A: I don't think we should aim for too much at this first meeting. I see it mainly as a chance to explore areas of agreement and disagreement.**
(aim for – erreichen wollen / … . Ich sehe die Sitzung in erster Linie als Möglichkeit, herauszufinden, wo wir übereinstimmen und wo nicht.)
B: I see it that way too. Let's leave serious bargaining for tomorrow.
(Ich sehe das auch so. Verhandeln wir die wesentlichen Punkte erst morgen.)

* **I don't think that we need a formal agenda.**
(agenda – Tagesordnung, Verhandlungsplan)

* **May I suggest that we first agree on the main points to be discussed today?**
(agree on – sich einigen auf / main point – Hauptpunkt)

DELIVERY, DELIVERY DATES AND TRANSPORT

Lieferung, Liefertermine und Transport

* **We can live with the other terms, but the delivery date is too tight.**
(terms – Bedingungen / delivery date – Lieferdatum, -termin / tight – knapp)

* **Couldn't you make it six weeks instead of eight? That would give us enough time to assemble the machine and meet the deadline set by our customer.**
(instead of – anstatt / enough – genug / assemble – zusammenbauen, montieren / meet deadline – Termin einhalten / set – festsetzen / customer – Kunde)

* **I don't think we can meet the delivery date you suggest.**
(suggest – vorschlagen)

* **Couldn't you extend the delivery period by a week or so? That would make things much easier for us.**
(extend – verlängern / delivery period – Lieferfrist / by – um)

* **Yes, I think we could bring the date forward by a week or so. But I'd have to check with Headquarters before I can give you a firm promise.**
(bring forward – vorziehen / check with sbdy. – bei jmdm. rückfragen / headquarters – [Firmen-]Zentrale / firm promise – feste Zusage)

* **Now, as far as delivery dates are concerned, there shouldn't be any problems.**
(Nun, was die Liefertermine betrifft, ...)

* **You mustn't let us down on delivery dates.**
(Sie dürfen uns bei den Lieferterminen nicht im Stich lassen.)

* **We can let you have the first batch in six weeks and the balance in about three months, from today, that is.**
(batch – Teilmenge, Stapel / balance – Rest; restliche Artikel / about – ungefähr / from today, that is – und zwar von heute an gerechnet)

* **O.K., that's agreed then. 20 in six weeks and the rest in early July.**
(Gut. Also abgemacht. . . . . / in early July – Anfang Juli)

* **We wouldn't mind paying a bit more, if you could let us have the material by the end of next week.**
(Wir hätten nichts dagegen, etwas mehr zu zahlen, ...)

* **You would have to give us a bit more time to make the modifications you require.**
(modification – Änderung / require – benötigen, verlangen)

* **I need the ball-bearings very urgently.**
(ball-bearing – Kugellager / urgent – dringend)

* **The import licence is valid only until March 31. This means that delivery would have to be effected by March 15 to leave some margin for unexpected delays.**
(valid – gültig / be effected – erfolgen / by – bis [spätestens] / margin – Spielraum / unexpected – unerwartet / delay -Verzögerung)

* **The only obstacle I see is availability of shipping-space. We have to book two months ahead.**
(obstacle – Hindernis / availability – Verfügbarkeit / shipping-space – Frachtraum / ahead – im vorhinein)

* **As I pointed out right at the beginning: we are working flat out and cannot promise more than two tonnes per month.**
(point out – feststellen / right – gleich / work flat out – voll ausgelastet sein / promise – versprechen)

* **Yes, we would be prepared to make some concessions as far as delivery dates are concerned.**
(be prepared – bereit sein / concession – Zugeständnis / concern – betreffen)

* **The penalty for late delivery is much too stiff. Our marketing people won't buy that.**
(penalty for late delivery – Pönale für Lieferverzug / stiff – geschmalzen, hoch / buy – akzeptieren)

* **I don't think I can get our people to accept the penalty clause.**
(get – dazu bringen / clause – Klausel, Paragraph)

* **A: Transport might be a problem. I don't think the machine would fit on a normal lorry.**
  (fit – passen / lorry – LKW)
  B: Don't worry about transport. It can be shipped in pieces.
  (worry – sich Sorgen machen / ship – versenden / in pieces – in [ihre] Bestandteile zerlegt)

* **There won't be any delay. The machine can be assembled and put into operation in a matter of hours.**
  (won't – will not / assemble – zusammenbauen, montieren / put into operation – in Betrieb nehmen / in a matter of hours – innerhalb von [wenigen] Stunden)

* **We'll arrange for somebody to accompany the consignment and to help you install the machine.**
  (Wir werden veranlassen, daß jemand die Sendung begleitet ....)

* **Delivery would have to be effected within two weeks of signing the contract.**
  (sign – unterzeichnen)

* **We'd prefer to collect the goods from your premises ourselves. So give us a quotation ex works.**
  (prefer – vorziehen / collect – abholen / premises – Geschäftsräume, Betriebsgelände / quotation – Preisangabe / ex works – ab Werk)

* **Both FOB and CIF terms would be acceptable to us.**
  (FOB – free on board | frei an Bord / CIF – cost, insurance and freigt | Kosten, Versicherung, Fracht)

* **No, we couldn't shorten the delivery date. It's not so much that we have a fairly full order book at the moment but that we depend on a subcontractor for some essential components.**
  (shorten – verkürzen / fairly – ziemlich / order book – Auftragsmappe, Auftragsbestand / depend on sbdy. for sthg. – hinsichtlich einer Sache auf jemanden angewiesen sein / subcontractor – Zulieferer, Subunternehmer / essential – wesentlich, wichtig / component – Bauteil)

* **A: Basically I'm in favour of part-shipments, but they will push up the cost of transport.**
  (basically – im Prinzip / in favour of – für / part-shipment – Teillieferung / push up – in die Höhe treiben)

B: You do have a point there, because the question is who will bear the higher transport charges.
(have a point – recht haben / question – Frage / bear – tragen, übernehmen / charges – Kosten)

* **The best plan would be to ship the dyes by air.**
(ship by air – als Luftfracht versenden / dye – Farbe)

QUANTITIES
Mengen

* **Could we now move on to discussing quantities?**
(move on to – dazu übergehen)

* **We'll probably need another 50 tonnes early next year.**
(probably – wahrscheinlich / another – weitere / early next year – Anfang nächsten Jahres)

* **Could you give us some idea of your annual requirements?**
(Könnten Sie uns eine ungefähre Vorstellung Ihres Jahresbedarfes geben?)

* **A: How many would you need?**
B: Fifty. Maybe sixty at the outside.
(at the outside – wenn's hoch kommt; im äußersten Fall)

* **I really can't say at this stage. Around 600 probably.**
(stage – Zeitpunkt / around – ungefähr)

* **500 is only an estimate, though. We cannot bind ourselves to this figure. It could be 10 per cent more or 10 per cent less.**
(estimate – Schätzung / though – jedoch / bind oneself – sich binden / figure – Zahl)

* **We'll need 300, give or take 10.**
(Wir brauchen 300, 10 auf oder ab.)

* **Quantities would be no problem. We could probably supply any number you might require from stock.**
(supply – liefern / require – benötigen / from stock – vom Lager; sofort)

* **Correct me if I'm wrong, but did you say the maximum you can supply in any given month would be 60?**
(be wrong – unrecht haben; sich irren)

* **We have prepared a detailed bill of quantities. Let me give everybody a copy.**
(prepare – erstellen, vorbereiten / bill of quantities – Mengengerüst)

PRODUCTS, QUALITY AND MODIFICATIONS

Produkte, Qualität und Modifikationen

(see also "Product Presentations")

* A: **If you can match the sample here, it's a deal.**
(Das Geschäft gilt, wenn Sie etwas diesem Muster hier Entsprechendes anbieten können.)
B: **Can I have a look at the specifications? … That should be no problem.**
(specifications – [technische] Angaben)

* **We have tested your machine. It's suitable for what we have in mind.**
(suitable – geeignet / have in mind – vorhaben; im Sinn haben)

* **This is a technical question which I would have to refer to our Production Department. I'll make a note of it.**
(refer to – weiterleiten an / make a note of sthg. – sich etwas notieren)

* A: **The feeder assembly would have to be modified.**
(feeder assembly – Beschickungsvorrichtung)
B: **I don't think that would be a problem. Production will come up with something.**
(come up with sthg. – sich etwas einfallen lassen)

* **No, you can forget the RX34. It's much too slow. We need something faster.**
(slow – langsam / fast – schnell)

* **A: We would need something with at least double the rated capacity of this model.**
(at least – zumindest / double – doppelt / rated capacity – Nennleistung)
B: Well, then I'd suggest the RTV-7, which is capable of turning out 600 units per hour.
(suggest – vorschlagen / be capable of – in der Lage sein / turn out – produzieren / unit – Stück)
C: Sorry to interrupt you Ben, but don't you think that the GTV-8 would be even more suitable?
(interrupt – unterbrechen / even – sogar noch)

TERMS OF PAYMENT

Zahlungsbedingungen

* **Our standard terms of payment are included in our General Terms of Sale. I don't think this point will require a lot of discussion.**
(terms of payment – Zahlungsbedingungen / General Terms of Sale – Allgemeine Geschäftsbedingungen / require – erfordern / a lot of – viel)

* **I'd appreciate it if you would pay for the first 10 machines in advance.**
(Ich wäre Ihnen verbunden, wenn Sie für die ersten zehn Maschinen im voraus bezahlen würden.)

* **I could allow you the usual terms, i.e. thirty days net, if you give us the usual references.**
(allow – einräumen, gewähren / usual – üblich / terms – Zahlungsbedingungen, Zahlungsziel / i.e. – that is / net – Kassa netto ohne Abzug / reference – Referenz, Referenzadresse)

* **Sorry, I've not been authorised to discuss credit terms.**
(authorise – ermächtigen / credit terms – Zahlungsziele)

* **I hope you will understand that I cannot offer you open account terms at once.**
(open account terms – offenes [d. h. unbesichertes] Ziel; Lieferung gegen offene Rechnung / at once – sofort)

* **I hope you don't mind paying in advance on this order.**

(Ich hoffe, es macht Ihnen nichts aus, bei diesem Auftrag im voraus zu bezahlen.)

* **Forget L/Cs. Too complicated and too expensive, you know. We'd be willing to pay in advance, if you reduce the price by two per cent.**
(L/C – Letter of Credit | Akkreditiv / expensive – teuer / pay in advance – im voraus zahlen / reduce by – senken um)

* **No, I'm sorry but D/A on your first order is out of the question. We don't want to set a precedent.**
(D/A – documents against acceptance | Dokumente gegen Akzept / be out of the question – nicht in Frage kommen / set precedent – Präzedenzfall schaffen)

* **A: How about 20 per cent in U.S. dollars and the balance in the form of premium vodka?**
(balance – Restbetrag / premium vodka – Spitzenwodka)
B: Sounds intriguing. But 20 per cent is not good enough. Wouldn't know what to do with so much vodka. Make it 40 per cent in dollars.
(sound – klingen / intriguing – interessant, verlockend / be good enough – reichen)
A: I couldn't go higher than 30 per cent. Where, do you think, are we going to get so many dollars? And even if you agree to 30, I would have to check with my boss.
(even – sogar / agree to – zustimmen / check with – rückfragen bei)

* **You must not forget that this machine would be built to your exact specifications. So we must insist on at least 40 per cent down when you place the order.**
(build – bauen / to specifications – nach Angaben / insist on – bestehen auf / down – als Anzahlung / place order – Auftrag erteilen)

* **A: May I suggest a compromise? 10 per cent when you place the order, another 10 per cent on delivery, and the remainder payable in eight semi-annual instalments.**
(suggest – vorschlagen / on delivery – bei Lieferung / remainder – Restbetrag / semi-annual instalment – Halbjahresrate)
B: Well, I suppose that's a reasonable compromise.
(Ja, das scheint mir ein vernünftiger Kompromiß zu sein.)

* A: **I have to insist on an advance payment guarantee issued by a reputable bank, though.**
(advance payment guarantee – Anzahlungsgarantie / issue – ausstellen / reputable – renommiert / though – jedoch, aber)
B: **My people would consider a guarantee a slur on their reputation.**
(consider – betrachten / slur – Flecken)

* **I would need more detailed specifications before I can quote a firm price.**
(quote – angeben, anbieten / firm – fest, bindend)

* A: **If I get you right, you are saying that if we agree to pay the bank charges, we have a deal?**
(Wenn ich Sie recht verstehe, so sagen Sie, daß wir ins Geschäft kommen, wenn wir uns bereit erklären, die Bankspesen zu übernehmen?)
B: **Yes. Maybe I've not expressed myself clearly enough. But that's what I've been saying all along.**
(express – ausdrücken / … . Aber das sage ich schon die ganze Zeit.)

❖

* **If you really insist on invoicing in your own currency, we would have no alternative but to call the whole thing off.**
(invoice – fakturieren / currency – Währung / but – als / call sthg. off – etwas abblasen)

* **We are not prepared to bear the exchange risk.**
(prepared – bereit / bear – übernehmen, tragen / exchange risk – Wechselkursrisiko)

* **Why don't we insert a currency escalator clause?**
(insert – einfügen / currency escalator clause – Kurssicherungsklausel)

PRICES AND COMMISSIONS

Preise und Provisionen

* **Let's concentrate on prices first.**

* **The next point is price then.**

* **Well, I think it's about time that we got down to discussing prices.**
(Ich glaube, es ist nun eigentlich an der Zeit, daß wir über die Preise zu reden beginnen.)

* **I want to make it quite clear from the very beginning that we are not authorised to negotiate a final price.**
(Ich möchte gleich zu Beginn eindeutig klarstellen, daß wir kein Pouvoir haben, einen endgültigen Preis auszuhandeln.)

* **Frankly, your prices are simply too high. I can get a much better deal from some of your competitors.**
(frankly – offen gesagt / simple – einfach / deal – Geschäft, Angebot, Preis / competitor – Konkurrent)

* **Sorry but I'll have to restrict negotiations to the simpler models. The more sophisticated ones with the additional features are right outside our range.**
(restrict – beschränken / sophisticated – kompliziert; technisch höherstehend / additional – zusätzlich / feature – Leistungsmerkmal / right – gänzlich / range – [Preis-]Bereich, Vorstellungen)

* **Quality is not the main consideration in our market. We sell – and therefore have to buy – on price.**
(main consideration – wichtigstes Verkaufsargument / market – Sparte / sell on price – über den Preis verkaufen)

* **I don't see why you can't match the prices quoted by your main competitors. You must have much the same cost structure.**
(Ich verstehe nicht, warum Sie nicht mit den Preisen Ihrer Hauptkonkurrenten mithalten können. Sie müssen doch in etwa dieselbe Kostenstruktur haben.)

* **If this is your last word on price, the deal's off, and, there won't be any more orders.**
(be off – geplatzt sein / won't – will not / order – Auftrag)

* **Well, I don't think I can go much lower.**

* **I need at least a small concession on price to show to Headquarters.**
(at least – zumindest / concession on price – Zugeständnis beim Preis / headquarters – [Firmen-]Zentrale)

* **I cannot accept your offer. Your prices are simply not competitive.**
(offer – Angebot / competitive – konkurrenzfähig)

* **There's a good chance that we shall place further orders if you can make some concession on price.**
(further – weiter / place orders – Aufträge erteilen)

* **Frankly, I'm a bit disappointed at what you are suggesting in terms of prices. Don't forget we are one of your best customers.**
(frankly – offen gesagt / disappointed – enttäuscht / in terms of – hinsichtlich / customer – Kunde)

* **Even for a good product the price is much too high.**
(even – sogar, selbst)

* **Yes, I admit that our prices are higher than those of our competitors. It would be silly to say otherwise. But you have to look at the overall situation. Just consider the savings in fuel and maintenance that our machines make possible.**
(admit – zugeben / silly – unsinnig / otherwise – etwas anderes / overall situation – Gesamtsituation / consider – betrachten; in Rechnung stellen / saving – Einsparung / fuel – Treibstoff / maintenance – Wartung)

* **I don't think that I can persuade Headquarters to accept your price. But I'll give it a try.**
(persuade – überreden / give sthg. a try – etwas versuchen)

* **Let me repeat what I said an hour ago: $400 per tonne is as far as we can go.**
(repeat – wiederholen)

* **I'll have trouble explaining that to my boss, but to show you our goodwill we'll reduce the price by another two per cent.**
  (trouble – Schwierigkeiten / explain – erklären / by another two per cent – um weitere zwei Prozent)

* **Well, we know pretty well what our competitors charge. Their prices for the small units range from £300 to £350.**
  (pretty – ziemlich / charge – berechnen, verlangen / unit – Gerät / range from … to … – zwischen … und … liegen)

* **If I go any lower, we'd make a loss on the deal.**
  (on – bei / deal – Geschäft)

* **This is about as far as we could go. Any further concessions would leave us no profit.**
  (concession – Zugeständnis / leave – lassen)

* **Please don't forget that I can't go beyond the limits set by Headquarters. I'm not a free agent.**
  (go beyond sthg. – über etwas hinausgehen / limit – Grenze / headquarters – [Firmen-]Zentrale / I'm not a free agent – ich bin gebunden)

* **You're driving a hard bargain. You don't want to see us go bankrupt, do you?**
  (drive a hard bargain – beinhart verhandeln / do you? – oder?)

* **A: No, you charge too much for this.**
  B: But against our higher price you must set the longer warranty period and the lower service charges we offer.
  (Aber unserem höheren Preis müssen Sie zum Vergleich die längere Garantiefrist und die niedrigeren Servicekosten, die wir bieten, gegenüberstellen.)

* **Don't you think that the higher quality justifies the slightly higher prices?**
  (justify – rechtfertigen / slightly – etwas, leicht)

* **$3,000 for 12 units sounds reasonable. I think I can accept that.**
  (unit – Stück, Gerät / sound – klingen / reasonable – vernünftig)

* **£450? Now you're talking.**
  (… ? Das läßt sich hören.)

* **Let's compromise. I think I can let you have the drills for $650 each, including packing and delivery.**
(compromise – Kompromiß machen | eingehen / drill – Bohrmaschine, Bohrer / each – pro Stück / including – einschließlich)

* **We seem to be deadlocked on price. What would you say to discussing something less controversial for a while and coming back to prices later?**
(be deadlocked – festgefahren sein / on – bei)

——— ❖ ———

* **The price is net of VAT.**
(net of – ohne, abzüglich / VAT – value-added tax | Mehrwertsteuer)

* **What else is included in the price?**

* **The price includes export packing and delivery to the Vienna Air Freight Terminal.**

* **Let's get this clear. Does this figure include delivery or not?**
(get sthg. clear – etwas klarstellen / figure – Zahl, Preis)

* **Could you itemise the price for the PX51 drilling machine? I'd like to see how it is made up.**
(itemise – aufschlüsseln / drilling machine – Bohrmaschine / be made up – zusammengesetzt sein)

* **I've prepared a detailed quotation for the scrubber. Here you are.**
(Ich habe ein detailliertes Angebot für die Rauchwaschanlage erstellt. Hier ist es.)

* **Packing would be charged at cost.**
(at cost – zum Selbstkostenpreis)

* A: **What about insurance? Is that included or not?**
(insurance – Versicherung)
B: **Our prices here are quoted FOB Hull. This means insurance would have to be covered by your firm.**
(Unsere Preise hier verstehen sich FOB Hull. .... / cover – abdecken)

* **Sorry, I seem to have got lost. Are we talking about the price of the basic model or of the souped-up version?**
(get lost – den Faden verlieren / basic model – Grundversion / soup up – auffrisieren)

—— ❖ ——

* **Five per cent on sales is not good enough. I need at least eight per cent to break even and 10 per cent for a slim profit margin.**
(sales – Umsatz / be good enough – reichen / break even – glatt aussteigen; ausgeglichen bilanzieren / slim – knapp, niedrig / margin – Spanne)

* A: **Our commission would be 10 per cent on net sales. But in addition you would have to agree to pay us a minimum of $5000 per month even if sales do not warrant it.**
(commission – Provision / in addition – zusätzlich / agree – sich verpflichten; sich bereit erklären / even – selbst, sogar / warrant – rechtfertigen)
B: **Let me make a counter-proposal: we'll give you 12 per cent, but without a guaranteed minimum.**
(counter-proposal – Gegenvorschlag)

DISCOUNTS
Preisnachlässe

* A: **What about a good discount for an old customer?**
(Wie wäre es mit einem anständigen Preisnachlaß ... ?)
B: **Well, we could give you the quantity discount we normally allow for 300 units and over. That would be six per cent.**
(quantity discount – Mengenrabatt / allow – gewähren, einräumen / unit – Stück, Gerät / over – darüber)
A: **Couldn't you make that 10 per cent?**
B: **No. 10 per cent is too high. Seven is as far as I can go. But there is always a two per cent cash discount if you pay within a week.**
(cash discount – Skonto)

* **Look, if you increase your order to 50 units, we could actually give you the 10 per cent you asked for.**
(increase – erhöhen / actually – tatsächlich)

* **Don't you run any special discounts for early purchases?**
(run – anbieten / special discount – Sonderrabatt / early – vorgezogen / purchase – Einkauf, Kauf, Bezug)

* **Normally we get a better discount on repeat orders. Three per cent really is not good enough.**
(repeat order – Nachbestellung)

* **Couldn't you give us a better discount for such a large quantity?**

* **A: Your discount period is a bit on the short side, just five days. Couldn't you make it ten?**
(discount period – Skontofrist / be a bit on the short side – eher kurz sein)
B: That's one of the things that might be a bit difficult to change because it's part of our General Terms of Business. But I'll see what I can do.
(change – ändern / General Terms of Business – Allgemeine Geschäftsbedingungen)

* **I'd have to check with Headquarters before I say yes or no.**
(check with – rückfragen in | bei / headquarters – [Firmen-] Zentrale)

* **I admit two per cent off doesn't sound much. But don't forget that in contrast to our competitors we have held last year's list price.**
(admit – zugeben / two per cent off – Preisnachlaß von zwei Prozent / sound – klingen / in contrast – im Gegensatz / competitor – Konkurrent / hold – halten; nicht ändern)

* **We can offer you a better discount if you decide to place your order before May 1.**
(decide – sich entschließen / place order – Auftrag erteilen)

* **A: What is your quantity discount?**
B: That depends on how much you order. Our discount system operates on a sliding scale. For one hundred units it would be six per cent, eight per cent if you order 200 or more.
(depend on – abhängen von / .... Unsere Rabatte werden nach einem Staffelsystem berechnet. ....)

* **I think I can meet you halfway: I can give you seven and a half per cent if you increase your order to 100 units.**
(meet sbdy. halfway – jmdm. auf halbem Wege entgegenkommen)

* **A: What are your discounts for selling to the trade?**
(trade – Handel, Wiederverkäufer)
B: Our trade discount to bona fide dealers is 35 per cent, plus an extra five per cent off the list price on orders for 400 units or more.
(trade discount – Wiederverkäuferrabatt, Stufenrabatt / bona fide dealers – Käufer, die ihren Händlerstatus nachweisen können; Käufer mit Gewerbeschein)

* **All our prices are net. We don't allow any cash discount.**
(Alle unsere Preise sind Nettopreise. Wir gewähren kein Skonto.)

TERM AND TERMINATION

Vertragslaufzeit und Beendigung des Vertragsverhältnisses

* **I have gone through the draft agreement you gave me yesterday. The only objection I have is that the agreement should run for an initial period of five years instead of four.**
(draft agreement – Vertragsentwurf / objection – Einwand / run for an initial period of … – eine anfängliche Laufzeit von … haben)

* **A: What about the period of notice? Is 12 months all right?**
(notice – Kündigung)
B: Yes, I think 12 months is standard for agency agreements.
(standard – Norm / agency agreement – Handelsvertretervertrag)

* **The main sticking point seems to be termination.**
(Es scheint sich hauptsächlich bei der Klausel über die Beendigung des Vertragsverhältnisses zu spießen.)

* **Don't worry, we have obtained a legal opinion on this point.**
(Da brauchen Sie sich keine Sorgen zu machen. Wir haben zu diesem Punkt ein Rechtsgutachten eingeholt.)

DRAFT CONTRACTS, LEGAL AND TECHNICAL POINTS

Vertragsentwürfe, juristische und technische Details

* **I've studied the draft contract you sent me. It's a good starting point, but no more than that.**
(draft contract – Vertragsentwurf)

* **Did I send you a copy? No? I've got one with me. Could you have it photocopied and study it for our next meeting on Thursday?**
(meeting – Sitzung)

* **May I call your attention to Clause 4 of the Draft Agreement?**
(call attention to – Aufmerksamkeit lenken auf / clause – Klausel, Paragraph)

* **I think there is a mistake in Section 3. The first sentence should read: "In the absence of any other clause ... ."**
(mistake – Fehler / section – Paragraph / read – lauten / in the absence of – mangels)

* **I have strong reservations about Paragraph b.**
(reservation – Vorbehalt / paragraph – Absatz, Abschnitt)

* **I hope you will understand that Subsection 8 will have to be amended.**
(subsection – Ziffer / amend – abändern)

* **A: I think Clause 5 is substantially the same as Clause 8. I think we could delete it. Any objections?**
(substantially – im wesentlichen / delete – streichen / objection – Einwand)
B: No. You're right of course.

* **In Clause 6 there is a reference to Schedule I in connection with the goods to be supplied under the Contract. I couldn't find Schedule I anywhere. You must have forgotten to attach it to the draft.**
(reference – Verweis / schedule – Vertragsanhang / connection – Zusammenhang / the goods to be supplied under the contract – die aufgrund des Vertrages zu liefernde Ware / attach – anheften, anfügen)

* **I think the wording of Clause 9 is misleading and should be changed. It seems to suggest that we would be responsible for collecting the goods.**
  (wording – Formulierung / misleading – irreführend / seem – scheinen / suggest – die Interpretation nahelegen / responsible – verantwortlich / collect – abholen)

* **I think we should include a Force Majeure Clause.**
  (include – inkludieren, hereinnehmen / force majeure – höhere Gewalt)

* **What struck me about Clause 10 is that no mention is made of demurrage.**
  (Was mir bei Paragraph 10 auffiel, ist, daß kein Liegegeld erwähnt wird.)

* **I think that Clause 1 does not reflect what we agreed last Friday.**
  (reflect – widerspiegeln, entsprechen / what – das / dem, was)

* **A: Don't you agree that the wording of Clause 1 is not very clear?**
  (Meinen Sie nicht auch, daß die Formulierung des Paragraph 1 nicht sehr klar ist?)
  B: Yes, you're right. I think it will have to be redrafted.
  (redraft – neu formulieren; umschreiben)

* **Could you explain what the last sentence on page four of the draft means? It doesn't seem to make sense.**
  (explain – erklären / page – Seite / mean – bedeuten / make sense – Sinn ergeben)

* **A: In my opinion we should add a standard arbitration clause. Is that O.K. with you?**
  (opinion – Meinung / standard arbitration clause – übliche Schiedsklausel)
  B: Yes, of course. Why don't we use the standard ICC clause?
  (ICC – International Chamber of Commerce / Internationale Handelskammer)

* **The next point to be discussed is Clause 6. I think it's on page four.**

BREAKS, NEXT MEETING, FINISHING

Pausen, die nächste Sitzung, Abschluß der Verhandlungen

* **I think we could all do with a break. Coffee, tea anybody?**
(do with – brauchen / break – Pause)

* **What about a coffee-break? That would give me a chance to call Headquarters about the contract currency.**
(what about – wie wär's mit / call – anrufen / headquarters – [Firmen-]Zentrale / contract currency – Vertragswährung)

* **We have reached agreement on a number of important points today. I think we could finalise the contract next Monday, if that's O.K. with you.**
(reach agreement – Übereinstimmung erzielen / number – Anzahl, Reihe / important – wichtig / finalise – finalisieren)

* **We seem to be fairly close to agreement on most of the points. I think we can finish the whole thing in a couple of hours. So why not meet again after dinner?**
(seem – scheinen / fairly – ziemlich / close to – nahe an / finish – beenden / a couple of – ein paar / dinner – Essen)

* **A: Would it be possible to have another meeting the day after tomorrow? I might be able to clarify some of the points you raised by then.**
(clarify – klären / raise point – Frage aufwerfen / by – bis [spätestens])
B: That would be Friday, wouldn't it? Yes, Friday would be O.K..
(wouldn't it? – nicht wahr?)
A: Two o'clock again?
B: Yes, two is fine.

* **See you again on Thursday then. Don't forget to bring the draft contract with you.**

* **Could you draft a suitable clause to cover this point for the next meeting?**
(draft – entwerfen, konzipieren / suitable – geeignet / cover – erfassen, abdecken)

* **I'll have the contract typed out. It will be ready for signature by about three this afternoon.**
(Ich werde den Vertrag tippen lassen. .... / ready for signature – unterschriftsreif / about – etwa)

* **I think that's all. I'll get our lawyers to check the draft to make sure we haven't overlooked anything.**
(get to check – veranlassen zu prüfen / lawyer – Jurist / make sure – sicherstellen / overlook – übersehen)

* **So, that's it then. Let's go and have a drink on it.**
(So, das wär's dann. Gehen wir einen darauf trinken.)

MEETINGS

Sitzungen

(see also "Conferences" and "General Presentations")

STARTING THE MEETING

Sitzungseröffnung

* **O.K., let's get started.**
(Okay, fangen wir an.)

* **Let's get started, shall we?**
(Fangen wir also an.)

* **Shall we begin?**
(Wollen wir anfangen?)

* **Right then. Let's get down to business, shall we?**
(Gut, fangen wir also an.)

* **May I have your attention, please, ladies and gentlemen?**
(Darf ich um Ihre Aufmerksamkeit bitten, ... ?)

* **I call the second meeting of the Investment Committee to order.**
(Ich eröffne hiermit die zweite Sitzung des Investitionsausschusses.)

* **I declare the meeting open.**
(Ich erkläre die Sitzung für eröffnet.)

* **We have a new member here today, Miss Briar from Auditing. I'd like to welcome her very cordially. Miss Briar is an experienced accountant and I'm looking forward to her contributions.**
(member – Mitglied / Auditing – Revisionsabteilung / cordially – herzlich / experienced – erfahren / accountant – [Bilanz-] Buchhalterin / look forward to – sich freuen auf / contribution – Beitrag)

* **Since most of the members don't know each other, I've asked my secretary to prepare name cards. Would you please check whether you have the right card in front of you?**
(since – da / prepare – vorbereiten, erstellen / whether – ob / in front of – vor)

* **May I remind you that we agreed last time not to smoke in meetings. I suggest that we have a break after an hour or so to give smoking members a chance to indulge in their vice in the adjacent room.**
(remind – [daran] erinnern / agree – sich einigen / suggest – vorschlagen / break – Pause / indulge in vice – Laster frönen / adjacent room – Zimmer nebenan)

* **What about the minutes of the last meeting ? Any queries? Can we take them as read?**
(Wie steht es mit dem Protokoll der letzten Sitzung? Irgendwelche Einwendungen? Gilt es als angenommen?)

* **I have received apologies for absence from Frank Finley and Anne Foley. They are both in London on business.**
(receive – erhalten / apology for absence – Entschuldigung wegen Abwesenheit / on business – geschäftlich)

* **I have received apologies from Jeff Wright, who is unable to attend because of other urgent commitments.**
(attend – teilnehmen / urgent – dringend / commitment – Verpflichtung)

SETTING THE AGENDA

Festlegung der Tagesordnung

* **We've three items of business on the agenda this morning.**
(Die Tagesordnung für die Sitzung heute morgen umfaßt drei Punkte.)

* **There are four main topics on the agenda.**
(main topic – Hauptthema)

* **There are four things we've got to discuss today.**

* **The agenda this morning consists of two items.**
(consist of – bestehen aus; umfassen)

* **First let's look at the request for more funds submitted by the Marketing Department.**
(look at sthg. – sich etwas anschauen; etwas behandeln / request – Ersuchen / funds – Mittel / submit – vorlegen, unterbreiten)

* **The big question we have to tackle today concerns the results of the cost-cutting drive.**
(question – Frage, Problem / tackle – angehen; sich befassen mit / concern – betreffen / cost-cutting drive – Kostensenkungsprogramm)

* **The major problem we've got to discuss is the high labour turnover in the Accounts Department.**
(major problem – Hauptproblem; wichtigstes Problem / labour turnover – Fluktuation / accounts department – Buchhaltungsabteilung)

* **I'd like to continue where we left off last week.**
(Ich möchte dort fortsetzen, wo wir letzte Woche aufgehört haben.)

* **There is still some unfinished business from the last meeting.**
(Es gibt da noch ein paar Punkte, die in der letzten Sitzung nicht abgeschlossen wurden.)

* **Any additions to the formal agenda?**
(addition – Zusatz; zusätzlicher Punkt)

INVITING CONTRIBUTIONS AND ASKING FOR OPINIONS

Bitte um Diskussionsbeiträge und Meinungsäußerungen

* **Now Mr. Rider has the floor.**
(Jetzt hat Herr Rider das Wort.)

* **It's your turn now, Ms. Green.**
(Sie sind jetzt an der Reihe, … .)

* **Yes, why don't you start, the floor is yours.**
(… , Sie sind am Wort.)

* **Would you like to comment on this, Peter?**
  (Möchtest du etwas dazu sagen, Peter?)

* **Is this O.K. with you, Susan?**
  (Geht das in Ordnung bei dir, Susan?)

* **What's your view on this, Fred?**
  (Was ist deine Ansicht dazu, Fred?)

* **How do you see this, Anne?**
  (Wie siehst du die Sache, Anne?)

* **How do you feel about this, Paul?**
  (Wie ist deine Meinung zu dieser Sache, Paul?)

* **What is your opinion about the new schedule, Mr. Baxter?**
  (Was halten Sie vom neuen Terminplan, Herr Baxter?)

* **Isn't there anybody who would like to say a few words in favour of the proposal?**
  (a few - ein paar / in favour of - zugunsten / proposal - Vorschlag)

* **Judith, could you outline the pros and cons of the project, please?**
  (outline - kurz umreißen / the pros and cons - das Für und Wider)

* **So what are <u>your</u> suggestions?**
  (Was schlagen <u>Sie</u> vor?)

* **Has anyone anything further to add?**
  (Hat noch jemand etwas dazu zu sagen?)

AGREEING AND DISAGREEING

Zustimmung und Ablehnung

* **I go along with that.**
  (Dieser Meinung | Diesem Vorschlag schließe ich mich an.)

* **I'm not sure I agree. We have to weigh the pros and cons more carefully.**
  (Ich bin mir da nicht ganz sicher, ob ich derselben Meinung bin. Wir müssen das Für und Wider sorgfältiger abwägen.)

* **I think you're right. We should put more emphasis on public relations.**
(put emphasis on sthg. – etwas betonen | in den Vordergrund stellen)

* **I couldn't agree more.**
(Da bin ich ganz und gar Ihrer Meinung.)

* **I agree.**
(Dem kann ich zustimmen. | Ich bin auch dieser Meinung.)

* **I disagree.**
(Da bin ich anderer Meinung. | Dem kann ich nicht zustimmen.)

* **I agree up to a point.**
(Dem kann ich bis zu einem gewissen Punkt zustimmen. | Dem kann ich mich mit gewissen Einschränkungen anschließen.)

* **I think we are in agreement on bringing forward the completion date.**
(Ich glaube, wir sind uns darin einig, das Fertigstellungsdatum vorzuziehen.)

* **The proposal to farm the job out to a specialist has my full support.**
(proposal – Vorschlag / farm out – extern vergeben / support – Unterstützung)

* **Do you agree that this is a non-starter?**
(be a non-starter – keinerlei Erfolgschancen haben; aussichtslos sein)

* **I don't accept that. In my view, we should go ahead.**
(in my view – meiner Ansicht nach / go ahead – anfangen)

* **I'm not sure whether I can go along with you here.**
(whether – ob / go along with sbdy. – mit jmdm. mitgehen; jmdn. unterstützen)

* **I'm afraid I don't agree with Harry.**
(Leider bin ich da anderer Meinung als Harry.)

* **I completely disagree. We can't wait. We have to act now.**

(Da bin ich gänzlich anderer Meinung. .... / wait – warten / act – handeln)

* **I'm not convinced that this is a good idea.**
  (convince – überzeugen)

* **I couldn't possibly support such a move.**
  (Ich könnte so einen Schritt nie unterstützen.)

* **On balance, I think it's not the right time for the move.**
  (on balance – per Saldo; alles in allem)

* **That's oversimplifying it.**
  (oversimplify – zu stark vereinfachen)

PERSUADING AND CONVINCING

Überreden und überzeugen

* **Couldn't you reconsider your stance, Frank?**
  (reconsider – noch einmal überlegen / stance – Standpunkt)

* **Can't this persuade you either?**
  (not ... either – auch nicht)

* **I think this is an irrefutable argument.**
  (irrefutable – unwiderlegbar)

* **Don't you think that it's time to do something about the loss of reach?**
  (loss of reach – Reichweitenverlust)

* **Have a look at this letter. Maybe this will convince you that we can't delay the decision any longer.**
  (letter – Brief / convince – überzeugen / delay – aufschieben / decision – Entscheidung)

* **Wouldn't you agree that the proposal is quite reasonable?**
  (proposal – Vorschlag / quite – durchaus, ganz / reasonable – vernünftig)

∗ **I can't understand why it should be so difficult to come round to our view.**
(come round to our view – sich unserer Meinung anschließen)

∗ **I do hope you will change your mind.**
(Ich hoffe wirklich, daß Sie Ihre Meinung ändern werden | daß Sie sich anders besinnen werden.)

∗ **Can't you give an inch just once?**
(Können Sie nicht wenigstens einmal nur ein bißchen nachgeben?)

SUGGESTIONS AND REACTIONS

Vorschläge und Reaktionen darauf

∗ **A: I suggest that we examine each of these plans in detail.**
(Ich schlage vor, daß wir jeden einzelnen dieser Pläne detailliert prüfen.)
B: Yes, I think that's a good idea.

∗ **A: I think we should take a closer look at the details.**
(Ich glaube, wir sollten uns die Details genauer ansehen.)
B: I'd say so, too.

∗ **A: I recommend that we take his objections very seriously.**
(Ich empfehle, daß wir seine Einwände sehr ernst nehmen.)
B: Yes, I agree. After all, he is the expert.
(after all – schließlich)

∗ **A: I recommend dropping the charge.**
(drop charge – Anschuldigung fallenlassen | nicht weiter verfolgen)
B: No, I couldn't go along with that. That would be a bit premature.
(go along with – mitgehen / premature – voreilig)

∗ **A: How about deferring the next item until we have clarified the details?**
(Wie wäre es, wenn wir die Behandlung des nächsten Tagesordnungspunktes aufschieben, bis wir die Einzelheiten geklärt haben?)
B: I don't think that would be a good idea.

* **A: What about offering them a special discount?**
(Wie wäre es, wenn wir ihnen einen Sonderrabatt anbieten?)
B: Well, I'm not sure whether that will clinch it. But it's worth a try.
(whether – ob / clinch sthg. – etwas zu einem endgültigen Abschluß bringen / worth a try – einen Versuch wert)

* **A: I propose calling in an expert.**
(Ich schlage vor, einen Experten beizuziehen.)
B: No, I think that would be a waste of time. The matter isn't all that important.
(Nein, ich glaube, das wäre Zeitverschwendung. So wichtig ist die Sache auch wieder nicht.)

* **A: What I would suggest is that the financial aspects of the deal should be investigated much more closely.**
(deal – Geschäft / investigate – untersuchen / close – genau)
B: Yes, that's what we should do.

* **A: Listen, why don't we send somebody over there to sort out the problem on the spot?**
(listen – zuhören / sort out – lösen / on the spot – an Ort und Stelle; vor Ort)
B: Yes, why not? Although I'm not sure whether the expense would be really justified.
(although – obwohl / expense – Aufwand / justified – gerechtfertigt)

* **A: My suggestion would be that we concentrate on the premium end of the market.**
(premium end – Hochpreissegment, Luxussegment)
B: Do you really think that would work? It might be a bit risky.
(work – funktionieren)

* **A: My suggestion is to call for a second opinion.**
(call for – einholen / opinion – Gutachten)
B: I'd support that.
(support – unterstützen)

* **A: Don't you think it would be better to waive the penalty?**
(waive – verzichten auf / penalty – Pönale)
B: With respect Peter, you have missed the point.
(Bei allem Respekt, Peter, aber du hast nicht verstanden, worum es geht / aber du hast den springenden Punkt nicht kapiert.)

CONCEDING POINTS

Zugeständnisse machen

* **I think you've got a point there. There is a strong case for not splitting the department.**
  (Ich glaube, da hast du recht. Es gibt starke Argumente, die gegen eine Aufspaltung der Abteilung sprechen.)

* **You may be right there, but we must not forget that interest rates have risen in the meantime.**
  (be right – recht haben / interest rate – Zinssatz / rise – steigen; sich erhöhen / meantime – Zwischenzeit)

* **You could have a point there. On the other hand I still think the financial aspects are more important.**
  (Da könntest du recht haben. Andererseits glaube ich trotzdem, daß die finanziellen Aspekte wichtiger sind.)

* **I think you're on to something here, but in my view the financial angle should be explored first.**
  (Ich glaube, da haben Sie den Finger auf einen wichtigen Punkt gelegt, … . / view – Ansicht / angle – Aspekt / explore – untersuchen, analysieren)

CLARIFYING

Klarstellungen

* **So, please, let me get this clear. We do not intend to merely license our invention.**
  (Ich möchte das bitte ganz klar zum Ausdruck bringen. Wir beabsichtigen nicht, unsere Erfindung bloß in Form von Lizenzen zu verwerten.)

* **Could you clarify what you have just said? I don't think I fully understand you.**
  (clarify – näher erläutern / just – gerade)

* **What exactly do you mean by "special requirements"?**
  (Was genau verstehen Sie unter „Sondererfordernissen"?)

* **Could you be a bit more specific?**
(specific – konkret, spezifisch)

* **I'm sorry, but could you explain this in a little more detail?**
(Entschuldigen Sie, aber könnten Sie das etwas genauer erklären?)

* **Sorry, probably I haven't made myself entirely clear.**
(Tut mir leid. Ich habe mich wahrscheinlich nicht ganz klar ausgedrückt.)

* **I'd like to make it quite clear that I will not support the scheme.**
(quite – ganz / support – unterstützen / scheme – Projekt, Aktion)

* **I'm afraid there seems to have been a slight misunderstanding. This isn't quite what I meant.**
(Ich fürchte, da scheint es ein kleines Mißverständnis gegeben zu haben. Das habe ich eigentlich nicht ganz so gemeint.)

* **Actually, what I was trying to say is that we need more information.**
(Was ich eigentlich sagen wollte, ist, ...)

* **From what you have just said I'm not quite sure whether you are in favour or against the proposal.**
(whether – ob / in favour – dafür / proposal – Vorschlag, Antrag)

INTERRUPTIONS AND DEALING WITH INTERRUPTIONS

Unterbrechungen und wie man damit umgeht

* **May I interrupt you for a moment? I think you have forgotten to allow for the period of grace.**
(interrupt – unterbrechen / allow for – berücksichtigen / period of grace – tilgungsfreier Zeitraum)

* **Excuse me. May I come in here?**
(Entschuldigen Sie. Darf ich an dieser Stelle etwas [dazu] sagen?)

* **Now hold on. Even if your projections are right, we won't reach the break-even point before 1995.**
(Moment mal. Selbst wenn Ihre Prognosen stimmen, werden wir die Gewinnschwelle erst 1995 erreichen.)

* **Excuse me. Before you go on, could I just say this?**
(Entschuldigen Sie. Bevor Sie fortfahren, könnte ich nur kurz etwas sagen?)

* **Excuse me for interrupting you. But before we go on, we have to clarify the cost position.**
(clarify – klären)

* **Can I just make a brief comment here?**
(Kann ich nur kurz etwas dazu sagen?)

——— ❖ ———

* **Excuse me, Miss Friar, I think Mr. Greer would like to make a point.**
(make a point – eine Anmerkung machen)

* A: **If you don't mind, Brian, could Anne just briefly tell us what she heard in the Ministry? I think that would be very relevant here.**
(if you don't mind – wenn es Ihnen nichts ausmacht / brief – kurz)
B: **Yes, certainly. Anne, go ahead.**
(Ja, natürlich. Schieß los, Anne.)

——— ❖ ———

* **Sorry, can I continue now? I haven't finished yet.**
(continue – fortfahren / .... Ich bin noch nicht fertig.)

* **I'll come back to this later, if you don't mind.**

* **That's an interesting point, but I'd rather deal with it later on.**
(I'd rather – ich möchte lieber / deal with – behandeln)

* **I'd rather comment on this later on.**
(Ich möchte mich lieber später dazu äußern.)

——— ❖ ———

* **Could you hold back until Peter has finished?**
(Könntest du warten, bis Peter fertig ist?)

* **Sorry Mr. Fisher, you'll have to wait a little. We must let Ms. Bunter finish first.**

* **Be brief Thomas, because strictly speaking Mr. Gower has the floor.**
  (Faß dich kurz, ... / strictly speaking – genaugenommen, eigentlich / have the floor – am Wort sein)

MOVING THE DISCUSSION FORWARD

Überleitung zum nächsten Tagesordnungspunkt

* **Well, let's move on to the environmental aspects of the project.**
  (Gehen wir jetzt zu den ökologischen Aspekten des Projektes über.)

* **Now, let's move on to item two on the agenda.**
  (Wenden wir uns nun dem zweiten Tagesordnungspunkt zu.)

* **Can we next deal with the legal implications of the move?**
  (Können wir als nächstes die juristischen Implikationen des Schrittes behandeln?)

* **Now, let's turn our attention to the question of discounts.**
  (Wenden wir uns nun der Frage der Preisnachlässe zu.)

* **Could we now discuss item three?**

* **I think this leads us to the next point.**
  (lead – bringen, führen)

* **The next item on the agenda is the Environmental Impact Assessment.**
  (Der nächste Tagesordnungspunkt ist die Umweltverträglichkeitsprüfung.)

* **Any objections to bringing Item 6 forward? I think it would be better to deal with it right now.**
  (Spricht etwas dagegen, daß wir den Punkt 6 vorziehen? ....)

KEEPING THE DISCUSSION ON TRACK

Wie man Abweichungen vom Thema verhindert

* **A: Excuse me, Frank, I know this is a very interesting question but it is not our main concern today.**
  (question – Frage / main concern – Hauptthema, Hauptanliegen)
  B: You're right of course. Let's leave it for the next meeting.
  (leave – lassen)

* **No, I don't agree. I think what I've been saying is very relevant to our main topic.**
  (main topic – Hauptthema)

* **Let's not stray too far from our main concern. Our time is limited anyway.**
  (stray – abschweifen / limited – beschränkt / anyway – ohnehin)

* **Let's not lose sight of the main point.**
  (lose sight of sthg. – etwas aus dem Auge verlieren)

* **I'm afraid we are getting side-tracked.**
  (Ich fürchte, wir kommen da auf ein Nebengeleis.)

* **May I remind you that the issue under discussion is the new marketing plan and not the marketing manager.**
  (remind – [daran] erinnern / issue – Thema)

HANDLING AWKWARD QUESTIONS AND BEING EVASIVE

Wie man mit unangenehmen Fragen umgeht und Ausflüchte macht

* **I'm afraid I can't give you a definite answer at present.**
  (Tut mir leid, aber ich kann Ihnen zum gegenwärtigen Zeitpunkt keine endgültige Antwort geben.)

* **It's hard to say at the moment. It all depends on how our competitors react to our move.**
  (depend on – abhängen von / competitor – Konkurrent / react to – reagieren auf / move – Schritt)

* **Sorry to sound evasive, but there is no straightforward answer to that.**

(Tut mir leid, wenn es nach einer Ausflucht klingt, aber die Frage kann nicht so einfach beantwortet werden.)

* **I'd need more information to answer your question.**

* **It's too soon for a final judgement.**
(final judgement – endgültige Bewertung; endgültiges Urteil)

* **I can't really say more at present. Anything I add might jeopardise the negotiations with the syndicate.**
(add – hinzufügen / jeopardise – gefährden / negotiation – Verhandlung / syndicate – Konsortium)

* **I hope you will understand, but to answer your question I would have to divulge classified information.**
(divulge – preisgeben / classified – geheim)

* **I'm sorry but I have not been authorised by the Board to disclose more.**
(authorise – ermächtigen / board – Verwaltungsrat; Führungsgremium einer brit./US-Kapitalgesellschaft / disclose – offenlegen, mitteilen)

* **You seem to be avoiding my question.**
(seem – scheinen / avoid – ausweichen)

SUMMARISING

Zusammenfassungen

* **In a nutshell, what I'm saying is that costs are too high.**
(Der langen Rede kurzer Sinn ist, daß … .)

* **To summarise, in my view, there are too many uncertainties.**
(Um das Ganze zusammenzufassen: meiner Meinung nach gibt es zu viele Unsicherheiten.)

* **Let me sum up what has been agreed so far.**
(sum up – zusammenfassen / agree sthg. – sich auf etwas einigen)

* **Let me recap on what has been decided so far.**
(recap on – zusammenfassen / decide – entscheiden, beschließen)

* **Let me pull together the main strands of the argument.**
(pull together – zusammenziehen / strand – Linie, Faden)

* **A: Does this summarise your present position?**
(present – gegenwärtig, aktuell)
B: Yes, that's an accurate summary.
(accurate – genau / summary – Zusammenfassung)

FORMAL MOTIONS AND VOTING

Formelle Anträge und Abstimmungen

* **I think everyone has had their say now. We cannot discuss the pros and cons interminably. Let's have a motion and vote on it.**
(Ich glaube, alle haben jetzt etwas dazu gesagt. Wir können das Für und Wider nicht endlos diskutieren. Irgend jemand muß einen formellen Antrag stellen, und dann stimmen wir ab.)

* **I don't think we see eye to eye on this at all. Let's put it to the vote.**
(Ich glaube nicht, daß wir die Sache auch nur im entferntesten gleich sehen. Stimmen wir also darüber ab.)

* **Mr. Chairman, I'd like to move that the project be postponed until the financial details have been clarified.**
(Herr Vorsitzender, ich möchte beantragen, daß das Projekt bis zur Klärung der finanziellen Einzelheiten aufgeschoben wird.)

* **I would like to propose that Ms. Gold should be asked to stay on.**
(propose – vorschlagen / stay on – in der Firma bleiben)

* **All right then. Let's put it to the vote.**

* **Perhaps we should take a vote on this.**
(take a vote on sthg. – über etwas abstimmen)

* **How many are in favour of postponing the project? How many against?**
(Wie viele sind für den Aufschub des Projektes? … ?)

* **All those in favour? … five. Those against? … four.**

* **Any abstentions?**
(Enthält sich irgend jemand der Stimme?/ Stimmenthaltungen?)

* **Can I ask for a show of hands?**
(Könnten Sie bitte aufzeigen?)

* **The motion to postpone the project has been carried by five votes to two.**
(Der Antrag, das Projekt aufzuschieben, ist mit fünf zu zwei Stimmen angenommen worden.)

* **The motion has been rejected.**
(reject – ablehnen)

* **Five in favour, five against. I'll have to use my casting vote. I'm against the proposal. This means that the motion has been defeated.**
(.... Ich muß von meinem Dirimierungsrecht Gebrauch machen. ..../ proposal – Antrag / mean – heißen, bedeuten / defeat – ablehnen)

* **It's a draw.**
(Die Abstimmung ist unentschieden ausgegangen.)

* **Are we all agreed on this then?**
(Sind wir da alle einer Meinung?)

* **Agreed.**
(Ja, einer Meinung.)

* **If everyone agrees ....**

* **A: Since this is a very sensitive matter I suggest that we have a secret ballot.**
(Da das eine sehr heikle Angelegenheit ist, schlage ich vor, daß wir geheim darüber abstimmen.)
B: I don't think the Rules of Procedure say anything about a secret ballot. I'm against it.
(Ich glaube nicht, daß die Geschäftsordnung eine geheime Abstimmung vorsieht. Ich bin dagegen.)

* A: **This motion cannot be put to the vote since nobody has seconded it.**
(second – formell unterstützen)
B: **Requiring formal support for a motion is British and not Continental practice.**
(Das Erfordernis einer formellen Unterstützung für einen Antrag ist nur in Großbritannien, nicht aber auf dem Kontinent üblich.)
A: **I see. Are you sure that there is nothing about this in the Rules of Procedure?**
B : **I'm positive. I drew them up myself.**
(Ganz sicher. Ich habe sie selbst erstellt.)

MINUTES
Das Protokoll

* **Don't put that in the minutes, please. It would make a bad impression on outsiders.**
(Schreiben Sie das bitte nicht ins Protokoll. Es würde einen schlechten Eindruck auf Außenstehende machen.)

* **Walter, will you draft suitable minutes about these two proposals, please?**
(Walter, würdest du bitte diese beiden Anträge für das Protokoll entsprechend formulieren?)

* **My suggestion is – and I want this to be minuted – that we first talk to the trade union representatives.**
(Mein Vorschlag ist – und ich möchte, daß das protokolliert wird –, daß wir zuerst mit den Gewerkschaftsvertretern reden.)

* **I must insist that my objections are put in the minutes. I want to make it quite clear where I stand on this matter.**
(Ich muß darauf bestehen, daß meine Einwände ins Protokoll aufgenommen werden. Ich möchte meine Haltung in dieser Sache eindeutig klarstellen.)

CLOSING THE MEETING

Wie man eine Sitzung schließt

* **All right. Time is getting on and I'd like to wind the meeting up now.**
(.... Es wird langsam spät, und ich möchte die Sitzung jetzt zu einem Abschluß bringen.)

* **I think it's time we finished.**
(Ich glaube, es ist Zeit, daß wir Schluß machen.)

* **Is there any other business?**
(Etwas unter Allfälliges?)

* **If we are all agreed then, I'd like to close the meeting.**
(close – schließen)

* **We are running out of time and I think we should break up now.**
(Die Zeit wird langsam knapp, und ich glaube, wir sollten jetzt Schluß machen.)

* **I suggest that we adjourn and leave the last two items on the agenda for the next meeting. There is no point in rushing them through. They can wait until next week.**
(adjourn – [sich] vertagen / leave – lassen / there is no point – es hat keinen Sinn / rush through – durchpeitschen)

* **Bye, see you all in two weeks' time.**

POST MEETING

Nach der Sitzung

* **Would you be willing to chair the next meeting, Mary? I have to attend a business function in Paris and I don't think I'll be able to make it.**
(chair meeting – bei Sitzung Vorsitz führen / attend – teilnehmen an / business function – geschäftlich wichtige Veranstaltung / make it – es schaffen)

* **Giles, could I have a copy of the minutes by tomorrow afternoon?**
  (by – bis [spätestens])

* **Geoffrey, could you get the minutes typed and distributed to the members as soon as possible?**
  (get sthg. typed – etwas tippen lassen / distribute – verteilen)

* **Could I have a word with you in my office, Anne?**

* **I don't think the meeting went too well. There was a lot of unnecessary bickering.**
  (a lot of – viel / unnecessary – unnötig, überflüssig / bickering – Gezänke)

* **Yes, some of the contributions were simply too long and partly irrelevant.**
  (contribution – Beitrag / simply – einfach / partly – teilweise)

* A: **Charles Miller can be a real pain in the neck.**
  (... kann einem wirklich auf die Nerven gehen.)
  B: **I agree. He is so stubborn and just refuses to see somebody else's point of view.**
  (stubborn – stur / just – einfach / refuse – sich weigern / point of view – Standpunkt)

* A: **Ah, that was a great meeting! Most of the participants were very constructive and spoke only to the point.**
  (participant – Teilnehmer / speak to the point – zum Thema sprechen)
  B: **Yes, but part of the credit goes to you. You handled the meeting very well. I particularly liked the way in which you dealt with the ramblings of Peter Read.**
  (part of the credit goes to you – das ist teilweise dein Verdienst / handle – führen, leiten / particularly – besonders / deal with – fertigwerden mit / ramblings – zielloses Geschwafel)

CONFERENCES

Konferenzen

(see also "Meetings" and "General Presentations")

REGISTRATION AND GENERAL INFORMATIONS

Anmeldung und allgemeine Informationen

* **I'd like to register for the Conference on the Internalisation of External Effects, please.**
(register – anmelden)

* **A: Could I have my tag and the copies of the conference papers?**
(tag – Namensschild / conference papers – Konferenzunterlagen)
B: Here you are, sir.
(Hier bitte!)

* **A: What? You can't find my name on the list? I registered months ago and paid the full fee.**
(fee – Gebühr)
B: When did you say you registered?

* **I wonder if you could tell me whether Mr. Vetter has already arrived, please.**
(Könnten Sie mir bitte sagen, ob Herr Vetter schon angekommen ist.)

* **No, you're right. I didn't book a hotel through your organisation because I'm staying with friends.**
(stay with – wohnen bei)

——— ❖ ———

* **Can you tell me where Dr. Minor's talk will be held?**
(talk – Vortrag)

* **Excuse me, could you tell me where the leaders of the working groups are meeting this afternoon?**
(leader – Leiter / working group – Arbeitsgruppe / meet – sich treffen)

* **When does the plenary session start this afternoon?**
(plenary session – Plenarsitzung)

* **I'd like to join the working party on Materials Management. Where are they meeting?**
(join – mitmachen bei / working party – Arbeitsgruppe / materials management – Materialwirtschaft)

* **A: Could you tell us where to register for the working groups, please?**
B: Yes, certainly. The office is on the second floor at the end of the corridor.
(certainly – gern / office – Büro / floor – Stock)

* **No, it can't be Room No. 34. I went there just a minute ago and it's occupied by the Cost Accounting people.**
(occupied – besetzt / cost accounting – Kostenrechnung)

* **A: Excuse me, is this the working party on Corporate Culture?**
(corporate culture – Unternehmenskultur)
B: No, we are the Operations Research people. The Corporate Culture people are meeting in Room 234. This is Room 134.

* **A: Excuse me, I'm afraid I'm a bit late. My plane was held up in Manchester because of fog. Could I still join your working party?**
(I'm afraid – ich fürchte / plane – Flugzeug / fog – dichter Nebel / still – noch)
B: Certainly. Come in and have a seat. What is your name?

* **A: What a pleasant surprise, Brian! I didn't know that you were coming, too. Great to see you again.**
(pleasant – freudig / surprise – Überraschung / great – schön)
B: Hello Andrew. Great to see you too. Didn't know myself that I'd be coming until a week ago. But the man my company originally wanted to send fell ill.
(originally – ursprünglich / fall ill – krank werden)

* **A: Yes, I'm going to read a paper on environmental audits.**
(read paper – Referat halten / environmental audit – Umweltbilanz)
B: I didn't know that you were an expert in that field.
(field – Gebiet)

OPENING CONFERENCES AND INTRODUCING SPEAKERS

Eröffnung von Konferenzen und Vorstellung von Vortragenden

* **Ladies and gentlemen, on this note, I declare the 4th Conference on "The Diffusion of Technology" open.**
  (on this note – in diesem Sinne / declare open – für eröffnet erklären)

* **Ladies and gentlemen, I have great pleasure in introducing Dr. Holmes, an expert on environmental matters and a specialist in business law.**
  (have great pleasure – sich sehr freuen; das Vergnügen haben / introduce – vorstellen / environmental matters – Umweltfragen, -angelegenheiten / business law – Wirtschaftsrecht)

* **It gives me great pleasure to welcome our next speaker, Mr. Van Dyke from Rotterdam.**

* **Our first speaker, Professor Blue, will talk on "The Cost Centre Concept".**
  (cost centre – Kostenstelle)

* **Ladies and gentlemen, we are pleased to have with us today Mr. Brown from the Confederation of British Industry. Mr. Brown's talk will be on "The British Strike Record".**
  (Confederation of British Industry – britischer Unternehmerverband / strike record – Streikbilanz)

* **Mr. Potter's subject today is "The Role of the Stock Exchange".**
  (subject – Thema / stock exchange – [Wertpapier-]Börse)

SPEAKER THANKS CHAIRMAN

Vortragende/r dankt Vorsitzender/m

∗ **Thank you very much for your kind words, although you've made it very difficult for me to meet the expectations you have aroused.**
(kind – freundlich / although – obwohl / meet expectations – Erwartungen erfüllen / arouse – erwecken)

∗ **That was very kind of you, Ms. Chairperson.**
(Ms. – neutrale Form für Miss oder Mrs. / chairperson – Vorsitzende/r)

SPEAKER INTRODUCES SUBJECT

Vortragende/r stellt ihr/sein Thema vor

∗ **The subject of my paper is "Countertrade with Bulgaria".**
(countertrade – Gegengeschäfte)

∗ **In the course of the next 30 minutes we shall be analysing some of thc ncw financial derivatives.**
(course – Verlauf / financial derivatives – derivative Finanzprodukte)

∗ **Ladies and gentlemen, as you have already heard, I'll be talking about "Cost Accounting Problems in Flexible Manufacturing Systems".**
(flexible manufacturing system – flexibles Fertigungssystem)

SPEAKER INTRODUCES FIRST POINT

Vortragende/r präsentiert ersten Punkt

* **I'd like to begin by giving you a brief outline of my paper.**
(brief outline – Kurzfassung / paper – Referat)

* **Let us begin with a summary of the major points I shall be considering.**
(summary – Zusammenfassung / major point – wichtigster Punkt / consider – erörtern, behandeln)

* **The first aspect to be considered is the motivation behind the new government policy.**
(government – Regierung / policy – Politik)

SPEAKER MOVES ON TO NEXT POINT/S

Vortragende/r leitet zum nächsten Punkt/zu den nächsten Punkten über

* **Let us move on to the next point then.**
(move on to – übergehen zu)

* **The second main point is how middle management can be involved in the scheme.**
(involve – einbinden / scheme – Projekt)

* **We are now in a position to consider the second major aspect, viz. the tax implications.**
(in a position – in der Lage / viz. – namely | nämlich / tax – Steuer)

* **The second element in the mix we shall investigate is off-shore manufacturing.**
(investigate – untersuchen / off-shore manufacturing – Produktion im Ausland)

* **Now I'd like to turn to the next point.**
(turn to – sich zuwenden)

CONCLUDING REMARKS
Schlußbemerkungen

* **Finally I'd like to summarise the chief points I've made.**
(finally – zum Abschluß / summarise – zusammenfassen / chief point – wichtigste Aussage)

* **By way of conclusion let me once again stress the importance of obtaining government support.**
(by way of conclusion – zum Abschluß / once again – noch einmal / stress – betonen / importance – Wichtigkeit / obtain – erhalten, erlangen / support – Unterstützung)

* **A few closing remarks .... .**
(closing remark – Schlußbemerkung)

* **I should now like to conclude by highlighting the crucial aspects once again.**
(conclude – schließen / highlight – herausstreichen / crucial – entscheidend)

* **Let me end on a note of optimism.**
(Ich möchte den Vortrag optimistisch ausklingen lassen. | Lassen Sie mich zum Schluß noch etwas Optimistisches sagen.)

* **In conclusion let me quote the doyen of marketing theory, Professor Kotler.**
(in conclusion – zum Abschluß / quote – zitieren / doyen – Doyen)

THANKING SPEAKER, INITIATING DISCUSSION, CLOSING CONFERENCE OR SESSION

Dank an die/den Vortragende/n, Eröffnung der Diskussion, Abschluß der Konferenz oder Sitzung

* **I'm sure I'm speaking for everyone when I say how grateful we are to Dr. Miller for his extremely interesting lecture.**
  (grateful – dankbar / extremely – äußerst / lecture – Vortrag)

* **I'd like to thank Mr. Fallow for his thoroughly provoking paper.**
  (thoroughly provoking – äußerst anregend / paper – Referat)

* **Are there any questions for the Speaker?**
  (question – Frage / speaker – Redner)

* **Yes, the gentleman at the far end of the room. Would you identify yourself, please?**
  (at the far end – ganz hinten / .... Würden Sie uns bitte Ihren Namen sagen?)

* **Mr. Fallow, would you like to answer this point?**
  (point – Einwurf, Frage)

* **Could the paper also be made available in German?**
  (make available – zur Verfügung stellen)

* **I now declare this meeting closed. We'll meet again in the plenary session here at 17.00 hours.**
  (Ich erkläre nun die Sitzung für beendet. .... / plenary session – Plenarsitzung / 17.00 hours – seventeenhundred hours)

GENERAL PRESENTATIONS (INCLUDING QUANTITATIVE STATEMENTS AND DIAGRAMS)

Allgemeine Präsentationen (unter besonderer Berücksichtigung von quantitativen Aussagen und Diagrammen)

(see also "Meetings" and "Conferences")

INTRODUCTIONS

Einleitende Worte

* **Good morning. For those of you who don't know me, I'm Richard Brinner from Marketing. I'm here today to report on the new developments in the American market.**
  (report on – berichten übcr / development – Entwicklung)

* **Right, ladies and gentlemen, for those who don't already know him from the fact-finding discussions in the past few weeks, I'd like to introduce Mr. Peter Soams of the Soams & Soams Consulting Agency. Peter, would you like to begin?**
  (fact-finding discussion – Sondierungsgespräch / in the past few weeks – in den letzten paar Wochen / introduce – vorstellen / consulting – Beratung)

* **Mr. Lenner, our CEO, has asked me to outline Marketing's views on our planned move into the East European markets.**
  (CEO – chief executive officer | etwa: Generaldirektor, Vorstandsvorsitzender / outline – umreißen; in groben Zügen darstellen / view – Ansicht / move – Schritt, Vorstoß)

* **Ladies and gentlemen, as you all know, R&D have completed their work on the new speed control. The question now is how to exploit this invention. It will be my task to present a number of options.**

(R&D – Research and Development [Department] | Forschung[s-] und Entwicklung[-sabteilung] / complete – abschließen / speed control – Geschwindigkeitsregler / question – Frage / exploit – verwerten / invention – Erfindung / task – Aufgabe / number – Anzahl, Reihe)

* **I'm going to present my case for raising the funds from a syndicate of major banks rather than from our shareholders.**
(case – Argumente / raise – aufnehmen, aufbringen / funds – Mittel / syndicate – Konsortium / major – größer / rather – statt / shareholder – Aktionär)

* **First I'd like to outline the present situation, then I'm going to present the possible alternatives open to us and finally I shall be recommending which of these alternatives we should take.**
(present – gegenwärtig / possible – möglich / finally – schließlich / recommend – empfehlen)

* **I've been commissioned by your President to analyse the purchasing activities of your company and to make some constructive suggestions on how to streamline the procurement function.**
(commission – beauftragen / president – [US] etwa: Generaldirektor, Vorstandsvorsitzender / purchase – einkaufen / suggestion – Vorschlag / streamline – durchrationalisieren / procurement function – Beschaffungswesen)

* **The recommendations which I will present are based on a careful analysis of the shipping department, including in-depth interviews with key people working there.**
(recommendation – Empfehlung / be based on – basieren auf / shipping department – Versandabteilung / in-depth – gründlich, ausführlich / key people – wichtige Leute)

* **I'm here today to report our findings and to present a number of options to help you formulate an appropriate strategy.**
(finding – Untersuchungsergebnis / appropriate – geeignet)

* **The question is what has gone wrong? I'd like to try and answer the question by looking at the current difficulties from two different angles.**
(go wrong – schiefgehen / try – versuchen / answer – beantworten / current – gegenwärtig / different – verschieden / angle – Gesichtspunkt, Blickwinkel)

TECHNICAL ASPECTS

Technische Aspekte

* **Just a moment, I can't seem to find the transparency showing the development of the contribution margin.**
(…, ich kann anscheinend die Folie, die die Entwicklung des Deckungsbeitrages zeigt, nicht finden.)

* **Can anyone show me how to focus the overhead projector, please?**
(focus – einstellen)

* **Why is this damn machine not working? Ah, here is the switch.**
(damn – verdammt / work – funktionieren / switch – Schalter)

* A: **You have to plug it in.**
(plug in – anstecken)
B: **Where's the wall socket?**
(wall socket – Steckdose)

* **There is a second switch at the back of the machine.**

* **I've run out of paper for the flip-chart and I'd also need a new marker, please.**
(sbdy. runs out of sthg. – jmdm. geht etwas aus / marker – Schreibstift)

* **Could somebody help me to adjust the flip-chart, please ? I don't want to ruin it!**
(adjust – einstellen, adjustieren)

* **Sorry, that's the wrong way round. … That's better now.**
(Entschuldigen Sie, aber das ist verkehrt herum. … .)

QUANTITATIVE STATEMENTS AND DIAGRAMS

Quantitative Aussagen und Diagramme

INTRODUCING DIAGRAMS

Einführung von Diagrammen

* **I'd like to support my findings by a number of charts.**
(support – stützen / finding – Ergebnis / number – Anzahl, Reihe / chart – Diagramm)

* **I'd like to begin by analysing the chart on page six of the hand-outs.**
(page – Seite / hand-out – [verteilte] Broschüre | Mappe)

* **Let me show you two charts to highlight some of the points I made.**
(highlight – herausstreichen / make point – Aussage machen; Feststellung treffen)

* **Here's a diagram illustrating what I've just said.**

* **This graph here relates advertising expenditure to sales.**
(graph – Graph, Linie, Graphik / relate – in Beziehung setzen / advertising expenditure – Werbeausgaben, -aufwand / sales – Umsatz)

* **In the first chart here annual sales from 1980 to 1990 are shown as bars.**
(annual sales – Jahresumsatz / show – darstellen / bar – Balken, Säule)

* **Let's move on to the next table, which compares the contribution margins of different product groups.**
(move on to – weitergehen zu / table – Tabelle / compare – vergleichen / contribution margin – Deckungsbeitrag / different – verschieden)

BREAKDOWNS AND PERCENTAGE SHARES

Aufgliederungen und Prozentanteile

* **This is a breakdown of our exports by country of destination, and this is an analysis according to commodity.**
(breakdown – Aufschlüsselung, Aufgliederung / by – nach / country of destination – Bestimmungsland / analysis – Aufgliederung, Aufschlüsselung / according to – nach / commodity – Ware)

* **As you can see, the share of exports in total sales has declined.**
(share of exports in total sales – Exportquote / decline – fallen, sinken)

* **The pie chart top left shows that exports account for just under fourteen per cent of total sales.**
(Das Kreisdiagramm links oben zeigt, daß nur knapp 14% des Gesamtumsatzes auf Exporte entfallen | daß Exporte nur knapp 14% des Gesamtumsatzes ausmachen.)

* **If you compare the blue segments in the two pie charts you will see that the share of services in total sales has increased.**
(share of x in y – Anteil von x an y / increase – sich erhöhen)

VARIABLE CHANGES OR REMAINS CONSTANT

Änderung oder Gleichbleiben einer Variablen

* **The broken line shows that exports of big-ticket items have been increasing since 1986.**
(broken line – strichlierte Linie / big-ticket items – Hochpreisartikel / have been increasing since – steigen seit)

* **May I call your attention to this blip in the curve. It represents the spurt in activity prior to the take-over.**
(call attention to sthg. – Aufmerksamkeit auf etwas lenken / blip – Ausschlag; kurzfristige Abweichung / spurt – scharfe, kurzfristige Erhöhung; „Explosion“ / prior to – vor / take-over – Firmenübernahme)

* **If I now put this overlay representing fiscal 1990 on top of the one for 1991, you will notice the dramatic increase in overheads.**

(overlay – Overlay, [darübergelegte Overheadfolie] / fiscal – Haushaltsjahr / on top of – über; auf ... darauf / notice – bemerken / increase in – Erhöhung bei / overheads – Gemeinkosten)

* **Now let's turn to page six of the booklet, where you can find a time series showing the development of the market shares of our competitors. Brior Corp.'s increased by all of 15 per cent.**
(turn to – sich zuwenden / booklet – Broschüre / time series – [statistische] Zeitreihe / development – Entwicklung / market share – Marktanteil / competitor – Konkurrent / Corp. – corporation I [US] etwa: Kapitalgesellschaft, Aktiengesellschaft / by all of 15 per cent – um ganze 15%)

* **The figures speak for themselves. Sales 30 per cent down on the year and pre-tax up 15 per cent.**
(figure – Zahl, Ergebnis / .... Der Umsatz ist gegenüber dem Vorjahr um 30% gefallen und der Gewinn vor Steuern um 15% gestiegen.)

* **As you can see, in early 1990 sales recovered.**
(early 1990 – Anfang 1990 / recover – sich erholen)

* **Our projection is that provisions will peak out next year.**
(projection – Prognose / provision – Rückstellung, Wertberichtigung / peak out – Höhepunkt überschreiten)

* **Inexplicably there was a bulge in orders in early May. That's the fifth bar in the chart.**
(inexplicably – unerklärlicherweise / bulge – plötzliche, starke Ausweitung / order – Auftrag / fifth – fünft / bar – Säule, Balken)

* **Surprisingly, our exports soared in the middle of a world-recession, as you can see from the time series on page five.**
(surprisingly – überraschenderweise / soar – stark steigen)

——— ❖ ———

* **Now let's look at column four in the table. This represents sales of large units. Not very encouraging, is it? Fell by more than ten per cent in both 1988 and 1989.**
(column – Spalte / table – Tabelle / unit – Gerät / encouraging – ermutigend / is it? – oder? / both ... and ... – sowohl ... als auch ...)

* **In 1989 we experienced a drastic fall in profits, as you can see from the dip in the line here.**
(experience – erleben / dip – [kurzes] Absacken)

* **In 1987 interest income plummeted, dropping by no less than 76 per cent. That's on page four.**
(interest income – Zinserträge / plummet – abstürzen / drop – zurückgehen, fallen)

* **Fortunately, sales bottomed out sooner than expected. As you can see, the decline began levelling out as early as June. They hit bottom in September and, as you can see, are now back to their 1989 level and rising.**
(fortunately – glücklicherweise / bottom out – Tiefpunkt erreichen und wieder steigen / expect – erwarten / decline – Rückgang / level out – abflachen; sich verflachen / as early as – schon / hit bottom – Tiefpunkt erreichen / level – Niveau / rise – steigen)

——— ❖ ———

* **The dividend has remained unchanged for the past five years. The development of dividends is shown on the last page of the booklet.**
(remain unchanged – unverändert bleiben / page – Seite / booklet – Broschüre)

* **The depreciation charge has been fairly constant in the past few years. You see the line's almost level.**
(depreciation charge – Abschreibungsaufwand / fairly – ziemlich / in the past few years – in den letzten paar Jahren / level – eben)

* **Sales have been flat in the past two years.**
(be flat – stagnieren)

RANKINGS

Rangordnungen

- ✻ **They have ranked first for the past five years.**
  (rank first – an erster Stelle rangieren)

- ✻ **The next graph shows that our company has fallen back to third place in terms of sales.**
  (graph – Graph, Graphik / in terms of – gemessen an)

- ✻ **If you refer to the bar chart on page five of the hand-out, you will see that we are no longer number one in our industry in terms of operating margins.**
  (refer to – sich zuwenden / bar chart – Säulendiagramm, Stabdiagramm / hand-out – ausgeteilter Zettel / industry – Branche / operating margin – Umsatzrentabilität auf der Basis des Betriebsergebnisses)

- ✻ **The ranking on page five is very interesting. It shows that Cern Corp. has moved up to fourth place, overtaking both us and our main competitor in the European market.**
  (ranking – Rangordnung / move up to – vorstoßen auf / overtake – überholen / main competitor – Hauptkonkurrent)

- ✻ **From the next chart it is quite clear that ATB will continue to head the list by a wide margin.**
  (quite – ganz / continue to head the list – weiterhin an erster Stelle liegen / by a wide margin – mit großem Abstand)

- ✻ **The next table is a projection for the next five years – and it raises an interesting point: although the division is expected to continue to rank first in terms of sales, it will no longer be number one in cash flow.**
  (projection – Prognose / raise point – Frage aufwerfen / although – obwohl / division – Sparte, Geschäftsbereich / expect – erwarten / continue to rank first – weiterhin an erster Stelle rangieren)

MISCELLANEOUS

Sonstiges

* **On the vertical axis you can see the total amount of capital employed. The horizontal axis measures the return, i.e. profits expressed as a percentage of total capital employed.**
  (amount – Betrag, Summe / capital employed – eingesetztes [Gesamt-]Kapital / measure – messen / return – Rentabilität / i.e. – that is / express – ausdrücken / percentage – Prozentsatz)

* **Now look here, where the two lines intersect. This is the point where the joint venture begins to show a better return on investment than the licensing strategy.**
  (intersect – sich überschneiden / return on investment – [Gesamt]Kapitalrentabilität)

* **I've plotted the inventory levels in a diagram to emphasise my argument.**
  (plot in a diagram – in ein Diagramm eintragen / inventory level – Höhe I Wert des Lagerbestandes / emphasise – unterstreichen, betonen)

* **From year five on, the curve slopes steeply upwards.**
  (slope steeply upwards – sich steil nach oben neigen)

* **The interesting point about the curve is its slope. It's very steep in periods one to five but then begins to level off and goes into a gentle decline after period ten.**
  (slope – Neigung, Steigung / level off – sich abflachen / go – übergehen / gentle decline – sanfter Rückgang)

* **As you can see from the broken line, in period two (1980 to 1985) overheads settled down at around 13 per cent of sales.**
  (broken line – strichlierte Linie / overheads – Gemeinkosten / settle down – sich einpendeln / around – rund)

* **The hatched area between the two curves requires further explanation.**
  (hatched – schraffiert / require – erfordern / further – weiter / explanation – Erklärung)

* **What does the shaded segment stand for?**
(shaded – getönt, dunkel, schraffiert)

* **The dotted line stands for sales, the solid line for operating expenses.**
(dotted line – punktierte Linie / solid line – durchgezogene Linie / operating expenses – betrieblicher Aufwand)

* **Now, let's take a closer look at the top-most ray emanating from the origin. It represents production process A.**
(take a closer look at sthg. – sich etwas genauer anschauen / top-most – oberst / ray – Strahl / emanate – ausgehen / origin – Ursprung)

* **Let's examine the price index on page three and the volume indices on page five in greater detail.**
(examine – näher betrachten / volume index – Mengenindex)

* **Very briefly, the matrix here shows the performance of our products in terms of market growth (on the vertical axis) and relative market share (on the horizontal axis).**
(brief – kurz / performance – Abschneiden, Leistung / growth – Wachstum / market share – Marktanteil)

* **The power drills are down here in the cash cow quadrant. But here in the top right-hand quadrant, we have our lawn-mowers with a negligible share of a rapidly expanding market segment.**
(power drill – Bohrmaschine / cash cow – Cashcow, Melkkuh / top right-hand – rechts oben / lawn-mower – Rasenmäher / negligible – geringfügig / share – Anteil)

MOVING THE PRESENTATION FORWARD
Überleitung zum nächsten Punkt der Präsentation

* **Right, ladies and gentlemen, those were the symptoms. Let's now move on to an examination of possible underlying causes.**
  (move on to – weitermachen mit; übergehen zu / examination – Analyse / possible – möglich / underlying – zugrundeliegend / cause – Ursache)

* **The second aspect that has to be considered is taxes.**
  (consider – untersuchen; näher betrachten / tax – Steuer)

* **This is the overall picture. Let's now consider the details.**
  (overall picture – Gesamtbild, Überblick)

* **Allow me to digress for a few minutes.**
  (digress – vom Thema abschweifen)

* **Let me get back to my main argument.**
  (main – Haupt…)

CLOSING THE PRESENTATION
Abschluß der Präsentation

* **This brings me to the final part of my presentation here this morning.**
  (final part – Schlußteil)

* **Let me summarise the chief points I've made.**
  (summarise – zusammenfassen / chief point – wichtigste Aussage)

* **Let me now draw the various threads of my argument together.**
  (Lassen Sie mich nun die verschiedenen Argumentationslinien zusammenführen.)

* **In conclusion, I'd like to remind you that analysis is an important step, but what really counts is action. In other words, we've got to tackle the underlying problems.**

(in conclusion – zum Abschluß / remind – [daran] erinnern / important – wichtig / step – Schritt / count – zählen / action – Taten / tackle – angehen, anpacken / underlying problems – Probleme, die dahinterstehen)

* **With hindsight it seems clear that the decision to acquire a stake in a small American distributor was wrong. The question now is how to minimise the losses.**
(with hindsight – im nachhinein / seem – scheinen / decision – Entscheidung / acquire – erwerben / stake – Beteiligung / distributor – Großhändler, Vertriebsberechtigter / question – Frage / loss – Verlust)

* **I've presented you with the facts. Now I'll leave it to you to draw the relevant conclusions from them.**
(leave – überlassen / draw – ziehen, ableiten / conclusion – Schlußfolgerung)

PRODUCT PRESENTATIONS

Produktpräsentationen

INTRODUCTION

Einleitung

* **Ladies and gentlemen, I'm pleased to present our new range of humidifiers.**
(be pleased – sich freuen / present – vorstellen, präsentieren / range – Sortiment / humidifier – Luftbefeuchter)

* **Ladies and gentlemen, thank you for giving me the opportunity to present our latest training package for salesmen.**
(opportunity – Gelegenheit / latest – neuest / training package – Ausbildungsprogramm / salesman – Verkäufer, Reisender)

* **I'm sure you will find our new range of skin care products interesting.**
(skin care – Hautpflege)

* **I'm Frank Brinner of Goller plc and I'm here today to demonstrate and explain our new range of copiers.**
(plc – public limited company I [brit.] etwa: Aktiengesellschaft / demonstrate – vorführen / explain – erklären)

* **Ladies and gentlemen, my company has come up with a radically new solution to your filing problems. Let me explain how the new ROMFI-system can assist you in reducing costs and improving efficiency.**
(come up with sthg. – sich etwas einfallen lassen / solution – Lösung / filing – Ablage, Registratur / assist – helfen / improve – verbessern)

* **My company has just introduced a new range of application programs for materials handling. I'd like to show you what the new programs can do for you.**
(introduce – einführen / application program – Anwendungsprogramm / materials handling – innerbetrieblicher Transport)

* **You might be wondering what something called "Ideofix" and produced by a chemical company could have to offer to a financial service company.**
(wonder – sich fragen / offer – bieten, anbieten)

MATERIALS AND COMPOSITION

Materialien und Zusammensetzung

* **The casing consists of a new type of bonded material, which is very strong and very light.**
(casing – Gehäuse / consist of – bestehen aus / bonded material – Verbundmaterial)

* **The cream contains only natural ingredients.**
(cream – Creme / contain – enthalten / ingredient – Bestandteil, Inhaltsstoff)

* **None of the ingredients has been tested on animals.**
(Keiner der Inhaltsstoffe ist in Tierversuchen getestet worden.)

* **We use only the best raw materials available.**
(available – erhältlich, verfügbar)

* **It's made of high-quality materials.**

* **The synthetic rubber used in the product is extremely hard-wearing.**
(rubber – Gummi / hard-wearing – strapazierfähig)

* **Our products are all hand-made from fir harvested from sustainably managed forests.**
(fir – Kiefernholz / harvest – schlägern / sustainably managed – nachhaltig bewirtschaftet / forest – Wald)

PROPERTIES AND QUALITY

Eigenschaften und Qualität

* **It's resistant to abrasion.**
  (resistant to abrasion – abriebfest)

* **The watch is waterproof to a depth of 90 feet.**
  (watch – Uhr / waterproof – wasserdicht / depth – Wassertiefe / foot – Fuß [30,48 cm])

* **The main benefits of the measuring device are its accuracy and speed.**
  (main – Haupt... / benefit – Nutzen / measuring device – Meßvorrichtung / accuracy – Genauigkeit / speed – Geschwindigkeit)

* **The "Securior" safe will certainly live up to its name.**
  (Der Securior-Safe hält sicherlich, was sein Name verspricht.)

* **The material will not warp, even if exposed to very high temperatures.**
  (warp – sich werfen / even if – selbst wenn / expose – aussetzen)

* **The cloth irons well.**
  (Das Tuch läßt sich gut bügeln.)

* **The soap is lighter than water and will float.**
  (will float – schwimmt)

* **The product is carefully finished down to the minutest detail.**
  (... bis ins kleinste Detail sorgfältig ausgeführt.)

* **What you will particularly like about the machine is its reliability.**
  (particularly – besonders / reliability – Verläßlichkeit)

* **I'd like to draw your attention to the excellent workmanship of our products.**
  (draw attention to – Aufmerksamkeit lenken auf / workmanship - Verarbeitung)

* **It's state of the art all the way.**

(Es entspricht in jeder Hinsicht dem neuesten Stand der Technik.)

* **The ink-jet printer is fully compatible with all leading software.**
  (ink-jet printer – Tintenstrahldrucker / leading – führend)

* **The computer runs on a new type of long-life battery.**
  (run on – betrieben werden mit)

* **The chip will accelerate the performance of practically all popular software packages by up to five times.**
  (accelerate – beschleunigen / performance – Leistung / by up to five times – bis um das Fünffache)

* **To demonstrate how confident we are of the quality and reliability the new product carries a three-year warranty.**
  (be confident of – fest glauben an / carry sthg. – mit etwas ausgestattet sein / warranty – Garantie)

* **We sell only premium wines.**
  (premium – Spitzen…)

* **The machine can be assembled and put into operation in a matter of hours.**
  (assemble – zusammenbauen / put into operation – in Betrieb nehmen / in a matter of hours – innerhalb weniger Stunden)

HANDY SIZE AND FLEXIBILITY

Praktische Größe und Flexibilität

* **The machine fits easily into your brief-case.**
  (fit into – hineinpassen in / brief-case – Aktentasche)

* **It can be folded and does not take up much storage space in winter.**
  (fold – zusammenlegen / take up – brauchen / storage space – Raum zum Aufbewahren)

* **The new filing system is very economical of space.**
  (filing system – Ablagesystem / economical of space – raumsparend)

* **The height can be adjusted very easily.**
  (height – Höhe / adjust – verstellen)

* **It adjusts to any height.**
(Es läßt sich auf jede beliebige Höhe – d. h. stufenlos – einstellen.)

* **The vehicle can be fitted with an additional shock absorber.**
(vehicle – Fahrzeug / fit – ausstatten / additional – zusätzlich / shock absorber – Stoßdämpfer)

* **The device plugs into any standard wall socket.**
(Das Gerät kann an jeder normalen Steckdose angesteckt werden.)

* **Our system allows you to link up computer products from different manufacturers.**
(link up – miteinander verbinden / different – verschieden / manufacturer – Erzeuger, Produzent)

BENEFICIAL ENVIRONMENTAL CONSEQUENCES

Positive ökologische Auswirkungen

* **The device could reduce your electricity bill by as much as 15 per cent.**
(electricity bill – Stromrechnung / by as much as 15% – um ganze 15%)

* **Another advantage is that the container can easily be recycled.**
(advantage – Vorteil / container – Behälter, Verpackung)

* **The product is environmentally benign.**
(Das Produkt ist umweltfreundlich.)

* **The standard model is fitted with a catalytic converter.**
(be fitted with – ausgestattet sein mit / catalytic converter – Katalysator)

* **A special filter reduces emissions to below the mandatory standard.**
(mandatory – gesetzlich vorgeschrieben / standard – Grenzwert)

* **The plastic used in the bag is biodegradable.**
(biodegradable – biologisch abbaubar)

CUSTOMER ACCEPTANCE

Kundenakzeptanz

* **The new lotion will go down well with your younger customers.**
(lotion – Gesichtswasser / go down well with – gut ankommen bei / customer – Kunde)

* **Test-marketing has shown that the new drink is very popular with teenagers.**

* **Your customers will love it.**

* **I'm sure it will find a ready market.**
(... wird sich gut verkaufen.)

* **The new brand has established itself in the market in an incredibly short time.**
(brand – Marke, Markenartikel / establish oneself – sich etablieren / incredible – unglaublich)

* **Our newly developed sprinkler sells very well in Germany and Austria.**
(develop – entwickeln / sprinkler – Sprinkler, Rasensprenger / sell – sich verkaufen)

* **Although it has been on the market for only three months, the glue has built a strong franchise.**
(although – obwohl / glue – Klebstoff / build franchise – Gefolgschaft aufbauen; Kundenakzeptanz erreichen)

* **The article will help you to build volume.**
(build volume – Absatzmenge steigern; Umsatzvolumen ausbauen)

* **The new stylus will satisfy even your most discriminating customers.**
(stylus – Abspielnadel / satisfy – zufriedenstellen / even – selbst / discriminating – kritisch, wählerisch)

PRICE AND PERFORMANCE

Preis und Leistung

* **The product is excellent value for money.**
  (Das Produkt ist äußerst preiswert.)

* **It is not very expensive.**
  (expensive – teuer)

* **You won't find a better product at this price.**
  (won't – will not)

* **And don't forget the low price.**

* **The two new cameras are very reasonably priced.**
  (be reasonably priced – einen vernünftigen Preis haben)

* **It has an excellent price-performance ratio.**
  (performance – Leistung / ratio – Verhältnis)

PACKING

Verpackung

* **The opener comes in a superbly finished leather-case.**
  (opener – Flaschenöffner / come – geliefert werden / finish – ausführen / leather-case – Lederetui)

* **It's supplied in a reusable container.**
  (supply – liefern / reusable – wiederverwendbar / container – Behälter, Verpackung)

* **We've reduced packaging to what is absolutely necessary to protect the article. I think that might help you win points with the green consumer.**
  (packaging – Verpackung, Aufmachung / necessary – notwendig / protect – schützen / points – Gutpunkte / with – bei / consumer – Konsument)

MEASUREMENTS AND WEIGHTS

Abmessungen und Gewichte

* **The casing measures 6" by 4" by 2".**
  (... six by four by two inches. / Das Gehäuse mißt 6 mal 4 mal 2 Zoll. [1 Zoll = 2,54 cm])

* **It is less than three feet wide and one foot high.**
  (wide – breit)

* **The screen measures 60 cm across.**
  (Der Bildschirm ist 60 cm breit.)

* **The machine weighs slightly over 50 kilos.**
  (slightly over – etwas mehr als)

* **The pipes are 3.5 cm in diameter.**
  (Der Durchmesser der Röhren beträgt 3,5 cm.)

IMPROVEMENTS

Verbesserungen

* **This is a much improved version of our standard XTX model.**
  (much improved – stark verbessert)

* **We have added a number of new features.**
  (Wir haben das Gerät mit einer Reihe von neuen Leistungsmerkmalen ausgestattet.)

* **The new model is even more economical in consumption.**
  (even – noch; sogar noch / economical – wirtschaftlich, sparsam / consumption – Verbrauch)

* **The new model is even more user-friendly than the old one.**
  (user-friendly – benutzerfreundlich)

* **The new features make the new model even better value than the old one.**
  (make sthg. better value – etwas preiswerter machen)

* **We have miniaturised several components and thus reduced the weight by as much as 50 per cent compared with the old version.**
(miniaturise – miniaturisieren, verkleinern / several – einige / component – Bauteil, Bestandteil / thus – so / weight – Gewicht / by as much as 50% – um ganze 50% / compare – vergleichen)

* **We have succeeded in reducing fuel consumption by all of 30 per cent.**
(Es ist uns gelungen, den Treibstoffverbrauch um ganze 30% zu verringern.)

* **We have shrunk the size of the machine so that it can easily be mounted on a rail carriage.**
(shrink – verringern / size – Größe / mount – montieren, befestigen / rail carriage – Eisenbahnwaggon)

VARIETY

Vielfalt des Angebots

* **The unit comes in three different sizes: small, medium, and large.**
(come – zu haben sein; geliefert werden / different – verschieden)

* **The model can be supplied in four different colours.**
(supply – liefern / colour – Farbe)

* **The basic design is available in three different materials.**
(basic design – Grundmodell / be available – zu haben sein)

* **We stock also a note-book size version.**
(stock – führen / note-book size – Taschenformat)

* **We are planning to introduce a model in a slightly different shade.**
(introduce – einführen / shade – Farbton, Farbnuance)

SUITABILITY AND MODIFICATIONS

Eignung und Modifikationen

* **I think this model, the PRS2, would be the most suitable for the application you have in mind.**
  (suitable – geeignet / application – Anwendung, Verwendungszweck / have sthg. in mind – an etwas denken; etwas im Auge | Sinn haben)

* **We can alter our standard model to your specifications.**
  (alter – ändern / to your specifications – nach Ihren Angaben)

* **We have a basic version which can be customised to meet individual requirements.**
  (Wir haben eine Grundversion, die modifiziert werden kann, um den individuellen Kundenwünschen zu entsprechen.)

* **I think this is exactly what you need.**

* **I think the X23 will fit your bill.**
  (Ich glaube, das Modell X23 wird Ihren Vorstellungen entsprechen.)

COMPARISON WITH COMPETING PRODUCTS

Vergleich mit Konkurrenzprodukten

* **Our product cannot be beaten for quality.**
  (... ist unübertrefflich, was die Qualität betrifft.)

* **The new PX4 is certainly much better than anything on the market.**
  (certainly – sicherlich)

* **Our new pump is second to none.**
  (Unsere neue Pumpe braucht keinen Vergleich mit einem Konkurrenzprodukt zu scheuen.)

* **You won't find a better valve at this price.**
  (won't – will not / valve – Ventil)

* **Our competitors will have a lot of catching up to do before they can match our printer.**
(Die Konkurrenz wird sich sehr anstrengen müssen, bevor sie mit unserem Drucker gleichziehen kann.)

* **Our new correction fluid compares well with anything on the market.**
(correction fluid – Korrekturflüssigkeit / compare well – bei einem Vergleich gut abschneiden)

* **The machine is much faster than competing products.**
(fast – schnell / competing product – Konkurrenzprodukt)

* **In contrast to most competing models ours requires next to no maintenance.**
(in contrast – im Gegensatz / require – erfordern / next to no – fast keine / maintenance – Wartung, Wartungsarbeiten)

* **It's definitely the best recorder on the market.**
(definitely – ganz entschieden)

DEMONSTRATIONS AND ILLUSTRATIONS

Vorführungen und Illustrationen

* **Now I'd like to demonstrate the new machine.**
(demonstrate – vorführen)

* **This is how you can control the speed. You just have to turn this knob.**
(control – regeln / speed – Geschwindigkeit / turn – drehen / knob – Knopf)

* **The controls are over there on the other side of the machine.**
(control – Steuervorrichtung)

* **Here's a short video showing the machine in operation.**
(in operation – in Betrieb)

* **Let me show you a few slides to illustrate what I've said about the new product.**
(slide – Diapositiv)

* **If you take a look at the leaflet which we have distributed, you will immediately see what I mean by "flexibility".**
(leaflet – Handzettel / distribute – verteilen / immediately – sofort / mean by – verstehen unter)

* **I'll now show you a few slides of the new model to give you an idea of what it looks like on the factory floor.**
(give an idea – einen Eindruck vermitteln / factory floor – Fabrik, Produktionsbereich)

* **May I refer you to the brochure for further technical details.**
(Nähere technische Details sind bitte der Broschüre zu entnehmen.)

* **If you come over here I can show you a scale-model of the URU-34.**
(scale-model – maßstabgetreues Modell)

TRADE FAIRS

Messen

ABOUT FAIRS AND FAIR PREPARATIONS

Gespräche über Messen und Vorbereitungsarbeiten

* **A: We are thinking of participating in the London International Menswear Fair.**
(participate – teilnehmen / menswear – Herrenbekleidung)
B: When is it?
A: I think it's always held in mid-September.
(hold – abhalten)

* **You shouldn't leave it too late before you apply for your space requirements. They were sold out by June last year.**
(leave sthg. late – sich mit etwas Zeit lassen / apply for – anmelden / space requirements – Platzbedarf / sold out – ausverkauft)

* **It's a large event with about 450 exhibitors from all over the world.**
(event – Veranstaltung / exhibitor – Aussteller)

* **They claim in their brochure that the show attracted over 5,000 trade visitors last year.**
(claim – behaupten / show – Schau, Ausstellung / attract – anlocken / trade visitor – Firmenkunde)

* **A: Has your company ever participated in the Hanover Fair?**
B: No, we actually prefer smaller events. They're more suitable for the type of goods we handle.
(company – Firma, Gesellschaft / ever – jemals / prefer – vorziehen / suitable – geeignet / handle – führen)

* **We would need about 3,000 square metres of uninterrupted exhibition space in a central location in London.**
(square metre – Quadratmeter / uninterrupted – durchgehend; ohne Trennwände / exhibition space – Ausstellungsfläche / central location – zentrale Lage)

* **A: I phoned the Austrian Trade Representative in London and he said that the London Arena would be a suitable venue for our trade show. What do you say?**
(phone – anrufen / Trade Representative – Handelsdelegierter der Bundeswirtschaftskammer / venue – Veranstaltungsort / trade show – Fachausstellung, Fachmesse)
B: I think he's right. I know the place because we staged an exhibition there once.
(stage – veranstalten / exhibition – Ausstellung / once – einmal)

* **It's centrally located and easily accessible by road and rail.**
(centrally located – zentral gelegen / be easily accessible by road and rail – gute Straßen- und Bahnverbindungen haben)

* **A: What about parking facilities?**
(Wie steht's mit den Parkmöglichkeiten?)
B: That should be no problem. They must have around 600 parking-spaces on site and there's a car-park within two minutes' walking distance from the main hall.
(around – ungefähr / on site – auf dem Gelände / car-park – Garage, Parkhaus, Parkplatz / main hall – Haupthalle)

* **Their catering service is also very good.**
(catering – Catering; Angebot an Speisen und Getränken)

* **What is the total cost per square metre?**

* **We might get a subsidy from our local Chamber of Commerce towards the cost of participating in the fair.**
(subsidy – Subvention / chamber of commerce – Handelskammer / towards – zur teilweisen Abdeckung)

* **I don't have any particular wishes regarding location, except maybe that the stand shouldn't be in a remote corner.**
(particular – besondere / wishes regarding location – Platzwünsche / except – außer / remote corner – entlegene Ecke)

* **I've still got one prime location. Look here on this layout plan. It's next to the main entrance.**
(still – noch / prime location – Vorzugsplazierung / layout plan – Lageplan, Grundriß / main entrance – Haupteingang)

* **I think we'll opt for the shell stand. It's obviously less original than a designer-built stand but ever so much cheaper.**
(opt for – sich entscheiden für / shell stand – Einheitskoje / obviously – offensichtlich / ever so much cheaper – um so viel billiger)

* **A: Where is the Organisers' Office, please?**
(organisers – Messeveranstalter)
B: It's at the other end of the exhibition site. It's a ten minutes' walk. Alternatively, you could phone them on 5678.
(exhibition site – Ausstellungsgelände / alternatively – oder … auch / phone on 5678 – unter der Nummer 5678 anrufen)

* **We would need the address of a fair contractor. Do you know a reliable firm you could recommend?**
(fair contractor – Messebaufirma / reliable – verläßlich / recommend – empfehlen)

ON THE STAND

Am Messestand

CONVERSATIONS WITH OTHER STAFF MEMBERS

Gespräche mit anderen Mitarbeitern

* **Make sure that there are at least two people on the stand at all times.**
(make sure – sicherstellen / at least – zumindest)

* **Could you please keep an eye on the exhibits while I go for a cup of coffee?**
(keep an eye on sthg. – etwas im Auge behalten / exhibit – Ausstellungsgegenstand, Exponat / while – während)

* **Will you call the Cleaning Service and make sure that they get their work finished before the Fair opens, please.**
(call – anrufen / cleaning service – Reinigungsdienst / finish – beenden)

CONVERSATIONS WITH VISITORS

Gespräche mit Besuchern

* **Can I help you? You seem to be interested in our new lawn-mower.**
(seem – scheinen / lawn-mower – Rasenmäher)

* **The engineer who actually designed this machine will be back on the stand in about an hour. He will be pleased to answer any technical questions you might have. Could you come back at around three?**
(engineer – Ingenieur / design – konstruieren / about – ungefähr / be pleased – sich freuen / question – Frage / at around – zirka um)

* **I'm authorised to grant a special discount of ten per cent on all orders placed during the fair.**
(Ich bin ermächtigt, auf alle während der Messe erteilten Aufträge einen Sonderrabatt von zehn Prozent zu gewähren.)

* **I think the best model for the application you have in mind is this one over here, the GRT-23.**
(application – Anwendung / have sthg. in mind – an etwas denken; etwas im Auge | Sinn haben)

* **May I offer you a glass of orange juice? Or maybe something a little stronger?**
(offer – anbieten)

* **Sit down for a moment. Mr. Primer, our chief design engineer, will be available when he has finished his phone call.**
(chief design engineer – Chefkonstrukteur / be available – zur Verfügung stehen)

* **I saw the machine at the Bristol Engineering Show last year, but you seem to have added several new features.**
(seem – scheinen / add – zusätzlich ausstatten mit / several – einige / feature – Leistungsmerkmal)

* **If you come back at three one of our engineers will be giving a demonstration of this machine.**
(demonstration – Vorführung)

* **We are going to have a reception for our most important customers at the Plaza Hotel tomorrow evening. We would be delighted if you could come.**
(reception – Empfang / important – wichtig / customer – Kunde / be delighted – sich sehr freuen)

* **We are planning to hold a short seminar for our customers at the Convention Centre tomorrow from six to eight p.m..**
(hold – abhalten / convention centre – Konferenzzentrum / p.m. – am Abend)

* **Can I give you my business card? We shall be pleased to welcome you to our company if you should ever go to Vienna.**
(business card – Visitenkarte / ever – je, jemals)

* **If you give me your telephone number, I'll call you right after the fair and arrange for one of our sales engineers to visit you.**
(right after – gleich nach / arrange for – veranlassen, daß / sales engineer – Verkaufsingenieur)

* **We actually have a second stand on the ground floor in the video section. Ask for Mr. Gummer, he's the expert.**
(ground floor – Erdgeschoß / video section – Videoabteilung)

* **I'm sorry about the mistakes in the brochure. We should have had it translated by a local service.**
(Tut mir leid wegen der Fehler in der Broschüre. Wir hätten sie von einem Büro vor Ort übersetzen lassen sollen.)

CONVERSATIONS WITH FAIR CONTRACTORS AND WORKERS

Gespräche mit Messebaufirmen und -arbeitern

* **We need a floral contractor to spruce up the stand a bit. Could you recommend a reliable firm?**
(floral contractor – Florist / spruce up – herausputzen / recommend – empfehlen / reliable – verläßlich)

* **Could you please get the X-4 up to our stand on the second floor as soon as the goods lift has been repaired.**
(get up – hinauftransportieren / floor – Geschoß, Stock / goods lift – Warenaufzug)

* **The lights on our stand don't work. Could you do something about them right away?**
(work – funktionieren / do about – sich kümmern um / right away – sofort; gleich jetzt)

* **A fuse must have blown. Where's the fuse-box?**
(fuse – Sicherung / blow – durchbrennen / fuse-box – Sicherungskasten)

* **Is there a bottle-bank anywhere on the site?**
(bottle-bank – Glascontainer / site – [Messe-]Gelände)

* **Can you arrange for the stand to be dismantled and shipped to Toronto ? We have booked a place there at the InterFur. Here's the address.**
(Können Sie veranlassen, daß der Stand abgebaut und nach Toronto geschickt wird? ....)

* **Please make sure that the exhibits are carefully packed.**
(make sure – sicherstellen / careful – sorgfältig)

POST MORTEM

Nach der Messe – Analyse und Bewertung

* **A: How was the trade fair in Brighton?**
B: Not too bad. About two hundred trade visitors contacted us and we managed to book a fairly large number of orders.
(trade visitor – Firmenbesucher / manage – können / fairly – ziemlich / order – Auftrag)

* **Well, the Pump Makers' Exhibition in Hull was a complete flop. We distributed tons of promotional material but we didn't make a single sale.**
(distribute – verteilen / promotional material – Werbematerial / sale – Verkauf)

* **I haven't analysed the records yet, but from what I saw at the stand I'd say that participating was a good investment.**
(not ... yet – noch nicht / records – Aufzeichnungen / participate – teilnehmen)

* **I was against taking part right from the beginning, but nobody listened to me. Now we are about ATS250,000 out of pocket and haven't much to show for it.**
(take part – teilnehmen / right from the beginning – von allem Anfang an / listen to – hören auf / .... Nun haben wir rund 250 000 Schilling ausgegeben und können kaum Resultate vorweisen.)

* **The exhibition itself was O.K., but we had so much trouble getting the exhibits back to Austria. There was something wrong with the ATA carnet and Customs wanted us to pay the normal import duty.**
(trouble – Schwierigkeiten, Mühe / exhibit – Ausstellungsgegenstand / ATA carnet – Carnet ATA; Dokument für den Vormerkverkehr / Customs – Zollbehörde / import duty – Importzoll)

* **We shouldn't have taken part in the group display. If you want to attract visitors you really need a separate stand.**
(group display – Gemeinschaftsstand / attract – anziehen / separate – eigen)

* **We didn't book too many orders during the fair but the press did give us a good write-up, so I'm still optimistic about the follow-up business.**
(press gives sthg. a good write-up – etwas hat eine gute Presse / still – noch immer / follow-up business – Nachmessegeschäft)

CONTACTS WITH ADVERTISING AGENCIES

Kontakte mit Werbeagenturen

REACTIONS TO SUGGESTIONS AND CONCEPTS

Reaktionen auf Vorschläge und Konzepte

* **We are not satisfied with your suggestions for the new campaign.**
(satisfied – zufrieden / suggestion – Vorschlag)

* **The visual concept is good, but I think the slogan you suggested needs to be improved.**
(visual concept – Bildidee / suggest – vorschlagen / need – müssen / improve – verbessern)

* **I think you will have to come up with something more lively.**
(come up with sthg. – sich etwas einfallen lassen / lively – lebendig, lebhaft)

* **I'm not sure, but maybe our sales promotion efforts should have been supported by a series of TV spots.**
(sales promotion – Verkaufsförderung / effort – Bemühung / support – unterstützen / series – Reihe)

* **We are not at all satisfied with the results of your latest campaign.**
(not at all – überhaupt nicht)

* **No, that's too flashy. We want to project a more sedate image. Don't forget we are selling industrial equipment.**
(flashy – knallig, protzig / project – ausstrahlen / sedate – gesetzt / industrial equipment – Anlagegüter, Investitionsgüter)

* **I think you still don't understand what our company stands for.**
(still – noch immer / company – Gesellschaft, Firma)

* **No, that wouldn't do for the type of product we sell.**
  (do – gehen; geeignet sein)

* **I think the copy is much too long. People don't have time to read a whole page of text.**
  (copy – Werbetext / page – Seite)

* **Splendid! That's the idea.**
  (Großartig! Genau das brauchen wir.)

* **Yes, I particularly like the new slogan. Brilliant idea.**
  (particularly – besonders)

* **That's exactly what we need to reach our target group.**
  (reach – erreichen / target group – Zielgruppe)

* **That looks like an award winner.**
  (Das sieht nach einer Auszeichnung aus.)

* **It's hilarious. I hope the audience won't forget that it's an ad for our product.**
  (hilarious – zum Schreien lustig / audience – Publikum / won't – will not / ad – advertisement | Annonce, Werbung)

DISCUSSING ADVERTISING POLICIES – MEDIA SELECTION

Diskussion werbepolitischer Konzepte – Medienauswahl

* **We are probably not putting enough emphasis on TV spots.**
  (probably – wahrscheinlich / put emphasis on – Nachdruck legen auf / enough – genug, ausreichend)

* **I don't think that advertising on TV would be suitable for this product, quite apart from the fact that it's much too expensive.**
  (advertising on TV – Fernsehwerbung / suitable – geeignet / quite – ganz / apart from – abgesehen von / expensive – teuer)

* **No, this channel wouldn't have the necessary reach.**
  (reach – Reichweite)

* **So far we have advertised only in the trade press. But for some of the products we've added to our range the national press might be more suitable.**

(advertise – werben, annoncieren / trade press – Fachpresse / range – Produktpalette / national press – die großen Tageszeitungen und Zeitschriften mit landesweiter Verbreitung)

* **No, not in the tabloids. That would hurt our image.**
(tabloids – Boulevardpresse / hurt – schaden)

* **Why don't we try radio commercials for a change? They are much cheaper and easier to produce than TV spots. If you give us the O.K., we could be on the air in a week.**
(try – versuchen / commercial – Werbespot, Werbesendung / for a change – zur Abwechslung / cheap – billig / be on the air – auf Sendung sein)

* **We'll shift part of our advertising budget into direct marketing.**
(shift – umschichten / advertising budget – Werbebudget)

* **A: Would you be interested in organising a mail shot for us?**
(mail shot – Mailing, Direktwerbung)
B: We don't do mail shots ourselves. But we have a trade investment in a company which specialises in that sort of thing. They are very reliable. Shall I put you on to them?
(trade investment – Beteiligung / reliable – verläßlich / put sbdy. on to sbdy. – für jmdn. Kontakt mit jmdm. herstellen; jmdn. an jmdn. weiterreichen)

* **We need to change our promotional mix and put more emphasis on direct mail shots.**
(need – müssen / promotional mix – kommunikationspolitisches Mix)

* **Why don't we try a teaser campaign?**
(teaser – Teaser, „Neckwerbung")

* **Let's start with the packaging. I think it will have to be redesigned. I don't like it any more. Looks too stolid.**
(packaging – Verpackung, Aufmachung / redesign – neu gestalten / stolid – fad, gesetzt)

* **Yes, I agree. You should develop a global advertising strategy.**
(agree – zustimmen, derselben Meinung sein / develop – entwickeln)

* **I'm against translating the copy. It should be recreated by a local copy-writer.**
(translate – übersetzen / recreate – neu kreieren / copy-writer – Werbetexter)

* **A: Don't you think that we need more information before we can decide on a new advertising strategy? We simply don't know enough about our target group.**
(decide on – sich entscheiden für / simply – einfach / target group – Zielgruppe)
B: Definitely, a new survey is an absolute must. The results of the old one are out of date. Also, if I remember correctly, it had a very low response rate.
(definitely – absolut richtig / survey – Erhebung, Studie / out of date – veraltet, überholt / remember – sich erinnern / response rate – Rücklaufquote; Prozentsatz der beantworteten Fragebögen)
A: Good. So we are agreed. Let's commission a new survey then and make sure that the questionnaires are designed very carefully.
(be agreed – einer Meinung sein; sich geeinigt haben / commission – in Auftrag geben / make sure – sicherstellen / questionnaire – Fragebogen / design – zusammenstellen, entwerfen / careful – sorgfältig)

TECHNICAL DETAILS, SCHEDULES AND DEADLINES

Technische Details, Zeitpläne und Termine

* **The deadline for the roughs is Monday.**
(deadline – letzter Termin / rough – Entwurf)

* **I know it will be tough to meet our deadline, but we have to be ready for the Christmas business.**
(tough – hart, schwierig / meet deadline – Termin einhalten / ready – bereit, fertig / business – Geschäft)

* **Why don't you let me have a look at the storyboard?**
(storyboard – Storyboard)

* **I mustn't forget to tell you: the meeting with the new account executive has been rescheduled for next Tuesday.**

(must not – nicht dürfen / meeting – Sitzung / account executive – Kontakter, Etatdirektor / reschedule for – verlegen auf)

* **Has the script already been submitted for approval?**
(script – Drehbuch / submit – vorlegen / approval – Billigung, Genehmigung)

* **The tape will be released to the radio stations a week from today.**
(tape – Band / release – zum Senden freigeben)

* **Can you let me have a sketch of the new poster?**
(sketch – Skizze / poster – Plakat)

* **My suggestion is to run the ad three times a week – Tuesdays, Thursdays and Fridays – for two months.**
(suggestion – Vorschlag / run ad – Annonce schalten / three times – dreimal)

TERMINATING AGREEMENT WITH AGENCY

Beendigung des Vertragsverhältnisses mit der Agentur

* **The latest campaign was a complete flop. So we have decided to put our account up for review.**
(decide – sich entschließen; beschließen / account – Account, [Werbe-]Etat / put account up for review – verschiedene Agenturen zu einer Wettbewerbspräsentation für einen Etat einladen)

* **I think we'd better part company. Our ideas of what the advertising for our firm should be like differ simply too much.**
(Ich glaube, das beste wäre, wenn wir uns trennen. ... . / differ – sich unterscheiden / simply – einfach)

* **Our agency has lost one of its best creative people. We are thinking of switching our account.**
(switch – anderweitig vergeben)

* **We are considering terminating the relationship with our agency.**
(consider – überlegen, erwägen / terminate – beenden / relationship – [Vertrags-]Verhältnis)

COMPLAINTS

Reklamationen

BUYER MAKES A COMPLAINT

Käufer beschwert sich | reklamiert

GENERAL | UNSPECIFIC COMPLAINTS

Allgemeine | Unbestimmte Reklamationen

* **A: I've got a complaint to make.**
(Ich habe eine Reklamation. | Ich muß mich beschweren.)
B: What is it about?
(Welche Sache betreffend? | Worum handelt es sich denn?)
A: It's about the brochures you printed for us.
(print – drucken)

* **A: I'm afraid I have a serious complaint to make.**
(I'm afraid – leider; ich furchte / serious – ernst, schwerwiegend)
B: I'm sorry to hear that. What's gone wrong?
(.... Was ist schiefgelaufen?)

*

A: I've got a complaint to make.
B: Oh, not again. What is it this time?
(this time – dieses Mal)

*

A: Listen, we are not satisfied with the way you handled our last order.
(listen – hören Sie mal / satisfied – zufrieden / way – Art und Weise / handle – erledigen, ausführen / order – Auftrag)
B: Sorry to hear that. What's the problem?

FAULTY OR DAMAGED GOODS

Mangelhafte oder beschädigte Ware

* **A: I have to complain about the pocket calculators you sent us last week.**
(complain about – sich beschweren über / pocket calculator – Taschenrechner)
B: What seems to be the trouble?
(Was ist denn das Problem?)
A: They are just not working. Not a single one.
(just – einfach / work – funktionieren / single one – einziger)

* **The last batch we received from you was faulty.**
(batch – Posten, Teilmenge / receive – erhalten / be faulty – Mängel aufweisen)

* **The goods arrived damaged.**
(Die Ware kam beschädigt an.)

* **The sugar content of the jam is way below what we had agreed. Here's the certificate of analysis by an independent agency.**
(sugar content – Zuckergehalt / jam – Marmelade / way below – weit unter / agree – sich einigen auf; vereinbaren / independent – unabhängig / agency – Stelle)

* **25 plates were found to be broken when we opened the case.**
(Wir stellten fest, daß 25 Teller zerbrochen waren, als wir die Kiste öffneten.)

* **The goods you sent us do not correspond with the sample we gave you. Our customers would never buy such poor-quality stuff.**
(correspond – übereinstimmen / sample – Muster / customer – Kunde / poor-quality – minderwertig / stuff – Zeug)

* **You sent us ten defective drive belts. That's not good enough!**
(defective – schadhaft / drive belt – Transmissionsriemen / .... So geht's wirklich nicht!)

* **Although your people have replaced several defective parts, the lathe is still not working properly.**
(although – obwohl / replace – ersetzen / several – einige / part – Teil / lathe – Drehbank / still – noch immer / proper – richtig, ordentlich)

* **The program you developed for us is full of bugs.**
(develop – entwickeln / bug – Fehler)

* **The report you sent us about our new customer is too superficial. We are very disappointed.**
(report – Bericht / superficial – oberflächlich / disappointed – enttäuscht)

WRONG GOODS

Falsche Ware

* **You don't seem to understand: you sent us the wrong goods. We didn't order any valves.**
(seem – scheinen / order – bestellen / valve – Ventil)

* **There's a serious problem. The case contained completely different goods from the ones we ordered.**
(serious – ernst / case – Kiste / contain – enthalten / different – andere)

* **You supplied a thicker material by mistake.**
(supply – liefern / by mistake – irrtümlicherweise)

* **You sent us DC5s instead of DC7s. It's a damn nuisance because we need them to complete a job for a very important customer.**
(instead of – anstatt / a damn nuisance – verdammt ärgerlich / complete – fertigstellen / job – Auftrag)

* **There seems to have been a mix-up. I ordered 26 of your heavy-duty RFC-I tyres and you sent me 62 of the much smaller RFC-Vs.**
(seem – scheinen / mix-up – Verwechslung / heavy-duty tyre – Hochleistungsreifen)

* **The containers are not the size and shape we ordered.**

(container – Gefäß, Behälter, Verpackung / size – Größe / shape – Form, Gestalt)

WRONG QUANTITY

Falsche Menge

* **Three typewriters are missing from the consignment.**
(typewriter – Schreibmaschine / be missing from – fehlen bei | aus / consignment – Sendung)

* **You haven't sent us all the goods we ordered.**

* **You've forgotten to include a manual.**
(manual – Handbuch)

* **I ordered 75 and you sent me 57. Are your shipping clerks dyslexic, or something?**
(shipping clerk – Expedient; Versandsachbearbeiter / dyslexic – legasthenisch / or something – oder was)

* **The last consignment has been shortshipped.**
(Die letzte Sendung wurde nicht vollständig geliefert.)

DELAYS IN DELIVERY

Lieferverzug

* **We haven't received the goods yet.**
(receive – erhalten / not ... yet – noch nicht)

* **Our order P2345/11/91 is already two weeks overdue. What's the matter?**
(overdue – überfällig / what's the matter? – was ist los?)

* **Can you tell me why the transparencies we ordered six weeks ago haven't arrived yet? I wish you'd keep the deadlines we have fixed.**
(transparency – Overheadfolie / arrive – ankommen / keep deadline – Termin | Frist einhalten)

* **The consignment we complained about last week did not arrive until today. We have no use for it any more.**
(did not arrive until today – kam erst heute an)

* **Our progress chaser has been unable to get an explanation as to why the ball bearings we ordered on May 2 have not been delivered yet. Could you look into the matter and report back by tomorrow?**
(Unserem Terminjäger ist es nicht gelungen eine Erklärung zu bekommen, warum die Kugellager, die wir am 2. Mai bestellten, noch nicht geliefert worden sind. Könnten Sie die Sache untersuchen und sich bis morgen wieder melden?)

* **We're wondering why there is such a long delay. Have the compressors left the factory yet?**
(Wir möchten gerne wissen, ... / delay – Verzug / leave – verlassen / factory – Fabrik / yet – schon)

* **You seem to have overlooked our order. We should have received the disk drives last week.**
(overlook – übersehen / disk drive – Platten-, Diskettenlaufwerk)

* **What's happened to our crank-shafts? We are still waiting for them. Yes, that's order No. 451/2/90.**
(happen to – geschehen mit / still – noch immer / crank-shaft – Kurbelwelle)

* **It's the third or fourth time that you've failed to meet the delivery date. The sales manager is furious.**
(the [third] time – das [dritte] Mal / fail to meet – nicht einhalten / furious – wütend)

PACKING
Verpackung

* **I have to complain about the really careless packing of the last consignment.**
(careless – schlampig; nicht sehr sorgfältig)

* **You've done it again. This time it's inadequate packing.**
(Sie können es nicht lassen! Diesmal ist es die unzureichende Verpackung.)

* **You did not secure the cartons with metal straps as we had suggested.**
(secure – verstärken / metal strap – Metallband / suggest – vorschlagen)

* **I'm surprised at the way in which you packed the machine.**
(surprised – überrascht / way – Art und Weise)

* **You should have used stronger cardboard boxes for such a heavy item.**
(cardboard – Pappe / box – Schachtel / item – Artikel)

* **Your packers apparently left out the padding and that's why the casing on the printer is cracked.**
(apparently – offenbar / leave out – weglassen, vergessen / padding – Füllmaterial / casing – Gehäuse / printer – Drucker / crack – bersten, springen)

* **The sacks were not strong enough. So some of them burst and the contents ran out.**
(enough – genug / burst – platzen / contents – Inhalt / run out – auslaufen)

* **The flaps on most of the cartons came unstuck. You must have used a poor-quality glue.**
(flap – Klappendeckel / come unstuck – aufgehen; sich lösen / poor-quality – minderwertig / glue – Klebstoff)

BUYER SUGGESTS PLAN OF ACTION

Käufer schlägt Regelung vor

* **Well, we have no use for the spanners you sent us. We can either return them at your expense or keep them until you have them collected.**
(have use for sthg. – etwas brauchen können / spanner – Schraubenschlüssel / either … or – entweder … oder / at sbdy.'s expense – auf jmds. Kosten / have sthg. collected – etwas abholen lassen)

* **We are returning the goods.**

* **The important thing is that you send us a replacement as soon as possible. We'll discuss the rest next week.**
(important – wichtig / replacement – Ersatzlieferung / as soon as possible – so bald wie möglich)

* **We must have the replacement by Tuesday at the latest. So you will have to send it by air – at your expense, of course.**
(by ... at the latest – bis spätestens / by air – als Luftfracht)

* **We would be prepared to keep the goods if you reduce the price by 15 per cent.**
(be prepared – bereit sein / keep – behalten / by – um)

* **We are willing to extend the delivery period by a week. But that's the limit. After that we would have to activate the penalty clause.**
(extend – verlängern / delivery period – Lieferfrist / penalty clause – Pönaleklausel)

BUYER MAKES THREATS

Käufer droht

* **If it happens again we'll simply have to look for another supplier.**
(happen – passieren / simple – einfach / look for – sich umsehen um / supplier – Lieferant)

* **This is no way to handle a first order! You will understand that we are no longer interested in doing business with you.**
(So kann man doch nicht mit einem Erstauftrag umgehen! .... / do business – Geschäfte tätigen)

* **I'm inclined to lodge a formal complaint with the Commercial Section of your Embassy.**
(be inclined – gute Lust haben / lodge – einbringen / commercial section – Handelsabteilung / embassy – Botschaft)

SELLER'S REACTION TO COMPLAINT, INVESTIGATION AND INSPECTION

Reaktion des Verkäufers auf Reklamation, Untersuchung und Inspektion

* **Well, that sounds serious. I'll send one of our service staff over first thing tomorrow morning.**
(sound – klingen / serious – ernst / staff – Personal / first thing – gleich)

* **I've come over to investigate your complaint personally.**
(come over – herüber [nach England] kommen / investigate – untersuchen)

* **Since you are such an important customer I jumped on the next plane. Here I am. Could I have a look at the defective home trainers?**
(Da Sie ein so wichtiger Kunde sind, nahm ich gleich das nächste Flugzeug .... / defective – schadhaft)

* **A: Can I inspect the consignment?**
(inspect – inspizieren / consignment – Sendung)
B: Yes, of course, it's in the warehouse by the factory gate.
(warehouse – Lagerhaus / factory gate – Fabrikstor)

* **A: Why don't you have a look yourself? The VDUs are over there.**
(VDU – visual display unit I Bildschirm; optische Anzeige)
B: You're absolutely right. They seem to have been banged about quite badly.
(.... Sie scheinen wirklich ziemlich unsanft behandelt worden zu sein.)

SELLER'S ADMISSION OF FAULT AND APOLOGIES

Verkäufer nimmt Schuld auf sich und entschuldigt sich

* **Sorry to hear that. Something obviously has gone wrong.**
(obviously – offensichtlich / go wrong – schiefgehen)

* **Your complaint is perfectly justified.**
(Ihre Reklamation ist absolut gerechtfertigt.)

* **We're very sorry for this delay. It won't happen again.**
(delay – Verzug, Verzögerung / won't – will not / happen – passieren, geschehen)

* **Yes, I think it was partly our fault.**
(partly – teilweise / fault - Schuld)

* **I do have to apologise. It seems that our shipping department is to blame for the scratches across the top of the desk.**
(Ich muß mich wirklich entschuldigen. .... / seem – scheinen / shipping department – Versandabteilung / to be to blame for sthg. – an etwas schuld sein / scratch – Kratzer / across – quer über / top – [Schreib-]Platte, Arbeitsplatte / desk – Schreibtisch)

* **Yes, it's our fault all right. But couldn't you waive the penalty?**
(Ja, es stimmt schon, daß es unsere Schuld ist. Aber könnten Sie nicht auf das Pönale verzichten?)

* **There has been a mistake at our end, I'm afraid. Let me explain what happened.**
(mistake – Fehler / at our end – bei uns hier / I'm afraid – leider / explain – erklären)

* **Yes, you were right. Our warehouse people are responsible for the delay.**
(be right – recht haben / warehouse – Lagerhaus, Lager / responsible – verantwortlich)

* **I do understand that you are angry.**
(Ich verstehe wirklich, daß Sie wütend sind.)

* **Sorry again. We'll make every effort to prevent similar mistakes in the future.**

(Nochmals Entschuldigung. .... / effort – Anstrengung, Mühe / prevent – verhindern / similar – ähnlich / future – Zukunft)

* **That was just not good enough. I'll have to have a word with the lads in the packing department.**
(Das war wirklich nicht in Ordnung. Ich werde mit den Burschen in der Versandabteilung ein ernstes Wort sprechen müssen.)

* **I must apologise. We really should have rung you up to tell you. But the lorry drivers are on strike so we can't get the goods to the airport.**
(apologise – sich entschuldigen / ring up – anrufen / lorry driver – Lastwagenfahrer / be on strike – streiken; im Ausstand sein)

SELLER SUGGESTS OR ANNOUNCES SETTLEMENT

Verkäufer schlägt Regelung vor oder kündigt eine an

* **Would it be acceptable if I sent somebody over to respray the consoles? In addition, we would offer you a five per cent reduction to compensate you for the trouble we have put you to.**
(respray – neu spritzen | lackieren / console – Konsole, Bedienungsplatz / in addition – zusätzlich / offer – anbieten / compensate – entschädigen / the trouble we have put you to – die Unannehmlichkeiten, die wir Ihnen bereitet haben)

* **We had a fire in the warehouse which destroyed most of our stock. We hope you don't mind if we send you only half the order next Monday. The balance would go out in two weeks' time.**
(warehouse – Lagerhaus / destroy – zerstören / stock – Lagerbestand / you don't mind – es macht Ihnen nichts aus / order – Auftrag / balance – Rest / go out – geliefert werden / in two weeks' time – in zwei Wochen)

* **What would you say to a 50 per cent price reduction if you agree to keep the unsuitable items?**
(agree – sich bereit erklären / keep – behalten / unsuitable – nicht geeignet / item – Artikel)

* **We are rushing out a new consignment today.**
(Wir beeilen uns und schicken Ihnen noch heute eine neue Lieferung.)

* **We are sending you a few extra units to make up for the inconvenience.**
(a few – ein paar / make up for – [jmdn.] entschädigen / inconvenience – Unannehmlichkeiten)

* **One of our customers has more of the components in question than he needs at the moment. I'll ask him to send you 50 right away so that you can continue production.**
(the components in question – die gegenständlichen Bauteile / right away – sofort / continue production – weiter produzieren)

* **Yes, we are willing to repair the machine free of charge, though, strictly speaking, the guarantee period has already expired.**
(free of charge – kostenlos / though – obwohl / strictly speaking – genaugenommen / expire – ablaufen)

* **Why don't you return the defective items carriage forward and we'll send you a credit note right away.**
(return – zurücksenden / defective – schadhaft / item – Artikel / carriage forward – unfrei / credit note – Gutschriftsanzeige)

* **The replacement should reach you by Friday at the latest.**
(replacement – Ersatzlieferung / reach sbdy. – bei jmdm. ankommen / by ... at the latest – bis spätestens ...)

BUYER REACTS TO SELLER'S SUGGESTIONS

Käufer reagiert auf Vorschläge des Verkäufers

* **Yes, that seems acceptable. But please make sure that it doesn't happen again.**
(seem – scheinen / make sure – sicherstellen / happen – passieren, geschehen)

* **No, we can't accept that. That's not good enough.**
(Wir können das nicht akzeptieren. Das ist nicht ausreichend.)

* **Well, I don't know. Ten per cent is not a very generous offer. It'll have to be at least 15.**
(generous – großzügig / at least – zumindest)

* **Well, I suppose I can accept that. Sounds reasonable.**
(suppose – glauben / sound – klingen / reasonable – angemessen, vernünftig)

SELLER DOES NOT ACCEPT COMPLAINT

Verkäufer weist Reklamation zurück

* **What was that? Deep scratches accross the top? I can't believe it.**
(scratch – Kratzer / across – quer über / top – Schreibplatte, Arbeitsplatte / believe – glauben)

* **We are surprised to hear that you are not satisfied with the last consignment we sent you. What's the matter?**
(surprised – überrascht / satisfied – zufrieden / consignment – Lieferung / what's the matter? – was ist los?)

* **The defect is quite clearly not due to faulty materials or workmanship. That's why it is not covered by our warranty.**
(quite – ganz / be due to – zurückzuführen sein auf / workmanship – Verarbeitung / cover – decken / warranty – Garantie)

* **We checked the material very carefully prior to shipment. Here's the inspection record.**
(careful – sorgfältig / prior to – vor / shipment – Versand / inspection record – Prüfprotokoll)

* **You don't seem to have followed our operating instructions carefully enough.**
(seem – scheinen / operating instructions – Bedienungsanleitung / enough – genug)

* **Well, we have been discussing your claim now for over two hours and I'm still not convinced that it is justified.**
(Nun, wir diskutieren Ihre Reklamation jetzt schon über zwei Stunden, und ich bin noch immer nicht überzeugt, daß sie gerechtfertigt ist.)

* **The inspection showed that your staff used the wrong kind of transparency for the copying job.**
(staff – Personal / kind – Art / transparency – Overheadfolie / job – Auftrag, Arbeit)

* **To be quite honest, I think you are making this complaint to get a reduction in price. It's really not justified.**
(quite – ganz / honest – ehrlich)

* **The goods seem to have been damaged in transit. Since they were sold ex works the damage can't well be our responsibility.**
(damage – beschädigen / in transit – während des Transportes / since – da / sell – verkaufen / ex works – ab Werk / responsibility – Verantwortung, Schuld)

* **We handled the case very carefully at our end. So it must be your or the carrier's fault.**
(handle – umgehen mit; behandeln / case – Kiste / at our end – bei uns hier / carrier – Frachtführer / fault – Schuld)

* **You seem to have forgotten to adjust the voltage before you switched on the machine.**
(adjust – umstellen / voltage – elektrische Spannung / switch on – einschalten)

* **There's no need to be worried. There is a second switch at the back of the machine.**
(Sie brauchen sich keine Sorgen zu machen. .... / switch – Schalter / back – Rückseite)

* **We can't understand the delay you're complaining about. The spare parts were dispatched by parcel post on March 23, and should have reached you long ago.**
(spare part – Ersatzteil / dispatch – versenden / by parcel post – als Postpaket)

SELLER'S OR BUYER'S SUGGESTIONS IF THERE IS NO AGREEMENT

Vorschläge seitens des Verkäufers oder Käufers im Falle der Nichteinigung

* **We don't seem to be able to agree on whose fault it is. So why don't we submit the whole thing to arbitration? I think there is something about this in the Contract of Sale anyway.**
(agree – sich einigen / submit sthg. to arbitration – etwas einem Schiedsgericht übergeben / contract of sale – Kaufvertrag / anyway – ohnehin)

* **If you really refuse to budge, I'll have to ask my lawyer what I should do. The amount of money involved is simply too large.**
(Wenn Sie sich wirklich weigern, auch nur ein kleines Zugeständnis zu machen, werde ich meinen Rechtsanwalt konsultieren müssen. Die Summe, um die es geht, ist einfach zu groß.)

Let's see if our respective lawyers can reach an agreement.
(respective – jeweilig / reach agreement – Einigung erzielen)

* **If you cannot come up with a better offer, I'm afraid we will have to place our orders elsewhere.**
(come up with sthg. – etwas auf den Tisch legen / be afraid – fürchten / place order – Auftrag vergeben / elsewhere – anderswo; an eine andere Firma)

* **If this is your last word, we shall have to hand the matter over to our solicitors.**
(hand over to – übergeben / matter – Sache, Angelegenheit / solicitors – Rechtsanwalt[-skanzlei])

* **We'll have to sue you for damages, I'm afraid.**
(sue for damages – auf Schadenersatz klagen)

* **I think we have no alternative left but to take you to court.**
(... es bleibt uns nichts anderes übrig, als Sie zu klagen.)

BUYER ACCEPTS RESPONSIBILITY

Käufer übernimmt Verantwortung

* **I have to admit that it was our fault.**
(admit – zugeben / fault – Schuld)

* **The foreman confessed that the workers dropped two of the heavy cases when unloading the consignment.**
(foreman – Vorarbeiter, Meister / confess – eingestehen / drop – fallen lassen / heavy – schwer / unload – abladen / consignment – Sendung)

* **I hope you don't bear us a grudge for blaming you first.**
(Ich hoffe, Sie tragen es uns nicht nach, daß wir Ihnen zuerst die Schuld gegeben haben.)

* **All I can do, apart from saying that I'm sorry, is promise a couple of large orders for next month. Though, to be quite honest, we would have placed them with you anyway.**
(apart from – abgesehen von / promise – versprechen / a couple of – ein paar / though – obwohl / place order with sbdy. – jmdm. einen Auftrag erteilen)

THE AUSTRIAN ECONOMY

Die österreichische Wirtschaft

ECONOMIC SITUATION

Konjunkturlage

* **A: What is the economic situation like in your country at the moment, Peter?**
(Wie ist die Konjunkturlage … ?)
B: Not too bad, actually. The economy is expanding at a satisfactory rate, unemployment is fairly low and so is inflation.
(satisfactory – zufriedenstellend / rate – Tempo / unemployment – Arbeitslosigkeit / fairly low – ziemlich niedrig)

* **I'd say that our economy is currently going through a difficult patch. If you look at gnp, it seems to have stopped growing for all practical purposes but prices are still rising.**
(currently – gegenwärtig / go through difficult patch – schwierige Zeit durchmachen / gnp – gross national product | Bruttonationalprodukt / seem – scheinen / grow – wachsen, steigen / for all practical purposes – praktisch / still – noch immer / rise – steigen)

* **I think it's fair enough to say that we've never been hit by a really serious slump in the post-war period.**
(Ich glaube, man kann mit Recht sagen, … . / hit – treffen / serious – ernst / slump – starke Rezession / post-war period – Nachkriegszeit)

* **You may not know this, but Austria has had a higher growth rate than most other OECD countries, of course with the exception of Japan.**
(growth rate – Wachstumsrate / OECD – Organisation for Economic Co-operation and Development / exception – Ausnahme)

* **I'm not entirely sure, but I think Austria ranks fairly high in terms of per-capita gnp, the usual measure of a country's standard of living.**
(entirely – ganz / rank – rangieren / in terms of – gemessen an / per capita – pro Kopf / usual – üblich / measure – Maßstab)

* **Some experts think that inflation will be in double figures next year.**
(in double figures – zweistellig)

* **The strange thing is that the unemployment rate has been moving up slowly but steadily in spite of satisfactory growth. It's still on the low side though by OECD standards.**
(strange – seltsam / steadily – stetig, unaufhaltsam / in spite of – trotz / on the low side – eher niedrig / though – doch / by OECD standards – gemessen an den OECD-Werten)

ECONOMIC SYSTEM AND INDUSTRIAL STRUCTURE

Wirtschaftssystem und Wirtschaftsstruktur

(see also "Politics")

* **A: What made you think that Austria has a centrally planned economy similar to the former East-bloc countries?**
(make – veranlassen / centrally planned economy – Zentralverwaltungswirtschaft / similar to – ähnlich)
B: How would you characterise your economic system, then?
A: Basically we have a free market economy, but one with a strong public sector. Also social security has always been very important in our system.
(basically – im Prinzip / social security – soziale Sicherheit / important – wichtig)

* **The Conservatives have come up with an interesting concept: their idea is to have a free market economy tempered with social and environmental considerations.**
(come up with sthg. – sich etwas einfallen lassen / temper – mildern / environmental – Umwelt... / considerations – Rücksichten)

* **The name of their programme is difficult to translate into English: "socially and environmentally oriented free market economy" is quite a mouthful, isn't it?**
(translate – übersetzen / quite – ziemlich / mouthful – langer, umständlicher | schwer auszusprechender Ausdruck / isn't it? – nicht wahr?)

* **In Austria, business firms are organised in Chambers of Commerce, workers in Chambers of Labour, and farmers in Chambers of Agriculture. What strikes most foreigners as odd is that membership in these organisations is compulsory.**
(chamber of commerce – Handelskammer / labour – Arbeiter [-schaft] / agriculture – Landwirtschaft / strike as odd – seltsam empfinden / foreigner – Ausländer / membership – Mitgliedschaft / compulsory – verpflichtend)

* **Parallel to this there are organisations with voluntary membership, such as the trade unions.**
(voluntary – freiwillig / trade union – Gewerkschaft)

❖

* **Actually, many people attribute the low rate of inflation to our system of industrial relations, the famous "social partnership", which has had a moderating influence on wage claims. Personally, I think they're right.**
(attribute – zuschreiben / industrial relations – Arbeitgeber-Arbeitnehmerbeziehungen / famous – berühmt / moderating – mäßigend, dämpfend / influence – Einfluß / wage claim – Lohnforderung / be right – recht haben)

* **A: What about your strike record?**
(Wie steht's mit eurer Streikbilanz?)
B: Well, there are hardly any strikes in Austria. Usually industrial disputes are settled by negotiations.
(hardly – kaum / industrial dispute – Arbeitskonflikt / settle – regeln, lösen / negotiations – Verhandlungen)

* **On the negative side, Austria probably has one of the most heavily regulated economies of all OECD countries. This is especially true in the field of business licensing.**
(probably – wahrscheinlich / heavy – stark / be true in – gelten für / field – Gebiet, Bereich / business licensing – etwa: Gewerberecht)

* **If we really join the EC, a lot of these regulations will have to go.**
(join – beitreten / EC – European Community | EG / a lot of – eine Menge; viele / regulation – [gesetzliche] Vorschrift / go – verschwinden; abgeschafft werden)

Talking about prices, quite a few are controlled in some way or other.
(quite a few – eine ganze Menge / control – regeln, lenken / in some way or other – auf irgendeine Art und Weise)

You won't be surprised to hear that our agriculture is heavily protected and subsidised. Whose isn't?
(won't – will not / surprise – überraschen / agriculture – Landwirtschaft / protect – schützen / subsidise – subventionieren)

PRIVATE SECTOR AND NATIONALISED INDUSTRIES

Privatwirtschaft und verstaatlichte Industrie

* **There aren't any really big privately-owned groups in Austria.**
(privately-owned – in Privatbesitz / group – Konzern)

* **You know, most Austrian companies are small or medium-sized.**
(company – Gesellschaft, Firma / medium-sized – mittelgroß)

* **In contrast to other countries, nationalised industries are still very important here. Austrian Industries, the holding company of Austria's nationalised industries, is easily the country's largest industrial group.**
(in contrast to – im Gegensatz zu / still – noch immer / important – wichtig / easily – bei weitem)

* **If you ask me, political meddling and management mistakes triggered a crisis in the nationalised industries in 1985. The group as a whole made a record loss of 14 billion Austrian schillings.**

(meddling – Einmischung / mistake – Fehler / trigger – auslösen / whole – ganz / loss – Verlust / billion – Milliarde)

* **Actually, the new management have done a good job refocussing our nationalised industries. The emphasis on basic materials like steel has gone. High-tech products with a higher percentage of value added are getting more attention now.**
(do a good job – erfolgreich sein bei / refocus – neu ausrichten / emphasis – Betonung / go – verschwinden / percentage – Prozentsatz / value added – Wertschöpfung / attention – Aufmerksamkeit)

* **Looking at the group as a whole, it's now actually back in the black, although some of its constituent companies are still running up losses.**
(back in the black – wieder in der Gewinnzone / although – obwohl / constituent companies – Konzerngesellschaften / run up losses – Verluste schreiben)

* **As you might expect, there has been some privatisation and some more is on the cards. But there won't be a sell-out and the state will still have the final say.**
(expect – erwarten / on the cards – im Bereich des Möglichen / sell-out – Ausverkauf / still – immer noch / the final say – das letzte Wort; ein entscheidendes Mitspracherecht)

* **Recently, several smaller companies have been privatised and some of the state-owned companies have gone into partnership with private-sector firms.**
(recently – in der letzten Zeit / several – mehrere, einige / state-owned – im Staatseigentum / go into partnership with sbdy. – sich mit jmdm. verbünden | zusammenschließen)

* **Well, you know, in many cases government has restricted private equity participation to 49 per cent or retained a golden share.**
(case – Fall / government – Regierung / restrict – beschränken / equity participation – Beteiligung / retain – zurückbehalten / golden share – goldene Aktie; Aktie, die Stimmenmehrheit sichert)

* **Actually, a lot of foreign companies have established subsidiaries in Austria. Many use them to serve the East European markets.**
(a lot of – eine Menge; viele / foreign – ausländisch / establish – errichten / subsidiary – Tochtergesellschaft / serve – bedienen, beliefern)

VARIOUS INDUSTRIES

Verschiedene Wirtschaftszweige

* **I don't know whether you know this, but we are completely dependent on imports for oil. I think we have to import 98 per cent of our requirements.**
(whether – ob / dependent on – abhängig von / requirements – Bedarf)

* **You probably did not realise that a lot of our electricity comes from hydro-electric power stations and to some extent from coal or oil-fired facilities.**
(probably – wahrscheinlich / hydro-electric power station – Wasserkraftwerk / to some extent – in einem gewissen Umfang / facility – Anlage)

* **As a matter of fact, we do have a nuclear power plant. It was completed in 1978 but never went on line.**
(as a matter of fact – eigentlich, genaugenommen / nuclear power plant – Atomkraftwerk, AKW / complete – fertigstellen / go on line – ans Netz gehen)

* **Dr. Kreisky – you may have heard of him – decided to hold a referendum on whether or not to start it up.**
(decide – beschließen / hold – abhalten / referendum – Volksabstimmung)

* **Surprisingly, the opponents to nuclear power came out ahead, if only by a small margin. Parliament then passed an act prohibiting the generation of electricity by nuclear fission.**
(surprisingly – überraschenderweise / opponent – Gegner / nuclear power – Kernenergie / come out ahead – gewinnen / if only – wenn auch nur / by a small margin – knapp / pass act – Gesetz verabschieden / prohibit – verbieten / generation – Erzeugung / nuclear fission – Kernspaltung)

* **Did you know that the basic oxygen process was developed in Austria? It's probably still the most important steel-making process. It has earned us a lot in licence fees as a matter of fact.**
(basic oxygen process – L.D.-Verfahren / develop – entwickeln / earn – einbringen, verdienen / fee – Gebühr)

* **We are also quite good at producing special metals.**
(quite – ganz)

* **Paper – as you might expect – is another important industry.**
(expect – erwarten)

INTERNATIONAL ECONOMIC RELATIONS

Internationale Wirtschaftsbeziehungen

* **Our economy is heavily dependent on foreign trade, both in goods and services.**
(dependent on – abhängig von / foreign trade – Außenhandel / both ... and ... – sowohl ... als auch ... / service – Dienstleistung)

* **Exports did very well last year, partly because our unit labour costs had risen less sharply than those of our competitors.**
(do well – gut abschneiden / partly – teilweise / unit labour costs – Lohnstückkosten / rise – steigen / competitor – Konkurrent)

* **Well, we've always had a fairly large trade deficit but have usually managed to offset it by selling enough services to foreigners.**
(fairly – ziemlich / trade deficit – Handelsbilanzdefizit / manage – es schaffen / offset – ausgleichen / enough – genug / foreigner – Ausländer)

* **Yes, tourism is of course very important. It brings in a lot of the foreign exchange we need to buy foreign goods.**
(foreign exchange – Devisen / foreign – ausländisch)

* **As a matter of fact, tourism in Austria contributes more to gnp than in any other country of the world, in percentage terms, of course.**
(contribute – beitragen / gnp – gross national product I Bruttonationalprodukt / in percentage terms – prozentmäßig)

* **We have no car industry worth speaking of and we import all of our cars, most of them from Germany and Italy.**
  (worth speaking of – nennenswert)

* **On the other hand, we are very strong in subcontracting to the German motor industry. As a matter of fact, our exports of components to that industry match our imports of German cars in value terms.**
  (on the other hand – andererseits / subcontracting – Zuliefergeschäft / motor industry – Autoindustrie / component – Bauteil, Bestandteil / match – entsprechen / in value terms – wertmäßig)

* **The composition of our exports has obviously changed a lot over the past ten years. Finished goods now account for a much higher percentage of the total.**
  (composition – Zusammensetzung / obviously – offensichtlich / change – sich ändern / a lot – sehr, stark / over the past ten years – während der letzten zehn Jahre / finished goods – Fertigwaren / account for – ausmachen / percentage – Prozentsatz / total – Gesamtsumme)

* **Did you know that timber is still one of our staple exports?**
  (timber – Holz / still – noch immer / staple export – Hauptausfuhrartikel)

* **Then we've got some star performers in highly specialised fields, like Plasser & Theurer, who are the world's main suppliers of railway-track equipment.**
  (star performer – Spitzenfirma / field – Gebiet, Sparte / main supplier – Hauptlieferant / railway-track equipment – Bahnbaumaschinen)

* **As you might imagine, a lot of our imports come from – and a lot of our exports go to – Germany.**
  (imagine [sthg.] – sich [etwas] vorstellen / a lot of – eine Menge)

* **Because of our geographical position we also do a lot of trade with East-European countries. That's why so many of the world's best countertrade specialists are based in Vienna.**
  (because of – wegen / do trade – Handel treiben / countertrade – Gegengeschäfte / be based in Vienna – [ihren] Sitz in Wien haben)

* **Foreign direct investment has increased considerably in the past few years, but we are still far behind comparable countries, like Switzerland, for instance.**
(increase – sich erhöhen, steigen / considerable – beträchtlich / be behind – liegen hinter / comparable – vergleichbar / for instance – zum Beispiel)

* **Well, actually more and more Austrian firms are setting up branches or subsidiaries abroad.**
(set up – errichten / branch – Zweigstelle / subsidiary – Tochtergesellschaft / abroad – im Ausland)

* **Of course, joint ventures are also very popular, especially in East-European countries.**

* A: **What about your currency?**
(Wie steht's mit Ihrer Währung?)
B: **Officially we are not a member of any currency bloc. In practice, the Austrian schilling is tied to the German mark.**
(member – Mitglied / be tied to – gebunden sein an)
A: **Does this mean that you pursue a hard currency policy?**
(mean – bedeuten, heißen / pursue – verfolgen)
B: **Yes, definitely. It has helped us to keep down inflation. And that has offset some of the negative impact on export prices.**
(definitely – ganz entschieden / offset – ausgleichen / impact – Auswirkungen)

* **I've got to admit that we do not spend all that much on aid to less developed countries. I'm ashamed even to mention the figure.**
(admit – zugeben / spend on – ausgeben für / all that much – allzuviel / aid – [Entwicklungs-]Hilfe / less developed country – Entwicklungsland / be ashamed – sich schämen / even – sogar / mention – erwähnen / figure – Zahl)

JOINING THE EC

Beitritt zur EG

* **The pros and cons of Austria joining the EC are the subject of a heated debate. The two big parties are in favour, while the Greens are against.**
  (the pros and cons – das Für und Wider / subject – Gegenstand / heated – hitzig / party – Partei / in favour – dafür)

* **There will be a referendum on the issue, just as there was in your country, wasn't there?**
  (referendum – Volksabstimmung / issue – Problem, Frage / just as – gerade so wie / wasn't there? – oder?)

* **If the polls are to be believed, more than 50 per cent of Austrians are in favour of joining.**
  (poll – Meinungsumfrage / believe – glauben)

* **The farmers are really worried because many of them are very small and they just would not survive EC competition.**
  (worried – besorgt / just – einfach / survive – überleben / competition – Konkurrenz)

* **Another important issue is transit. Austria's geographical position makes it necessary for a lot of the trade between Italy and the northern members of the EC to pass through Austria.**
  (necessary – notwendig / trade – Handel / member – Mitglied / pass through – gehen über)

* **Some people argue that as an EC member Austria would find it much more difficult to restrict the movement of lorries through its territory. Free movement of goods and all that, you know.**
  (argue – argumentieren / restrict – beschränken / movement through – Durchfahrt durch / lorry – LKW / free movement of goods – Freizügigkeit des Warenverkehrs / and all that – und so weiter)

* **You must agree that the lorries of course do a lot of harm to the environment and to the health of the people living along the motorways.**
  (Sie werden zugeben, ... / do a lot of harm – großen Schaden anrichten / environment – Umwelt / health – Gesundheit / motorway – Autobahn)

* **You mustn't forget that we already have a free trade agreement with the EC. Since the end of the transitional period in 1977, trade in industrial goods has been duty-free. Of course, there are exceptions.**
(must not – nicht dürfen / agreement – Abkommen / transitional period – Übergangszeit / duty-free – zollfrei / exception – Ausnahme)

* **I'm not sure whether the new EEA regime will really facilitate our entry into the EC.**
(whether – ob / EEA – European Economic Area | Europäischer Wirtschaftsraum / regime – Regelung / facilitate – erleichtern / entry into – Beitritt zu)

* **No, the EEA is not a customs union, but it adds the free movement of capital, services and labour to the existing agreement between EFTA and the EC.**
(customs union – Zollunion / add – hinzufügen / free movement of capital – Freizügigkeit des Kapitalverkehrs / labour – Arbeitskräfte / EFTA – European Free Trade Association | Europäische Freihandels-Assoziation)

FINANCIAL MARKETS

Finanzmärkte

* **Unfortunately, our banking system is pretty fragmented. We've got too many banks with too many branches. There are bound to be several mergers before we enter the EC.**
(unfortunately – leider / pretty – ziemlich / fragmented – zersplittert / branch – Filiale / there are bound to be ... – es muß zwangsläufig ... geben / several – einige / merger – Fusion / enter – beitreten; eintreten in)

* **The Vienna Stock Exchange is tiny by international standards, although it has expanded dramatically in the past five years.**
(stock exchange – Wertpapierbörse / tiny – winzig / by – gemessen an / although – obwohl / in the past five years – in den letzten fünf Jahren)

* **Austrian companies are fairly small and tend to rely on bank finance.**
(fairly – ziemlich / tend – tendieren; dazu neigen / rely on – sich stützen auf)

* **It's a good thing that our companies are now putting more emphasis on equity finance. As a result, a couple of interesting firms have gone public.**
(put emphasis on – Nachdruck legen auf / equity finance – Eigenkapitalfinanzierung / a couple of – ein paar / go public – an die Börse gehen)

* **A: I assume that Vienna is the financial centre of Austria.**
(assume – annehmen)
B: Yes, all the big banks are based there and so is, of course, the Vienna Stock Exchange and the new futures and options exchange.
(be based – [ihren] Sitz haben / futures and options exchange – Termin- und Optionenbörse)

ECONOMIC AND SOCIAL POLICIES

Wirtschafts- und Sozialpolitik

* **Currently, our government is trying to reduce the budget deficit to around 3.5 per cent of gdp both by increasing taxes and cutting expenditure. The same old story.**
(currently – zum gegenwärtigen Zeitpunkt / government – Regierung / try – versuchen / around – ungefähr / gdp – gross domestic product | Bruttoinlandsprodukt / both ... and ... – sowohl ... als auch ... / increase – erhöhen / tax – Steuer / cut – senken / expenditure – Ausgabe, Ausgaben / story – Geschichte)

* **Can't imagine that the policy will really work.**
(imagine [sthg.] – sich [etwas] vorstellen / work – funktionieren)

* **Our national debt is around one trillion Austrian schillings, that's equivalent to about 50 billion British pounds or 100 billion US dollars.**
(national debt – Staatsschuld / trillion – Billion, 10^{12} / that's equivalent to – das entspricht einem Gegenwert von; das sind umgerechnet / about – zirka / billion – Milliarde, 10^{9})

* **As a matter of fact, the official budget deficit is not too high, although, like in most other countries, there is a lot of off-budget financing.**
(although – obwohl / a lof of – eine Menge / off-budget – außerbudgetär)

* **I think the government should take reflationary measures.**
(reflationary measures – konjunkturbelebende Maßnahmen)

* **What really worries me is that a large chunk of government expenditure goes on public-sector wages, subsidies to the social security system, and the debt service. Only a small portion is still discretionary.**
(worry – Sorgen machen / chunk – Brocken / go on – entfallen auf / public – öffentlich / wages – Löhne & Gehälter / subsidy – Subvention / social security – soziale Sicherheit / debt service – Schuldendienst / portion – Teil / still – noch / discretionary – frei disponierbar)

* **We have an incredibly large number of civil servants.**
(incredible – unglaublich / number – Anzahl / civil servant – Staatsbeamter, Bundesbeamter)

* **The present government is certainly not prepared to fight unemployment at all costs. You can imagine that the trade unions are not too happy about this.**
(present – jetzig, gegenwärtig / certainly – sicherlich / prepared – bereit / fight – bekämpfen / at all costs – um jeden Preis / trade union – Gewerkschaft)

* **As everywhere, public opinion and the government have moved to the right.**
(public opinion – öffentliche Meinung / move – schwenken)

* **One hotly debated issue is unemployment benefits. Most people seem to think that the system encourages "scroungers".**
(issue – Problem / unemployment benefits – Arbeitslosenunterstützung / seem – scheinen / encourage – begünstigen, ermutigen / scrounger – Schmarotzer)

* **Our monetary policy shadows what the Germans do. For instance, when the German central bank pushes up interest rates we usually follow suit.**
(monetary policy – Geld- und Währungspolitik / shadow – sich eng halten an / for instance – zum Beispiel / push up – erhöhen / interest rate – Zinssatz / follow suit – nachziehen)

* **Only lately have we become a bit more independent, mainly because our inflation rate is lower at the moment.**
(lately – in der letzten Zeit / independent – unabhängig / mainly – hauptsächlich)

TAXES

Steuern

* **Taxes are much too high in my country, and there are too many of them.**
(tax – Steuer, Abgabe, Gebühr)

* **Of course, we've got a progressive income tax. The top tax rate is 50 per cent . It used to be 62 per cent. But there was a major tax reform a couple of years ago. They got rid of a lot of the exceptions and reduced the rates.**
(top tax rate – Spitzensteuersatz / used to be – war früher einmal / major tax reform – größere Steuerreform / a couple of – ein paar / get rid of – streichen / a lot of – viele / exception – Ausnahmeregelung / rate – [Steuer-]Satz)

* **Moreover, our tax brackets are not linked to the inflation rate. This means there are hidden tax increases every year.**
(Überdies sind unsere Progressionsstufen nicht an die Inflationsrate gebunden. Das heißt, daß es jedes Jahr versteckte Steuererhöhungen gibt.)

* **As for company profits, we used to have a mitigated form of double taxation. But they changed this a couple of years ago. Dividends and retained earnings now attract approximately the same tax rate.**
(Was die Gewinne von Gesellschaften betrifft, so hatten wir früher eine gemilderte Form der Doppelbesteuerung. .... / change – ändern / retained earnings – nichtausgeschüttete Gewinne;

thesaurierte Gewinne / attract – unterliegen / approximately – ungefähr)

* **Our corporation tax system is different from what you have in Britain, although it also avoids the double taxation of dividends.**
(corporation tax – Körperschaftsteuer / although – obwohl / avoid – vermeiden)

* **Our VAT is a bit on the high side: the standard rate is 20 per cent and there is a so-called "luxury tax", e.g. on motor cars.**
(VAT – value-added tax | Mehrwertsteuer / a bit on the high side – eher hoch / standard rate – Normalsteuersatz / e.g. – for example | zum Beispiel)

* **Our VAT rates will have to be adjusted before or when we enter the EC. That would be part of a general harmonisation exercise, which would affect many other fields as well.**
(adjust – anpassen, ändern / enter – beitreten; eintreten in / EC – European Community | Europäische Gemeinschaft | EG / harmonisation exercise – Harmonisierungsprogramm / affect – betreffen / field – Gebiet, Bereich / as well – auch)

* **We have a large public sector in Austria. So it's not surprising that our taxes should be fairly high.**
(.... Daher ist es nicht überraschend, daß unsere Steuern ziemlich hoch sind.)

ENVIRONMENTAL MATTERS

Umweltaspekte

ENVIRONMENTAL REGULATIONS

Umweltvorschriften

* **A: What are environmental regulations like in your country?**
  (Wie sind die Umweltvorschriften in Ihrem Land?)
  B: Well, actually I think they are a lot tougher than here in Britain.
  (a lot – viel / tough – streng)

* **We'll simply have to resign ourselves to tougher environmental standards.**
  (simple – einfach / resign oneself to – sich abfinden mit / standard – Norm, Grenzwert)

* **We decided to add a specialist on environmental law to our legal department. You simply need somebody to monitor the new developments in this field.**
  (decide – sich entschließen / add – zusätzlich einstellen / environmental law – Umweltrecht / legal department – Rechtsabteilung / monitor – überwachen, verfolgen / development – Entwicklung / field – Gebiet)

* **It cost us ATS20 million to meet the stricter emission standards. But we developed most of the equipment in-house and this has given us a lead in filter technology.**
  (ATS – Austrian schilling[s] / meet standard – Norm erfüllen; Grenzwert einhalten / develop – entwickeln / equipment – Geräte, Ausrüstung / in-house – firmenintern; in der eigenen Firma / lead – Vorsprung)

* **Under the new Clean Air Act we have had to install filters in all our production facilities. It has cost a bomb.**
  (under – aufgrund, gemäß / clean air act – Luftreinhaltegesetz / production facility – Produktionsstätte / bomb – Menge Geld)

* **I think you need somebody working closely with the design and manufacturing departments to look after the environmental aspects of the operation.**
(work closely with – eng zusammenarbeiten mit / design department – Konstruktionsabteilung / manufacturing department – Produktionsabteilung / look after – sich kümmern um / operation – Betrieb, Projekt)

* **We are considering transferring our manufacturing activities to Taiwan, where there are fewer environmental regulations.**
(consider – denken an; erwägen / transfer – verlegen / manufacture – fertigen, produzieren)

* **Doing business is no fun anymore. You need a permit for this and a permit for that. Government and citizens' groups are constantly breathing down your neck.**
(business – Geschäfte / no fun anymore – kein Spaß mehr / permit – Genehmigung / government – Regierung / citizens' group – Bürgerinitiative / breathe down sbdy.'s neck – jmdm. auf die Zehen steigen)

* **As far as I know, the new law will require an environmental impact assessment for all major projects.**
(require – verlangen, fordern / environmental impact assessment – Umweltverträglichkeitsprüfung / major – größer)

* **We have come to the conclusion that installing filters and scrubbers at the end of each pipe or smoke-stack is the wrong approach.**
(conclusion – Schluß, Schlußfolgerung / scrubber – Naßabscheider / pipe – Röhre, Leitung / smoke-stack – Fabriksschlot / approach – Methode, Vorgangsweise, Ansatz)

* **I think a much better idea would be to redesign the whole production process. This will not only cut emissions but may save raw materials and labour.**
(redesign – neu gestalten; neu konstruieren / cut – senken / save – einsparen / labour – Arbeitskräfte)

* **You know what the real problem is? The lack of uniformity in environmental legislation. Take Switzerland, for instance: it has outlawed metal containers, which are perfectly legal in most other countries.**
(lack – Fehlen, Mangel / uniformity – Einheitlichkeit / legislation – Gesetzgebung / for instance – zum Beispiel / outlaw – verbieten / container – Gefäß, Behälter, Verpackung)

* **We commissioned one of these new environmental consulting firms to carry out an environmental audit. It was a real eye-opener.**
(commission – beauftragen / consulting firm – Beratungsfirma / carry out – erstellen, durchführen / environmental audit – Umwelt-Audit, Umweltbilanz; erweiterte Wirtschaftlichkeitsrechnung)

* **A: What is your company doing for the environment?**
B: Not much, I'm afraid. Our management haven't really woken up to the fact that doing nothing may help reduce costs in the short term but is probably bad business in the long run.
(I'm afraid – leider / wake up to sthg. – etwas kapieren / in the short term – auf kurze Sicht / probably – wahrscheinlich / in the long run – auf lange Sicht)

WASTE

Abfall

* **We are quite proud of the fact that we now recycle close to 50 per cent of the solid waste generated in our plants.**
(quite – ziemlich / proud – stolz / recycle – wiederverwerten / close to – knapp / solid waste – feste Abfallstoffe / be generated – anfallen / plant – Werk, Anlage)

* **It's a shame that so much of our waste ends up in an incinerator. A lot of it could be recycled, I'm sure.**
(shame – Schande / end up – schließlich kommen / incinerator – [Müll-]Verbrennungsanlage / a lot of – ein Menge; viel)

* **We have been very careful with our liquid wastes since leakage from a storage tank contaminated the ground water and we ended up having to pay a heavy fine.**

(careful – vorsichtig / liquid wastes – flüssige Abfallstoffe / leakage – ausgelaufene Flüssigkeit / storage tank – Behälter / contaminate – verseuchen / end up doing sthg. – schließlich etwas machen / heavy fine – hohe Strafe; hohe Strafgebühr)

* **One of our engineers came up with the idea of capturing the waste heat from our kilns for heating purposes. Clever! Cut our fuel bill by more than 40 per cent and paid for itself within three years.**
(come up with idea – Idee haben / capture – auffangen, nutzen / waste heat – Abwärme / kiln – Brennofen / for heating purposes – für Heizzwecke / clever – brillant, schlau / cut – senken / fuel bill – Brennmaterialrechnung, -kosten / it pays for itself – es amortisiert sich)

* **Just imagine, Green Peace came along and plugged up a pipe discharging toxic effluents into a small river. It was all on TV and knocked our image sideways.**
(Stellen Sie sich das nur vor, ... / plug up – zustopfen / pipe – Rohr / discharge – einleiten / toxic effluents – giftige Abwässer / river – Fluß / knock sideways – ramponieren; Schlag versetzen)

* **We had to act really fast, because the local authorities threatened to withdraw our business licence if we didn't stop discharging untreated effluents into the local river.**
(Wir mußten wirklich schnell reagieren, weil die Lokalbehörde drohte, uns die Konzession zu entziehen, wenn wir nicht das Einleiten unbehandelter Abwässer in den örtlichen Fluß einstellten.)

* **Unfortunately our new waste-water treatment facility was very expensive.**
(Leider war unsere neue Kläranlage sehr teuer.)

* **We are lucky because we have a small landfill of our own where we can dump most of our solid waste. Only the small amount of hazardous waste we produce goes to a special reprocessing facility.**
(be lucky – Glück haben / landfill – Deponie / of one's own – eigen / dump – deponieren, ablagern / hazardous waste – gefährliche Abfallstoffe / reprocessing facility – Wiederaufbereitungsanlage)

* **We used to export most of our toxic waste, but under the new regulations this is no longer possible.**
(we used to export – früher einmal exportierten wir / toxic waste – Giftmüll / under – aufgrund)

* **We are looking into the possibility of using a deposit scheme for our containers. I think it would be good for our image.**
(look into sthg. – etwas überprüfen / possibility – Möglichkeit / deposit scheme – Pfandsystem / container – Behälter, Verpackung, Gefäß)

PROMOTIONAL ASPECTS
Kommunikationspolitische Aspekte

* **Our new advertising manager revamped our promotional activities to increase their appeal to the green consumer.**
(advertising manager – Werbeleiter / revamp – völlig neu gestalten / promotional activities – kommunikationspolitische Aktivitäten / increase – erhöhen / appeal – Attraktivität)

* **One of his ideas was that we should sponsor an environmental exhibition next year.**
(exhibition – Ausstellung)

* **We got the World Wildlife Fund to endorse some of our products.**
(get sbdy. to do sthg. – jmdn. dazu bringen, etwas zu tun / endorse – unterstützen)

* **The consultant suggested that we redesign our packages to enhance their appeal to the environmentally sensitive segment of our customers.**
(consultant – Konsulent, Berater / suggest – vorschlagen / redesign – neu gestalten / package – Verpackung / enhance – erhöhen, verstärken / sensitive – bewußt, sensibel / customer – Kunde)

* **A: We publish an annual report on our environmental activities as part of our Social Audit.**
(publish – veröffentlichen / annual report – Jahresbericht / social audit – Sozialbilanz)
B: What do you put in there?
A: Well, for instance we show the percentage of paper which is

recycled, the value of services supplied to firms producing pollution-control equipment, the percentage of employees coming to work by bus, the percentage coming in car pools, and things like that.
(for instance – zum Beispiel / percentage – Prozentsatz / value – Wert / supply – erbringen / pollution-control equipment – Umweltschutztechnologie, -geräte / employee – Arbeitnehmer / car pool – Fahrgemeinschaft)

* **In the end, we called in an environmental consultant to help us sort out our environmental problems. A lot of what he recommended was just public relations, but he did have some useful ideas as well.**
(in the end – schließlich / call in – beiziehen / sort out – lösen, regeln / recommend – empfehlen / just – nur, lediglich / useful – sinnvoll, nützlich / as well – auch)

PRODUCTS

Produkte

* **Last year we introduced a line of phosphate-free detergents to the market. They were a success because they attracted a lot of new customers and we can sell them at premium prices.**
(introduce – einführen / line – Produktlinie / detergent – Waschmittel / success – Erfolg / attract – anziehen / a lot of – eine Menge / premium price – hoher Preis; Hochpreis)

* **We stopped selling CFC aerosol cans two years ago.**
(CFC – Chlorofluorcarbon | FCKW | Fluorchlorkohlenwasserstoff / aerosol can – Sprühdose)

* **To begin with, we developed a quiet electric lawn-mower for the German market. It was awarded the Blue Angel eco-label.**
(to begin with – als erstes / develop – entwickeln / quiet – leise, Flüster... / lawn-mower – Rasenmäher / be awarded sthg. – etwas verliehen bekommen / eco-label – Umweltgütesiegel; ökologisch orientierte Warenauszeichnung)

* **Tell me more about your eco-labelling schemes.**
(scheme – Programm)

* **You won't believe it, but we are thinking of diversifying and buying into a health-food chain.**
(won't – will not / believe – glauben / buy into – Beteiligung erwerben an / health food – Vollwertnahrung / chain – Kette)

* **My company has started importing green products from Germany. They are selling very well, according to our Sales Department.**
(sell – sich verkaufen / according to – nach Angaben / sales department – Verkaufsabteilung)

* **We obtain some of the food for our works canteen from an organic farmer. Actually, it's a worker co-operative.**
(obtain – beziehen / food – Lebensmittel / organic farmer – Biobauer / worker co-operative – Betrieb in Arbeiterselbstverwaltung; Produktivgenossenschaft)

* **R & D have succeeded in developing a biodegradable plastic, which could be used as an environmentally benign packing material.**
(R & D – Research and Development [department] | Forschung[s-] und Entwicklung[-sabteilung] / succeed – gelingen / biodegradable – biologisch abbaubar / environmentally benign – umweltfreundlich)

* **We are doing quite a lot to make our products more environment-friendly. For one thing, we have switched to water-based paints for our metal goods.**
(quite – ziemlich / a lot – viel / for one thing – zum einen / switch to – umsteigen auf / water-based – auf Wasserbasis / paint – Farbe, Lack)

TRANSPORT

Transport

* **We bought a couple of the new fuel-efficient lorries last year.**
(a couple of – ein paar / fuel-efficient – treibstoffsparend / lorry – Lastwagen)

After months of discussions we decided to fit all our delivery vans with catalytic converters. Since there is a tax incentive for this it didn't cost us that much.
(decide – beschließen / fit – ausrüsten / delivery van – Lieferwagen /

catalytic converter – Katalysator / since – da / tax incentive – steuerlicher Anreiz / that – so)

* **All our company cars run on unleaded petrol.**
(Alle unsere Firmenautos fahren mit bleifreiem Benzin.)

* **You know, the ban on the night-time movement of lorries has created a really bad logistics problem for our firm.**
(ban on night-time movement – Nachtfahrverbot / create – verursachen)

* **Unfortunately the piggyback service offered by Austrian Railways is not particularly fast and efficient.**
(unfortunately – leider / piggyback service – Huckepackverkehr; rollende Landstraße / offer – anbieten / particular – besonders / fast – schnell)

* **If rail transport is ever to become competitive with road transport, they will have to invest a lot in new tracks, terminals and rolling stock.**
(rail – Eisenbahn / competitive – konkurrenzfähig / road – Straße / tracks – Gleisanlagen / rolling stock – rollendes Material)

* **I think in the long run we'll have to switch to rail transport, at least for the heavy equipment.**
(in the long run – langfristig gesehen / switch to – umsteigen auf / at least – zumindest / heavy – schwer / equipment – Ausrüstung, Geräte)

* **If they really decide to put this tax on road transport, JIT will become a less attractive proposition.**
(put tax on sthg. – etwas mit einer Steuer belegen / JIT – just in time I Lagerbestandsminimierungsstrategie / proposition – Sache, Angelegenheit)

INDEX

Accidents s. Emergencies

Advertising Agencies s. Contacts ...

Air Travel 119
- Between Check-in and Departure 125
- Booking and Other Arrangements 119
- On Board the Aircraft 126
- Post Flight 128

Apologies and Reactions 41

Asking the Way and Public Transport 110
- Bus/Coach 115
- General 110
- Tram 118
- Underground 113

Austrian Economy 401
- Economic and Social Policies 412
- Economic Situation 401
- Economic System and Industrial Structure 402
- Financial Markets 411
- International Economic Relations 407
- Joining the EC 410
- Private Sector and Nationalised Industries 404
- Taxes 414
- Various Industries 406

Bars s. Restaurants, Bars etc.

"Bitte" and "danke" in English 34

Car Accidents s. Emergencies

Car Rental s. Motoring

Chemist s. Health

Cinema 207

Company 282
- Current Conditions 288
- Human Resources/Employees 296
- Organisational Structure and Management 286
- Premises 298
- Products and Activities 285
- Type, Size, Location, Ownership, History, etc. 282

Complaints 386
- Buyer Accepts Responsibility 399
- Buyer Makes a Complaint 386
- Buyer Makes Threats 392
- Buyer Reacts to Seller's Suggestions 396
- Buyer Suggests Plan of Action 391
- Seller's Admission of Fault and Apologies 394
- Seller does not Accept Complaint 397
- Seller's or Buyer's Suggestions if there is no Agreement 398
- Seller's Reaction to Complaint, Investigation and Inspection 393
- Seller Suggests or Announces Settlement 395

Computers 300

Concerts 216

Condolences s. Sympathy ...

Conferences 343
- Concluding Remarks 348
- Opening Conferences and Introducing Speakers 345
- Registration and General Information 343
- Speaker Introduces First Point 347
- Speaker Introduces Subject 346
- Speaker Moves on to Next Point/s 347
- Speaker Thanks Chairman 346
- Thanking Speaker, Initiating Discussion, Closing Conference or Session 349

Congratulations and Good Wishes 44

Contacts with Advertising Agencies 381
- Discussing Advertising Policies - Media Selection 382
- Reactions to Suggestions and Concepts 381
- Technical Details, Schedules and Deadlines 384
- Terminating Agreement with Agency 385

Credit Cards s. Personal Banking

Dentist s. Health

Doctor s. Health

Educational Background 271
- Access to Universities 272
- Conditions at University 278
- Degrees 273
- Extracurricular Activities 280
- Finance 276
- Post University 280
- Secondary Education 271
- Studies and Examinations 274
- Studying Abroad 279
- Study Record 278

Emergencies 90
- Accidents 92
- Car Accidents 92
- In Hospital 91
- Lost Property 90

Environmental Matters 416
- Environmental Regulations 416
- Products 421
- Promotional Aspects 420
- Transport 422
- Waste 418

Eurocheques s. Personal Banking

Exclamations 53

Family 63

Formal Occasions 195
- Announcements 197
- Celebrations 198
- Thanking for Invitation 199
- Thanking People 200
- Toasts - Best Wishes for the Future 196
- Toasts - Congratulating People 197
- Toasts - General 195
- Toasts - Thanking Somebody 195
- Welcoming People 199

General Presentations 350
- Closing the Presentation 360
- Introductions 350
- Moving the Presentation Forward 360
- Quantitative Statements and Diagrams 353
- Technical Aspects 352

Greeting People 22

Health 83
- At the Chemist's 86
- At the Dentist's 88
- At the Doctor's 87
- General; Minor Illnesses 83

Hospital s. Emergencies

Hotel 151
- At the Reception 155
- Breakfast 160
- Business Facilities 164
- Checking out 162
- Complaints 161
- Hotel Services 158
- Inquiries, Reservations, etc. 151

Job 259
- Compensation 266
- Job Description and Duties 262
- Job Satisfaction 264
- Joining the Company 259
- Leaving the Company and Looking for a New Job 265
- Promotion 268
- Superiors, Subordinates and Colleagues 261
- What do you Do for a Living? 259
- Working Hours and Working Conditions 260
- Your Business here in Britain 269

Jokes 62

Language Problems 55

Leisure Time Activities s. Sports ...

Meeting People 17
- Introducing Other People 19
- Introducing Yourself 17

Meetings 324
- Agreeing and Disagreeing 327
- Clarifying 332
- Closing the Meeting 341
- Conceding Points 332
- Formal Motions and Voting 338
- Handling Awkward Questions and Being Evasive 336
- Interruptions and Dealing with Interruptions 333
- Inviting Contributions and Asking for Opinions 326
- Keeping the Discussion on Track 336
- Minutes 340
- Moving the Discussion Forward 335
- Persuading and Convincing 329
- Post Meeting 341
- Setting the Agenda 325

- Starting the Meeting 324
- Suggestions and Reactions 330
- Summarising 337

Motoring 137
- Asking the Way 140
- At the Petrol Station 141
- Breakdowns and Minor Repairs 143
- Car Ferry 147
- Car Rental 137
- Miscellaneous 148
- Parking 145
- Taxi 149

Museums 218

Negotiating Contracts 303
- Breaks, Next Meeting, Finishing 322
- Chat Phase 303
- Delivery, Delivery Dates and Transport 305
- Discounts 317
- Draft Contracts, Legal and Technical Points 320
- Opening the Discussion 304
- Prices and Commissions 313
- Products, Quality and Modifications 309
- Quantities 308
- Term and Termination 319
- Terms of Payment 310

Opera 215

Parking s. Motoring

Parties s. Visits and Parties

Personal Banking 247
- Changing Money 250
- Credit Cards 258
- Deposits 253
- Eurocheques 249
- Opening and Closing an Account 252
- Opening Hours 247
- Ordinary Cheques 249
- Overdrafts 257
- Statements and Balance of Account 257
- Transfers 255
- Travellers' Cheques 247
- Withdrawals 254

Petrol Station s. Motoring

Politics 74
- Elections 79
- International Aspects 81
- Political Parties 78
- Political Past 80
- Political System 74
- Present Political Situation and Attitudes 76

Post Office 231

Product Presentations 362
- Beneficial Environmental Consequences 366
- Comparison with Competing Products 371
- Customer Acceptance 367
- Demonstrations and Illustrations 372
- Handy Size and Flexibility 365
- Improvements 369
- Introduction 362
- Materials and Composition 363
- Measurements and Weights 369
- Packing 368
- Price and Performance 368
- Properties and Quality 364
- Suitability and Modifications 371
- Variety 370

Public Transport s. Asking the Way ...

Radio s. TV

Rail Travel 130
- At the Station 133
- General 136
- Inquiries and Tickets 130
- In the Train 134

Regrets and Consolation s. Sympathy ...

Requests and Replies 30

Restaurants, Bars, etc. 177
- After the Meal 192
- At the Bar 183
- At the Reception 182
- Booking a Table 181
- Complaints 190
- During the Meal 187
- Invitations 177
- Ordering 183
- Out on the Town 193
- Pubs/Pub Lunch 179
- Smoking 189
- The Bill 190

Saying Goodbye 26

Shopping ____ 224

Sports and Other Leisure Time Activities ____ 219

Season's Greetings ____ 48

Sympathy, Regrets and Consolation, Condolences ____ 49

Taxi s. Motoring

Telephoning ____ 235
- Answering the Switchboard ____ 235
- Caller Identifies himself/herself in Reply to a Request for Identity ____ 236
- Caller Requests a Particular Person or Service ____ 237
- Caller States his/her Business ____ 239
- Difficulties in Understanding the Other Party ____ 242
- Person Called Answers the Phone ____ 236
- Person Wanted is not Available ____ 240
- Reacting to Unavailability of Party Called ____ 241
- Reaction to Caller's Request for a Particular Person ____ 238
- Requesting Identity ____ 235
- Ringing off ____ 244
- Spelling Words, Numbers and Other Details ____ 243
- Talking about the Telephone ____ 245

Theatre ____ 211

Time ____ 94
- Age ____ 107
- Appointments ____ 94
- Deadlines ____ 99
- Miscellaneous ____ 108
- Other Expressions Indicating Time ____ 103
- Pressed for Time ____ 100
- Time of Day ____ 102

Trade Fairs ____ 374
- About Fairs and Fair Preparations ____ 374
- On the Stand ____ 376
- Post Mortem ____ 379

Travellers' Cheques s. Personal Banking

TV, Radio, Video, etc. ____ 202

Underground s. Asking the Way ...

Video s. TV ...

Visits and Parties ____ 166
- After the Meal ____ 173
- Arrival ____ 168
- At a Party ____ 174
- At the Table ____ 171
- Drinks ____ 169
- Invitations ____ 166
- Leaving and Thanking for Hospitality ____ 175
- Tea/Coffee ____ 170

Weather ____ 66

REGISTER

Apotheke s. Befinden ...

Arzt s. Befinden ...

Aufforderungen s. Bitten

Ausrufe 53

Auto 137
- An der Tankstelle 141
- Autofähre 147
- Autovermietung 137
- Erkundigung nach dem Weg 140
- Pannen und kleinere Reparaturen 143
- Parken 145
- Sonstiges 148
- Taxi 149

Autounfälle s. Notfälle

Autovermietung s. Auto

Bankgeschäfte 247
- Abhebungen 254
- Einzahlungen 253
- Eröffnung (Schließung) eines Kontos 252
- Euroschecks 249
- Geld wechseln 250
- Kontoauszüge, Kontostand 257
- Kontoüberziehungen 257
- Kreditkarten 258
- Öffnungszeiten 247
- Reiseschecks 247
- Überweisungen 255

Bars s. Restaurants ...

Bedauern s. Mitgefühl ...

Befinden und Gesundheit 83
- Allgemeines Befinden; Wehwehchen 83
- Beim Arzt 87
- Beim Zahnarzt 88
- In der Apotheke 86

Begrüßung 22

Beileid s. Mitgefühl ...

Besuche und Parties 166
- Bei Tisch 171
- Einladungen 166
- Eintreffen 168
- Getränke 169
- Nach dem Essen 173
- Verabschiedung und Dank für Gastfreundschaft 175

Bildungsweg 271
- Akademische Grade 273
- Außeruniversitäre Aktivitäten 280
- Finanzierung des Studiums 276
- Höhere Schulen, „Mittelschulen“ 271
- Nach dem Studienabschluß 280
- Studienbedingungen 278
- Studienergebnisse 278
- Studium im Ausland 279
- Studium und Prüfungen 274
- Zulassung zum Universitätsstudium 272

Bitten/Aufforderungen 30

„Bitte“ und „danke“ in Englisch 34

Computer 300

Einkaufen 224

Eisenbahn 130
- Allgemeines 136
- Auf dem Bahnhof 133
- Auskünfte und Fahrkarten 130
- Im Zug 134

Entschuldigungen 41

Erkundigung nach dem Weg und öffentliche Transportmittel 110
- Allgemeines 110
- Bus/Überlandbus 115
- Straßenbahn 118
- U-Bahn 113

Euroschecks s. Bankgeschäfte

Familie 63

Fernsehen, Radio, Video 202

Firma 282
- Art, Größe, Standort, Eigentumsverhältnisse, Geschichte 282
- Gegenwärtige Lage 288
- Organisationsstruktur und Management 286
- Personalressourcen/Mitarbeiter 296
- Produkte und Tätigkeitsbereiche 285
- Räumlichkeiten, Betriebsstätten 298

Flugzeug 119
- Buchungen 119
- Einchecken 123
- Im Flugzeug 126
- Nach dem Flug 128
- Zwischen Einchecken und Abflug 125

Gesundheit s. Befinden ...

Gratulationen, Genesungs- und sonstige Wünsche 44

Hotel 151
- Abreise 162
- Am Empfang 155
- Anfragen, Zimmerreservierungen 151
- Beschwerden 161
- Frühstück 160
- Leistungsangebot für Geschäftsleute 164

Job 259
- Arbeitszeit, Arbeitsbedingungen 260
- Arbeitszufriedenheit 264
- Ausscheiden aus der Firma und Suche nach neuem Arbeitsplatz 265
- Beförderung 268
- Beschreibung des Arbeitsplatzes und Aufgaben 262
- Eintritt in die Firma 259
- Entlohnung 266
- Vorgesetzte, Untergebene, Kollegen 261
- Wie verdienen Sie sich Ihren Lebensunterhalt? 259
- Zweck Ihres Aufenthaltes in Großbritannien 269

Kino 207

Konferenzen 343
- Anmeldung, allgemeine Informationen 343
- Dank an Vortragende/n, Eröffnung der Diskussion, Abschluß 349
- Eröffnung, Vorstellung von Vortragenden 345
- Schlußbemerkungen 348
- Vortragende/r dankt Vorsitzendem 346
- Vortragende/r leitet zum nächsten Punkt über 347
- Vortragende/r präsentiert ersten Punkt 347
- Vortragende/r stellt Thema vor 346

Kontakte mit Werbeagenturen 381
- Beendigung des Vertragsverhältnisses 385
- Diskussion werbepolitischer Konzepte – Medienauswahl 382
- Reaktionen auf Vorschläge und Konzepte 381
- Technische Details, Zeitpläne, Termine 384

Konzerte 216

Krankenhaus s. Notfälle

Kreditkarten s. Bankgeschäfte

Messen 374
- Am Messestand 376
- Gespräche über Messen und Vorbereitungsarbeiten 374
- Nach der Messe - Analyse und Bewertung 379

Mitgefühl, Bedauern und Beileid 49

Museen 218

Notfälle 90
- Autounfälle 92
- Im Krankenhaus 91
- Unfälle 92
- Verlust von Sachen 90

Offizielle Anlässe 195
- Allgemeine Toasts 195
- Ankündigungen und Verlautbarungen 197
- Dank für Einladung 199
- Feiern 198
- Gratulationen 197
- Jemanden begrüßen 199
- Toasts in Verbindung mit Dank 195
- Toasts in Verbindung mit Gratulationen 197
- Toasts in Verbindung mit Wünschen 196
- Wie man sich bedankt 200

Oper ____ 215

Österreichische Wirtschaft ____ 401
- Beitritt zur EG ____ 410
- Finanzmärkte ____ 411
- Internationale Beziehungen ____ 407
- Konjunkturlage ____ 401
- Privatwirtschaft, verstaatlichte Industrie ____ 404
- Steuern ____ 414
- Verschiedene Wirtschaftszweige ____ 406
- Wirtschaftssystem, Wirtschaftsstruktur ____ 402
- Wirtschafts- und Sozialpolitik ____ 412

Parken s. Auto

Parties s. Besuche ...

Politik ____ 74
- Gegenwärtige Lage und persönliche Einstellung ____ 76
- Internationale Aspekte ____ 81
- Parteien ____ 78
- System ____ 74
- Vergangenheit ____ 80
- Wahlen ____ 79

Post ____ 231

Präsentationen ____ 350
- Abschluß ____ 360
- Einleitende Worte ____ 350
- Quantitative Aussagen und Diagramme ____ 353
- Technische Aspekte ____ 352
- Überleitung zum nächsten Punkt ____ 360

Produktpräsentationen ____ 362
- Abmessungen und Gewichte ____ 369
- Eigenschaften und Qualität ____ 364
- Eignung und Modifikationen ____ 371
- Einleitung ____ 362
- Kundenakzeptanz ____ 367
- Materialien und Zusammensetzung ____ 363
- Positive ökologische Auswirkungen ____ 366
- Praktische Größe und Flexibilität ____ 365
- Preis und Leistung ____ 368
- Verbesserungen ____ 369
- Vergleich mit Konkurrenzprodukten ____ 371
- Verpackung ____ 368
- Vielfalt des Angebots ____ 370
- Vorführungen und Illustrationen ____ 372

Radio s. Fernsehen ...

Reiseschecks s. Bankgeschäfte

Reklamationen ____ 386
- Käufer beschwert sich/reklamiert ____ 386
- Käufer droht ____ 392
- Käufer reagiert auf Vorschläge des Verkäufers ____ 396
- Käufer schlägt Regelung vor ____ 391
- Käufer übernimmt Verantwortung ____ 399
- Reaktion des Verkäufers auf Reklamation, Untersuchung und Inspektion ____ 393
- Verkäufer nimmt Schuld auf sich, entschuldigt sich ____ 394
- Verkäufer schlägt Regelung vor oder kündigt eine an ____ 395
- Verkäufer weist Reklamation zurück ____ 397
- Vorschläge seitens Verkäufers oder Käufers bei Nichteinigung ____ 398

Restaurants, Bars ____ 177
- Beschwerden ____ 190
- Bestellung ____ 183
- Einladungen ____ 177
- Nach dem Essen ____ 192
- Nachtleben ____ 193
- Rechnung ____ 190
- Tischreservierung ____ 181
- Während des Essens ____ 187

Sitzungen ____ 324
- Ablehnung, Zustimmung ____ 327
- Abweichungen verhindern ____ 336
- Anträge, Abstimmungen ____ 338
- Bitte um Diskussionsbeiträge und Meinungsäußerungen ____ 326
- Eröffnung ____ 324
- Festlegung der Tagesordnung ____ 325
- Klarstellungen ____ 332
- Nach der Sitzung ____ 341
- Protokoll ____ 340
- Schließung ____ 341
- Überleitung zum nächsten Tagesordnungspunkt ____ 335
- Überreden und überzeugen ____ 329
- Unangenehme Fragen, Ausflüchte ____ 336
- Unterbrechungen ____ 333
- Vorschläge und Reaktionen ____ 330
- Zugeständnisse machen ____ 332
- Zusammenfassungen ____ 337

Sport und andere Freizeitbeschäftigungen ____ 219

Sprachliche Probleme ____ 55

Tankstelle s. Auto

Taxi s. Auto

Theater 211

Telefonieren 235
- Angerufene/r meldet sich 236
- Anrufer/in gibt Grund an 239
- Anrufer/in nennt Namen 236
- Anrufer/in verlangt Person oder Abteilung 237
- Beendigung des Gesprächs 244
- Bitte um Namensnennung 235
- Buchstabieren von Wörtern, Zahlen 243
- Gespräche rund um das Telefon 245
- Gewünschte Person ist nicht erreichbar 240
- Reaktion auf Nichterreichbarkeit 241
- Reaktion auf Wunsch, jemanden bestimmten zu sprechen 238
- Schwierigkeiten, den Partner zu verstehen 242
- Zentrale meldet sich 235

Transportmittel s. Erkundigung ...

U-Bahn s. Erkundigung ...

Umweltaspekte 416
- Abfall 418
- Kommunikationspolitische Aspekte 420
- Produkte 421
- Transport 422
- Vorschriften 416

Unfälle s. Notfälle

Verabschiedung 26

Vertragsverhandlungen 303
- Abschluß 322
- Eröffnung der Diskussion 304
- Lieferung, Liefertermine und Transport 305
- Mengen 308
- Pause, nächste Sitzung 322
- Preise und Provisionen 313
- Preisnachlässe 317
- Produkte, Qualität, Modifikationen 309
- Vertragsentwürfe, Details 320
- Vertragslaufzeit, Beendigung des Vertragsverhältnisses 319
- Vorgeplänkel 303
- Zahlungsbedingungen 310

Video s. Fernsehen ...

Vorstellung 17
- Jemand anderen vorstellen 19
- Sich selbst vorstellen 17

Weihnachts- und Neujahrswünsche 48

Werbeagenturen s. Kontakte mit ...

Wetter 66

Witze 62

Wünsche s. Gratulationen ...

Zahnarzt s. Befinden ...

Zeit und Zeitangaben 94
- Altersangaben 107
- Sonstiges 108
- Sonstige Zeitangaben 103
- Termine und Fristen 99
- Terminvereinbarungen und Verabredungen 94
- Unter Zeitdruck 100

DIE AUTOREN

Univ.-Prof. Mag. Dr. Wolfgang Obenaus

Jahrgang 1953; Mag. rer. soc. oec. (Wirtschaftsuniversität Wien, 1976); Universitätsassistent am Institut für Englische Sprache / Wirtschaftsuniversität Wien (seit 1976); Forschungsstipendium / Georgetown University und Export-Import Bank in Washington, D.C. (1978); Dr. rer. soc. oec. (Wirtschaftsuniversität Wien / Wirtschaftsenglisch 1979); Lehrbeauftragter für Wirtschaftsenglisch an der Wirtschaftsuniversität Wien seit 1980; Forschungsstipendium / Georgetown University und Overseas Private Investment Corporation in Washington, D.C. (1982); 1990 Habilitation (»Die amerikanische Terminologie des Wechselkursrisikos und der Kurssicherungstechniken«); Forschungsstipendium / Harvard University in Cambridge, Mass. (Sommer 1990); seit März 1991 Universitätsprofessor für das Fach »Englische Wirtschaftssprache« an der Wirtschaftsuniversität Wien; Vortragender und Trainer auf dem Gebiet des Wirtschaftsenglischen im Rahmen von Managementseminaren für Praktiker; Veröffentlichungen und Übersetzungen auf dem Gebiet des Wirtschaftsenglischen, unter anderem Wolfgang Obenaus, Josef Weidacher: Englische Wirtschaftssprache, Übungen zur Grammatik, Wien, 3. Aufl. 1992; Wolfgang Obenaus, Josef Weidacher: Handbook of Business English. Keywords in Context, 4. überarbeitete und erweiterte Auflage, Wien 1990; Wolfgang Obenaus: Handbuch der amerikanischen Terminologie des Wechselkursrisikos und der Kurssicherungstechniken, Wien 1990; alle im Verlag Ueberreuter erschienen.

ao. Univ.-Prof. Dr. Josef Weidacher, M.A.

Jahrgang 1935; Stipendium / University of Minnesota (1959); Master of Arts (University of Minnesota 1961); Lehramt für Anglistik, Germanistik, Philosophie (Universität Wien, 1961); Ergänzungsprüfung aus Wirtschaftsenglisch (1963); Lehrtätigkeiten an Handelsschulen und -akademien (1961 bis 1968); Bundeslehrer / Lektor für Wirtschaftsenglisch (Hochschule für Welthandel / Wirtschaftsuniversität Wien seit 1968); Dr. phil. (Universität Wien / Wirtschaftslinguistik 1971); Seminarleiter an der Diplomatischen Akademie Wien (1979 bis 1984); Verleihung des Berufstitels »Außerordentlicher Universitätsprofessor« (1990); Veröffentlichungen, Übersetzungen und Vorträge auf dem Gebiet des Wirtschaftsenglischen, unter anderem Wolfgang Obenaus, Josef Weidacher: Englische Wirtschaftssprache, Übungen zur Grammatik, Wien, 3. Auflage 1992. Wolfgang Obenaus, Josef Weidacher: Handbook of Business English. Keywords in Context, 4. überarbeitete und erweiterte Auflage, Wien 1990; alle im Verlag Ueberreuter erschienen.